A PHILOSOPHY OF HAVRUTA

UNDERSTANDING AND TEACHING
THE ART OF TEXT STUDY
IN PAIRS

Elie HOLZER

with

Orit KENT

Jewish Identity in Post-Modern Society

ACADEMIC
STUDIES
PRESS

A PHILOSOPHY OF HAVRUTA

UNDERSTANDING AND TEACHING THE ART OF TEXT STUDY IN PAIRS

Elie HOLZER

with

Orit KENT

BOSTON /2014

Library of Congress Cataloging-in-Publication Data:
The bibliographic data for this title is available from the Library of Congress.

ISBN 978-1-61811-290-3 (cloth)
ISBN 978-1-61811-291-0 (electronic)
ISBN 978-1-61811-385-6 (paperback)

Cover design by Ivan Grave

Published by Academic Studies Press in 2013, paperback edition 2014.
28 Montfern Avenue
Brighton, MA 02135, USA
press@academicstudiespress.com
www.academicstudiespress.com

ACKNOWLEDGMENTS

The research for this book and its publication were made possible by the generous support of the Jack, Joseph and Morton Mandel Center for Studies in Jewish Education, a partnership between Brandeis University and the Jack, Joseph and Morton Mandel Foundation.

It was also assisted by a generous grant from the Lookstein Center for Jewish Education, Bar Ilan University.

Rabbi Ishmael the son of Rabbi Yossei says: One who learns Torah in order to teach, is given the opportunity to learn and teach. One who learns in order to do, is given the opportunity to learn, teach, observe and do.

Ethics of our Fathers, 4:5

Real learning gets to the heart of what it means to be human.

Peter Senge

Any meeting of personalities requires great bravery. One who attempts to communicate with another endangers his own life, for to do this he must reveal what is in his heart. Such an act is potentially dangerous because one does not know ahead of time if he will find a receptive ear. There is always the possibility that the ear of the listener will be impervious. Any real communication, then, is a dangerous leap. But if one never screws up the courage to jump, he will wither away in silent isolation.

Yochanan Muffs

TABLE OF CONTENTS

PREFACE

Sharon Feiman-Nemser

Since its founding in 2002, the Mandel Center for Studies in Jewish Education at Brandeis University has become *the* address for serious research on teaching and learning in Jewish education. One of the signature projects at the Mandel Center is the Beit Midrash Research Project, which investigates the purposes, pedagogy and practices of text study in havruta (pairs). Elie Holzer and Orit Kent have been conceptualizing, teaching, researching, and writing about this central mode of Jewish learning for over a decade. This is the first book based on their work.

Holzer's and Kent's devotion to classical Jewish texts and the transformative power of text study is rooted in their own autobiographies and professional interests, but the research and teaching they describe here originated in the unique institution that they created for the DeLeT teacher education program at Brandeis.

For ten years, I served with Holzer and others on the faculty of the Mandel Teacher Educator Institute, a professional development seminar for instructional leaders in Jewish education. A central activity in MTEI involved studying short rabbinic texts, mostly narratives, concerned with issues of teaching and learning. As we studied in havruta under Holzer's guidance, I saw clear parallels between his approach to text study and the inquiry stance toward teaching that MTEI and DeLeT embraced. I wanted the DeLeT fellows, future day school teachers, to experience this kind of text study; I hoped it would deepen their attachment to Jewish learning and help build intellectual and relational skills needed for teaching. I invited Holzer to come to Brandeis in the summer of 2003 to create a Beit Midrash for Teachers (BMT) as a central component of the DeLeT program.

Orit Kent, a doctoral student in Jewish education at the time, had been studying how people learn in havruta and wanted to pursue this inquiry further. She joined Holzer in creating and teaching in the

Beit Midrash, which served as a laboratory for her ground-breaking dissertation research. Together they framed a complementary agenda of conceptual and empirical studies, and the Mandel Center's Beit Midrash Research Project was born.

The Beit Midrash researchers developed and tested a distinctive model of text study in havruta based on a dynamic relationship among three partners—two people and a text. According to this model, the human partners give voice to the text and to their own and each other's ideas, and the text inspires and constrains their interpretations. This "theory" of havruta learning, rooted in philosophical hermeneutics and sociocultural learning theories, emerged from and was refined through ongoing teaching and research in the Beit Midrash for Teachers and in other settings.

Holzer and Kent champion the idea that havruta text study is not an automatic practice which springs up naturally when two people sit together to study a text. It can and should be taught and learned. Moreover, when the skills and dispositions required for "good" text study in havruta are taught, the learning and the learners are transformed.

And now we have this wonderful book to help us understand the particulars of how havruta text study works, and how to unlock its transformative power through teaching. Holzer wrote this book, except for Chapter Six, which was written by Kent, but the use of "we" throughout signals their longstanding collaboration, and much of this book emerged from their joint work.

Few books combine philosophical analysis and pedagogical guidance and present both with such clarity. Teachers at all levels interested in the study of texts and the power of collaborative learning will find conceptual and practical tools to enhance their students' learning and inspire their teaching. Even more, Holzer and Kent's model of paired text study, with its emphasis on big ideas and concern for evidence, critical and imaginative thinking and humane interactions, is a microcosm of liberal learning at its best.

Torah is acquired by study, attentiveness,
orderly speech (...) the give and take of colleagues (...)
loving reproof (...) concentrating on one's studies, asking
and answering questions.

Ethics of the Fathers, 6:6

CHAPTER ONE:
CONTEXTUAL FOUNDATIONS

Havruta text study is considered an ancient mode of Jewish learning, most commonly described as the study of traditional Jewish texts by a pair of learners.[1] In our own view it can be best conceptualized as the opening of a dialogue with a text together with a havruta partner. For many years, we, the authors of this book, have been actively engaged in promoting havruta text study outside traditional yeshiva settings.[2] Like many Jewish educators in recent decades, we are drawn to this ancient learning style's authentic "feel." At the same time, we have come to appreciate the complexity of havruta text study as a rich praxis, as well as the challenge of cultivating a supportive environment in which it can flourish.[3] The premise of our work and the

---

[1]   *Havruta* means companionship or friendship. It is an extension of the Hebrew word *haver,* companion or friend. In its common use, the word havruta can refer to the learning pair, to the learning partner, and/or to the practice of paired learning itself. In using the term "havruta text study," we mean to refer to the symbiotic interaction between a text and two havruta learning partners.

[2]   A yeshiva is an academy in which people dedicate themselves mainly to the study of Talmud and other traditional rabbinic literature. Since its inception around the first century in Israel, and later in Babylonia, the institution of the yeshiva has gone through many changes. See *Encyclopedia Judaica,* the entries on "Academies in Babylonia and Erez Israel" and "Yeshivot."

[3]   Praxis is hereby understood as an informed committed action. It indicates the reflective relationship between theories and action that occurs in a interactive process between experiences, the refinement of old theories and the development of new ones. For Aristotle, praxis is guided by the moral disposition to act truly and rightly, a concern for furthering human well-being and the good life. It is not simply action based on reflection. It is

impetus for this book is our belief that educators have much to gain by helping others become proficient havruta learners, and that havruta text study is a praxis that can be taught.

Over the years, we have learned that students and educators alike hold different opinions about what havruta text study looks like as well as differing ideas regarding its purposes and benefits. For example, some emphasize that havruta learning helps students understand that a text is inherently open to multiple perspectives and interpretations. Others may think about havruta learning in more instrumental terms, arguing that it can produce a better understanding of the material at hand; still others value this traditional learning format for the sake of historical continuity. But in our view, many of these responses are often uncritical, or at best pre-critical, with regard to havruta learning's epistemological, pedagogical, and educational aspects.

Having two learners talk, ask questions, and offer interpretations of a text does not adequately summarize what an optimal havruta study would be. Following Apel and Habermas' works on conversation, we believe that for havruta communications to be successful, partners need to possess a set of shared norms about the forms and purposes of their communication, even if these norms are implicit and unnoticed.[4] Our experience has taught us that the establishment of such norms and engagement in meaningful havruta text study does not necessary happen naturally or spontaneously. Participants

---

action which embodies certain qualities. These include a commitment to human well-being, respect for others, and the ability to make wise practical judgment about how to act in a particular situation. See Wilfred Carr and Stephen Kemmis, *Becoming Critical: Education, Knowledge and Action Research* (Lewes: Falmer, 1986), 190. Richard Bernstein's discussion of praxis as a form of knowledge and its connection to philosophical hermeneutics provides the epistemological background of our approach to havruta text study discussed in Chapter Two of this book. See Richard J. Bernstein, *Beyond Objectivism and Relativism: Science, Hermeneutics and Praxis* (Oxford: Basil Blackwell, 1983); see also Moacir Gadotti, *Pedagogy of Praxis: A Dialectical Philosophy of Education* (New York: SUNY Press, 1996).

[4]   Karl-Otto Apel, "The Problem of Philosophical Foundations in Light of Transcendental Pragmatics of Language," in *After philosophy: End or transformation?*, ed. Kenneth Baynes and James Bohman (Cambridge, MA: MIT Press, 1987), 250–299; Jurgen Habermas, *The Theory of Communicative Action* (Boston: Beacon Press, 1984).

in havruta study require opportunities to learn what the conversation ideally entails, and to acquire the skills and attitudes necessary to conduct it.

This book presents a particular model of havruta text study that developed through a decade of teaching, design and research. It is the outcome of practice-based research in which havruta text study has been conceptualized, designed, taught, and adapted to fit the context of contemporary teacher education. This book makes a unique contribution by framing havruta text study in the context of philosophical hermeneutics. That discipline offers an epistemology grounded in an interpretive and dialogical view of understanding and of the self, particularly in the encounter with texts and dialogical partners. We have also been influenced by theories from other disciplines, such as literary, educational, sociocultural, and psychological theory.

The main laboratory for most of the work presented here has been the Beit Midrash for Teachers,[5] a central component in the DeLeT/ MAT, a graduate program at Brandeis University that prepares teachers for Jewish day schools. This setting differs from the traditional beit midrash in that its primary purposes are to provide prospective teachers the opportunity to study classical Jewish texts about teaching and learning and to explore the elements of good havruta text study.[6] We conducted our design research under the auspices of The Beit Midrash Research Project, supported by the Mandel Center for Studies in Jewish Education,[7] the first extensive and intensive, conceptual and empirical investigation of havruta text study in Jewish education.

By articulating and developing a comprehensive understanding of havruta text study, we hope to fill a void in the pedagogical literature and to be of both practical and conceptual help to educators looking to adopt this ancient learning format. Our research reflects our belief that people can learn, and learn to cultivate, the elements of successful havruta text study. It has grown out of our practical experiences as

---

[5]   Literally, "house of study"; here, a reference to a learning setting in which havruta text study plays a central role.

[6]   For a detailed and conceptual discussion of the Beit Midrash in the context of the DeLeT program see Sharon Feiman-Nemser, "Beit Midrash for Teachers: An Experiment in Teacher Preparation," *Journal of Jewish Education* 72.3 (2006): 161–81.

[7]   See http://www.brandeis.edu/mandel.

teachers and researchers as we conceptualized, designed and taught the norms and practices of havruta text study in various settings, to help our students become effective havruta learners.

Despite the professional character of the setting in which this research took place, this book is written for teachers (and teacher educators) at all levels and in all settings who are interested in helping students learn havruta text study. It is also written for scholars with an interest in research on collaborative learning, interpretive discussion, and other dialogical approaches to textual interpretation.

It is not our aim to present a finite set of techniques, nor are we advocating a particular protocol for teaching havruta learning. Rather, our goal is to help teachers and teacher educators think about havruta text study in new ways, and design settings and strategies for teaching core practices that are indispensable for havruta learners. While we offer here a systematized model of havruta text study, it is not meant to supplant the teachers' individual experience or preferences, nor to neutralize the need for teachers to factor in contextual elements like a student's age, skills, and background.

In this introductory chapter, we will discuss the historical evolution of the havruta text study paradigm, explain how we, the authors, became interested in studying and promoting havruta text study, and describe how this book came about and what it offers.

Historical Roots

From a historical and conceptual perspective, havruta text study reflects two longstanding characteristics of Jewish education: the centrality of text-based study and the collaborative nature of that study.

With the emergence of rabbinic Judaism around the turn of the first century, *talmud torah*, the formal duty for every (male) Jew to study Jewish teachings and texts, became a central tenet of Judaism, if not always as a sociological reality than at least as one of its stated cultural values.[8] Though once reserved primarily for the Temple clergy in pre-rabbinic times, in the wake of the Temple's destruction Torah study became *the* formative activity of rabbinic leadership. Torah academies organized around text study flourished in Israel and Babylon between

---

8   See for example the concept of "The study of Torah [is] above all [other values]," Mishnah Peah, 1:1.

the second and fifth centuries CE. Throughout the centuries, text study has prevailed as a central form of Jewish learning, though the choice of texts and the types of discussions generated during study have often taken different and competing forms. Up until the changes that occurred due to the Emancipation, Torah study occupied a vital role in the cultivation of Jewish communities throughout Europe and elsewhere, though economic realities made full-time study prohibitive for the majority.

Prior to the written recording of the Mishnah and later the Talmud, the oral transmission of the rabbinic tradition contributed to the emergence of a learning culture with a strong dialogic and inter-personal character, which continued even after these works' official redaction. A significant component of traditional Jewish learning is indeed characterized by a dialogical element that is expressed in rabbinic literature itself as well as its study.

The Talmud is written and edited as a series of discussions, not merely a list of opinions (which is more characteristic of the Mishnah). In the world of the Talmud, learning takes place through interpersonal exchange; multiple voices and opinions are expressed and interpretations of earlier texts are offered and analyzed. Even if many of the talmudic discussions are literary constructs and not historical renditions of actual conversations, the very texture of the edited talmudic text as a presentation of debates, arguments, and counterarguments highlights the role of dialectical exchange in the development and acquisition of knowledge. With the invention of the printing press, the text of the Talmud was printed (first in 1522), with surrounding commentaries in which the authors refer to and argue with each other beyond the borders of time and geography, thus adding further dimensions to the dialogical character of the textual culture of rabbinic Judaism.[9] This character was not limited to the literary realm, but over the centuries impacted the culture of learning as well.[10]

---

[9]   Ephraim E. Auerbach, *Hazal-Pirke emunot vedeot* (Jerusalem: Magnes, 1969); Marvin J. Heller, *Printing the Talmud: A History of the Earliest Printed Editions of the Talmud* (Brooklyn, New York: Am Hasefer, 1992); Yaakov S. Spiegel, *Amudim betoledot hasefer haivri: Hagahot umagihim* (Ramat Gan: Bar-Ilan University Press, 1996).

[10]   Simha Assaf, *Mekorot letoldot hahinukh beYisra'el: mitehilat yemehabenayim ad tekufat hahaskalah* (Tel Aviv: Devir, 1925); Shaul Stampfer, *Hayeshivah hal-*

Traditional Jewish texts offer a very limited glimpse into the frequency, formats, and uses of what we might identify as havruta learning in Jewish communities throughout the early centuries of rabbinic Judaism. We cannot say with any certainty whether such learning was confined to pairs, or if it required a formal set of skills. The talmudic literature does, however, provide us with a favorable view of collaborative learning in statements such as the following: "Torah is acquired only in a group"[11] — the word for group used here, *havurah*, is related to havruta. Most prominently, we have the example of Rabbi Akiva, a legendary and heroic character of the rabbinic tradition, who was said to have had 12,000 *pairs* of students in his beit midrash.[12]

A number of statements by rabbis of the Talmud articulate the advantages provided by learning with peers: "Just as in the case of iron, when one implement sharpens another, so, too, do two Torah scholars sharpen each other when they discuss questions of halakhah together (...) Just as fire cannot be made to burn with one piece of wood alone, so too the words of Torah cannot be retained by someone who studies alone."[13] Some rabbis go so far as to state that scholars who engage in solitary study will be cursed, grow foolish, and ultimately fall into sin.[14] Special metaphors are used to capture the dynamic of interpersonal and argumentative learning — for example, "the war of Torah."[15] Specific practices of collaborative learning such as careful listening are also praised and highlighted in various talmudic sources.[16]

Contemporary researchers like Helmreich and Heilman consider the interpersonal and deliberative aspect of learning that prevails in traditional talmudic academies today to be a direct continuation

---

itait behithavutah (Jerusalem: Zalman Shazar, 1995); Samuel C. Heilman, *The People of the Book, Drama, Fellowship, and Religion* (Chicago: University of Chicago Press, 1987); William Helmreich, *The World of the Yeshiva: An Intimate Portrait of Orthodox Jewry* (New Haven: Yale University Press, 1982).

11   Babylonian Talmud, Tractate Brachot 63b. Unless indicated otherwise, Talmud references refer to the Babylonian Talmud.

12   Talmud, Tractate Yevamot, 62b.

13   Talmud, Tractate Ta'anit 7a.

14   Ibid., 21a.

15   Talmud Tractate Sanhedrin, 42b, 93b, 111b; Megilah 15b; Sotah 42a; Brachot 64a, 68a.

16   For example in Talmud, Tractate Shabbat 63a.

of this ancient Jewish tradition—though, undoubtedly, how learners over the centuries have understood their roles and responsibilities in the learning encounter has been shaped by prevailing cultural norms, however unconscious.[17] In contrast, historian Saul Stampfer claims that havruta learning only became predominant in Eastern Europe yeshivot towards the end of the nineteenth century, when pairing new underprepared students with more advanced students was simply considered efficient.[18] This argument cannot eclipse the textual expressions of the importance of learning as a social activity that have been found over the course of the centuries. Stampfer's research warns us, however, not to draw from those general expressions a hasty conclusion about the specific historical reality of paired text study over the centuries.

Contemporary Expressions

Over the last two to three decades, havruta text study has spread outside traditional yeshivot to a variety of settings of Jewish learning in the United States and Israel. These include but are not limited to day schools, professional preparation programs for teachers and rabbis, and adult education settings. In these new educational environments, havruta learning continues to exhibit key features of the now-traditional havruta model: pairs of learners face or sit next to each other and engage in the study of a Jewish text, alternating between reading, interpreting, and exchanging ideas. Some contemporary institutions have also embraced the concept of the traditional beit midrash, allocating a space where many havruta pairs engage simultaneously in text study. In such cases, the hum of learning sounds familiar to anyone who has ever visited a traditional yeshiva.

At the same time, we can also identify some differences between modern and traditional havruta learning. Unlike traditional yeshiva study, texts are not limited to the Talmud and its commentators, but include other works such as the Hebrew Bible, biblical commentaries, or even modern Hebrew poetry. Besides signaling a possible shift in what constitutes a canonical Jewish text, this change suggests that

---

[17]   Helmreich, *The World of the Yeshiva: An Intimate Portrait of Orthodox Jewry*; Heilman, *The People of the Book, Drama, Fellowship, and Religion*.

[18]   Stampfer, *Hayeshivah halitait behithavutah*.

contemporary havruta learning may satisfy new purposes and expectations, creating its own dynamics. For generations, it was assumed
that the primary reason that students sought a havruta partner (rather
than studying alone) was the inherent complexity of the talmudic text.
In studying less complex works, havruta partners may spend less time
deciphering the literal meaning of the text and focus instead on discussing its implications. Unlike traditional yeshivot, newer academic
institutions may not necessarily follow havruta study with a frontal
lecture. Rather, a session of paired learning may often lead to group
discussion, which evolves organically from individual dialogues.
Finally, one of the landmarks of contemporary expressions of havruta
text study is the inclusion of women, which, according to recent
research, may bring about new modes of engagement with both the
text and the havruta partner.[19]

Researchers' Journeys

Like any researchers, we bring our own biographies to our work. In
this case, our interest in havruta text study developed over many
years of experience as both students and teachers of Jewish texts. As
classroom teachers, we promoted havruta text study among our students and later, as teacher educators, we developed ways to introduce
havruta learning to our colleagues. Through these different experiences, we have come to question, reflect on, and problematize havruta
text study as well as what might be involved in helping others to
become havruta learners. The following biographical descriptions
have a double purpose: to disclose where we come from and what we
bring to this research, and to share with the reader how we each came
to view havruta text study as something to be investigated, critically
analyzed, theorized, and taught in its particulars.

---

[19]   Esti Barel, *Vetalmud torah keneged kulam: Mabat migdari al limud hatorah bemi-
       drashot beisrael* (Doctoral dissertation Bar-Ilan University, Ramat Gan, 2009);
       Ruti Feuchtwanger, *Becoming a Knower: Acquisition of Knowledge and Status
       by Religious Women Studying Talmud in Order to Teach* (Doctoral disserta-
       tion Bar-Ilan University, Ramat Gan, 2011); Esty Teomim-Ben Menachem,
       Women Study: Characterizing Conversation and Learning in Women's Havrutot
       (Doctoral dissertation Bar-Ilan University, Ramat Gan, forthcoming).

Elie's Journey

I grew up in Antwerp, Belgium in a familial and communal environment that cherished Jewish learning. There, I attended a coed Jewish day school with a rigorous program of both general and Jewish studies, the latter taught in Hebrew. My first memory of havruta study goes back to seventh grade, our first year of Talmud study. We studied the Babylonian Talmud, Tractate Baba Metzia, focusing on the laws of lost objects. After several classes, the teacher told us to sit in pairs and prepare the next couple of lines of the tractate. He labeled this activity "havruta learning." Since we used the original Aramaic with no diacritics, we had the challenge of determining where sentences began and ended in addition to deciphering the literal meaning of the text. We received no guidelines or suggestions about how to study together. I clearly remember taking the lead, attempting to read the text first for myself and then to explain it to my partner. My partner's contribution to the learning was more or less limited to following along. I remember how empowered I felt.

Over the next two years, I studied Talmud privately with a rabbi, twice a week. During these lessons, I found myself in the opposite role, the less experienced learner, but the exchange was nevertheless clearly one of havruta. We sat at the table facing each other; the rabbi often asked me probing questions. More than anything else, I recall the informal and pleasant atmosphere of learning, which was so different from school.

In tenth grade, I entered the Ets Haim Yeshiva High School in Montreux, Switzerland, where I was immersed in a different experience of Jewish learning that incorporated havruta learning extensively. Our rabbis there modeled the value of finding meaning in our learning, and of seeking rational, existential, and philosophical explanations of the traditional texts we studied as well as giving voice to our own questions and views. In retrospect, it was my time there that shaped my affective attachment to this type of study. We devoted five to seven hours a day, six days a week, to Talmud study, most of the time in the beit midrash, not in the classroom. Our havruta study served several purposes. First, it gave us an opportunity to review material from the previous lessons. This included reading and explaining the text, and reviewing various interpretations offered by both the commentators and the teacher. It also helped us prepare for daily Talmud class, which included the sharing of our personal understanding of the Talmud text.

Perhaps most significantly, havruta study was a venue that encouraged independent learning. During the evening hours, most students paired up with a havruta partner, often from a different grade, and met for an hour or two in the beit midrash, either to study another tractate of the Talmud, various rabbinical works, or the weekly Torah portion. No specific learning task was assigned and no class was to follow.

Through this formative engagement in havruta study, I came to adopt an approach to Jewish learning that is deeply grounded in text-based discussion with a partner. I came to the realization that articulating my thoughts to someone else shaped my own understanding of what I was trying to say. I saw that searching for the right words or a good example to convey my thoughts to my partner deepened my comprehension of the material at hand.

After high school, I attended the Har Etzion Yeshiva in Israel, a post-high school yeshiva. In the evenings, I studied Talmud with a much older and more advanced student, but this was not a positive experience. He did the reading and led the interpretation, though he would sometimes ask me to lead or inquired about my views; I often felt that he was merely talking to himself. I remember wondering if this was how one was "supposed" to study, but there was no forum or culture to discuss such questions or any deeper or meta questions about havruta text study.

Yet during my years in yeshiva, I also experienced how intensive havruta text study can foster real friendship. Not only did my "day" havruta partner and myself become acquainted with each other's skills and learning habits, we also grew to know each other as people. I admit we spent some of the time allocated to havruta learning in personal conversation, but I believe those conversations contributed a spirit of trust to our learning relationship. To be sure, this did not eliminate elements of competition, but most of our interactions were infused with mutual support and appreciation.

I joined the Beit Midrash of the Hartman Institute in Jerusalem in 1989 and studied there for six years, three half-days a week, spending most of my time in havruta study of Talmud and Jewish thought. The Hartman Institute encourages the study of Jewish texts as one way to inform how we confront the challenges facing contemporary Jewry. Since the Hartman Beit Midrash attracted a diverse group of religious and secular Israelis, I had an opportunity to study with partners from significantly different backgrounds than my own. I studied with havruta partners who asked questions, offered interpretations, and expressed attitudes that were antithetical to many of my own beliefs and assumptions. Some of these interactions led me to amend or reframe my beliefs. Other times, the need to articulate my opinions led to greater clarity and deeper understanding of my own belief system and of the assumptions I brought to the reading of these texts.

These years of havruta text study also heightened my awareness of the role that Jewish texts can play in critical, reflective thought. Often, the texts served as triggers for our discussions and, ultimately, our own intellectual growth. We returned to the same texts repeatedly, arguing and "responding" to them, as if the text itself was a partner in the discussion.

Despite all these years spent in havruta learning, I cannot recall any of my teachers ever discussing or instructing us in havruta text study per se. Nor did they show any interest in my own evolving thinking about havruta text study, nor in my development as a successful havruta partner. While havruta text study remained a central part of my life, it was not a topic that was subject to inquiry or analysis.

As a teacher, I taught Jewish studies (mainly Talmud) for several years in two different environments: a high school and a post-high school yeshiva, both in Jerusalem. In the high school, I enjoyed double teaching periods, which allowed my tenth and eleventh graders to devote short blocks of time (thirty to forty minutes) to havruta study. It was during my early years as a teacher that I found myself reflecting on the role of havruta text study from a pedagogic perspective: how was the practice of havruta building on what I was teaching in the classroom? Was havruta learning a good way to teach the basic skills of Talmud study, such as becoming familiar with the Talmud's key rhetorical devices and learning how to identify answers and associate them with their original questions? How could havruta learning support the aims of the future lessons?

It was while teaching at Heichal Elyahu, a post-high school yeshiva, that I developed a much more proactive interest in havruta text study. My students, ranging in age from nineteen to twenty-three, had at least two hours to prepare for each of my classes, which took place four times a week. I began to develop a more refined interest in various aspects of my students' interactions with the text. For example, I soon realized that my students were not making effective use of their long beit midrash hours of preparation, so I began to hand out study guidelines. These guidelines included specific tasks, such as preparing an articulation and comparison of various views presented in the text or asking the students to take a stance on a particular opinion. A significant part of my ensuing class was devoted to discussing what students had come up with during their havruta sessions.

Over time, I began to explore more critically the potential benefits of written guidelines for working in havruta. I asked myself what kinds of guidelines might help my students improve their efforts to engage with the texts. How, for example, could I use questions to direct them to re-associate the various post-talmudic commentaries they were studying with the corresponding original Talmud text?

As I observed my students' learning during these long beit midrash hours, I was fascinated by the diverse interpersonal dynamics that emerged in havruta text study. One of the challenges involved assigning pairs to learn together. Some students did not get along well. Typically, the more advanced Talmud students would agree only to study with someone on their proficiency level. My aim in fostering effective havruta dynamics required me to consider various potential matches, weighing how each individual's strengths and weaknesses might balance another's.

I also began to become more aware of what I would later identify as features of productive and unproductive learning interaction in havruta text study. Who were the students who only seldom took turns reading and explaining the text? Who were the pairs who signaled me rather quickly that they were "done studying the text?" I also became increasingly involved in my students' learning during the time allocated to havruta study. Rather than wait for them to come up to me with questions, I often challenged their explanations or asked them for more textual evidence to support their interpretations. In addition, I continued to seek ways to help students develop a stance toward the study of Jewish traditional texts that would not be confined to the accumulation of information, to a formal fulfillment of a religious duty, or to the pleasure provided by overcoming intellectually challenging texts. Most important in my view was helping students become learners who search for meaning, and who have learned to add their own personal voice to the sounds created by the study of traditional texts. I often wondered: what might that look like, especially in havruta text study?

In 1998, I joined the faculty of the Mandel Teacher Educators Institute (MTEI), which prepares senior Jewish educators to lead professional development for teachers in Jewish schools and institutions across North America.[20] There, I was fortunate to work with and learn from a number of educators and researchers including Gail Dorph, Sharon Feiman-Nemser, Deborah Ball, and Barry Holtz. Beyond their various fields of expertise, my colleagues brought to their education work a deep intellectual passion and a grounded, inquiry-based approach to teaching and learning. The preparation at MTEI is based on a concept of teacher development that emphasizes learning in and from practice.[21] I began to see parallels between the interpretive work that takes place in havruta text study and the collaborative interpretive work of "reading teaching" through the investigation of classroom videotapes and samples of student work.[22]

Perhaps due to their greater professional and life experience as well as the diversity of their backgrounds, my fellow faculty members pushed me to re-examine my understanding of text study and havruta learning. For example, through our many discussions, I came to realize the key role played by cultural environments in students' learning experiences. I had come from learning environments in Israel, where it was natural for students to challenge each other's interpretations during havruta learning. At MTEI, however, I was teaching havruta text study to a Jewish American audience, for whom challenging someone else's opinion was not as culturally accepted. Indeed, many came from backgrounds in which questioning another's statements was frowned upon. It was in this context that I developed a new educational identity.

---

[20] Barry W. Holtz, Gail Z. Dorph, and Ellen B. Goldring, "Educational Leaders as Teacher Educators: The Teacher Educator Institute — A Case from Jewish Education," *Peabody Journal of Education* 72.2 (1997): 147–66; Gail Z. Dorph, Barry W. Holtz, "Professional Development for Teachers: Why Doesn't the Model Change?" *Journal of Jewish Education* 66.2 (2000): 67–76; Elie Holzer, "Conceptions of the Study of Jewish Texts in Teachers' Professional Development," *Religious Education* 97.4 (2002): 377–403; Susan Stodolsky, Gail Z. Dorph, and Sharon Feiman-Nemser, "Professional Culture and Professional Development in Jewish Schools: Teachers' Perceptions and Experiences," *Journal of Jewish Education* 72.2 (2006): 91–108.

[21] Deborah L. Ball and David K. Cohen, "Developing Practice, Developing Practitioners, Toward a Practice-Based Theory of Professional Education," in *Teaching as The Learning Profession: Handbook of Policy and Practice*, ed. Linda Darling-Hammond and Gary Sykes (San Francisco: Jossey-Bass, 1999), 3–32.

[22] Elie Holzer, "Conceptions of the Study of Jewish Texts in Teachers' Professional Development.".

I no longer considered myself a teacher of Jewish texts who happened to use havruta text study. Rather I began to see myself as a teacher—and student—of havruta text study itself.

What for years had been the beginnings of ideas began to gain terminology and conceptualization as I asked myself the following questions: How am I conceptualizing the purposes, core characteristics, and outcomes of havruta text study? How can I help process havruta text study in such a way that does not lead directly to consensus and agreement? How can I craft havruta text study so that participants will capitalize and benefit from their potentially differing views? What tools should I develop to help them learn the dynamics of the learning conversation between two partners and a text? Slowly, the first contours of a genuine model of havruta text study began to emerge.

Last but not least, after years of text-centered Jewish learning and teaching, I felt a deep need to investigate and evaluate the fundamental philosophical aspects of text interpretation. I wondered if there could be any inherent existential and spiritual value in the very practice of text interpretation and text-based discussion. I was also looking for a broad philosophical basis from which I could make sense of these central activities in Jewish education—one that would transcend what I experienced at times as the narrow limitations of twentieth-century Jewish educational discourse, in which pedagogical discourse seemed confined by either beliefs in the divinely-inspired authorship of texts or the fundamental priority of the learner's critical thinking and autonomy. I became acquainted with intellectual traditions and theories in education and philosophy, especially philosophical hermeneutics, in which text interpretation and human dialogues are addressed not only as methods but also as epistemological theories, and as the basis for an existential philosophy. These bodies of theoretical knowledge have helped me to examine, revise, and conceptualize my understanding of "good" havruta study and the practices of text interpretation and interpersonal learning that go along with it. They have deeply influenced my pedagogical work, that is, my various efforts to help students become havruta text learners and to gradually uncover broader educational values that might be embedded in this learning format.

In 2003, I was invited by Sharon Feiman-Nemser, the director of the Mandel Center for Studies in Jewish Education at Brandeis University, along with Orit, who was then a doctoral student in

Jewish education, to extend and further develop this work in the context of DeLeT, a graduate program that prepares teachers for Jewish day schools. Over five summers, I had the privilege of designing and teaching in DeLeT's Beit Midrash for Teachers. Building on that experience, and following the end of my term as co-director and researcher in the Beit Midrash Research Project, I continued to develop practical tools as well as conceptual aspects of this work. I designed additional teaching tools and developed new learning experiences for students' and teachers' learning of havruta practices in a number of learning institutions and programs in Israel, the United States, and Europe. I learned to appreciate how, despite the cultural differences of these contexts, a proactive pedagogy for the learning of havruta text study holds great educational potential and elicits learners' strong intellectual and emotional interest.

In my research, I continued to draw on philosophical hermeneutics to expand my understanding of the potential for transformative learning that is provoked by the study of ancient and culturally diverse texts.[23] With my colleague Miriam Raider-Roth, I came to appreciate how key concepts of relational psychology combined with principles of philosophical hermeneutics can illuminate the relational aspects of havruta text study. We articulated several transformative aspects of this work in empirical research that highlighted how havruta text study helped participants (all classroom teachers) revise their beliefs about the "autonomous learner," fostered trust and nurtured the learning relationship with their havruta partners, and impacted their own classroom teaching practices.[24]

---

[23]   Elie Holzer, "Allowing the Text to Do Its Pedagogical Work: Connecting Moral Education and Interpretive Activity," *Journal of Moral Education* 36.4 (2007): 497–514; Elie Holzer, "Educational Aspects of Hermeneutical Activity in Text Study," in *Modes of Educational Translation: Studies in Jewish Education,* ed. Jonathan Cohen and Elie Holzer (Jerusalem: Magnes Press, 2009), 205–40; Elie Holzer, "Choosing to Put Ourselves 'at Risk' in the Face of Ancient Texts: Ethical Education through the Hermeneutical Encounter," in *International Studies in Hermeneutics and Phenomenology,* ed. Andre Wiercinski (Berlin: LIT Verlag, 2013).

[24]   Miriam Raider-Roth and Elie Holzer, "Learning to be Present: How Hevruta Learning Can Activate Teachers' Relationships to Self, Other and Text," *The Journal of Jewish Education* 75.3 (2009): 216–39.

Orit's Journey

I grew up in a home imbued with Jewish texts. Picking up a Jewish book or source and learning it, both on my own and with others (and it was never an either/or) was a natural part of my daily life. From my very young years, I understood that these texts were something of value and that they were mine to explore, learn, struggle with, and love. Both at home and in school, I had opportunities to gain the knowledge and skills to comfortably access texts. My grandmother, in whose home I spent a great deal of my childhood, instilled in me a sense that part of the process of making sense of Jewish texts was to discuss them with others, and in particular to discuss different perspectives on the text in question. Most significantly, she did this by modeling this approach continually, engaging everyone in ongoing discussions about texts. She often took different positions in order to explore all possible facets of a particular text. In her eyes, reading the text was simply the very beginning of a process of uncovering its meaning, a process that could go on for a lifetime.

While none of us at that time were familiar with ideas such as "interpretive discussion," "active reading," "creating a text world," "adopting multiple perspectives," "gap-filling," or "accountable talk," this is exactly what we did. My grandmother also shared stories of her rabbinic family engaging with texts for the purpose of determining the right course of action for the many people who came to them with a *shaylah* (a question of religious practice). As she told these stories, it was clear that rabbis determined halakhah not only based on their study of sources, but also on conversations with the particular people asking the questions. The meaning of the text was determined through the conversation and the particulars of each case.

In these early years, my learning was "whole"[25] in the sense that it involved all of me—intellectually, socially, emotionally, and spiritually—and involved me with real and rich materials that mattered in my life. For me, Judaism, Jewish texts, and community were inseparable. The texts took on meaning in conversation and lived experience with others. This experience resonated with the idea of sociocultural theories of learning that "[l]earning and developing occur as people participate in the sociocultural activities of their community,

---

[25]   David Perkins, *Making Learning Whole* (San Francisco: Jossey Bass, 2009).

transforming their understanding, roles, and responsibilities as they participate."[26] It is through participation in the central activities of a given community that people learn and develop roles for themselves within those communities. When I later encountered this particular idea, which so beautifully captures my own early learning experience, the question became for me: How do educators create learning environments that foster this kind of rich and real participation and honor and involve the whole person?

In day school, I was introduced to both Talmud study and havruta learning. I was lucky enough to have an incredibly skilled teacher who worked with us on our technical and conceptual skills, and found the right balance between supporting us enough so that we did not feel lost and giving us the space to develop our own capacities and ideas. We were not instructed in how to do havruta or even explicitly introduced to strategies for studying the talmudic page, but our teacher modeled for us in our full-class discussions a give-and-take that we carried over to our havruta time, as we thought out loud and puzzled through the text with a peer.

As the school years went on and I found myself having havrutot with many more people, I found quite naturally that some of my havrutot were far better than others. There were those that really felt like a good workout, in which I came out on the other end with far more insight than I had started with, and there were those that did not seem to go anywhere. This continued to be the case during the time I spent learning in Israel, at Bravenders, Matan, and the Hartman Institute, and through my own independent havruta learning. I had a sense that this might be related to the particular expertise we each — that is, my partner and I—brought to the table and our capacities to not only sift through the details of the text but also link these details to larger questions and issues, but I did not have a language for explaining this further or figuring out how to use my good havruta experiences to improve the others.

For a decade I worked as a community organizer, helping people come together to identify their common concerns and work

---

26   Barbara Rogoff, Eugene Matusov, and Cynthia White, "Models of Teaching and Learning: Participation in a Community of Learners," in *The Handbook of Education and Human Development*, ed. David R. Olson and Nancy Torrance (Cambridge, MA: Blackwell, 1996), 390.

collectively to address them. The approach to community organizing that I took sought to develop "relational culture" through intentionally creating space for community members to connect and, together, discover new ways to approach the world. Practically, this made people more accountable to and for each other and helped them effectively work together. But bit by bit, I also came to see the spiritual impact of this work.

After organizing low-income neighborhoods, I began to organize with synagogues in the Greater Boston area, developing Jewish leaders who could bring their communities along with them as they partnered with other communities to address pressing social problems. As community members increasingly asked how their work was "Jewish," we introduced havruta text learning to their meetings as a way to help create a learning community, giving people more space to explore and develop different ideas that they could share with each other and learn from. While I surely should not have been, I was surprised by the extent to which people responded to the texts, drawing new energy and insight not only from the texts, but from each other as they grappled together with the text in front of them.

Participants reported seeing things anew, gaining new insight and inspiration (the delight of hearing alternative ideas and puzzling through significant questions) and a growing sense of value and respect for the text and what was to be gleaned from it through close study with others. Not just people's work, but their community and their own "selves" began to transform when they learned together, when they began to make meaning. Sharon Parks writes, "William Perry… often remarked that the purpose of an organism is to organize, and what human beings organize is meaning. Meaning making is the activity of composing a sense of the connections among things: a sense of pattern, order, form, and significance."[27]

These learnings were reinforced by the Jewish teaching I did during my organizing years. I taught in formal and informal settings, my students both adults and teens, beginners and more advanced. Regardless of the setting, one theme that often emerged was that people sought out Jewish education because they felt disengaged both

---

[27]   Sharon Daloz Parks, *Big Questions, Worthy Dreams: Mentoring Young Adults in Their Search for Meaning, Purpose, and Faith* (San Francisco: Jossey-Bass, 2000), 19.

from Jewish content and the Jewish people—or, if they were not, they wanted to make sure their children would not be. Beyond conveying content, my teaching had to help foster real engagement with both Jewish texts and the Jewish people. I tried to help students create a learning community, so that they would be comfortable expressing their ideas and asking their questions, and feel connected to the larger Jewish community and to the text itself, seeing it as something with real meaning and integrity rather than simply a useful jumping off point for talking about the real issues. None of this was easy, and I did a better job in some cases than others. Havruta was one of many strategies I used. It was clear that in some groups, using havruta would not work and actually made students feel quite uncomfortable. In other groups, usually those that had more text experience or were together for longer periods of time, havruta was a wonderful tool for engaging with new ideas and people and keeping the text central.

I also came to see that, regardless of the setting, I needed to provide more scaffolding to all of my students when I sent them to study in havruta. With more experienced students, it was initially easier for me to make assumptions about what they could and could not do and simply teach them by mimicking the methods by which I had been taught. With less experienced students, it was clear from the beginning that they would need something more. They would frequently stop to ask more questions and I could not assume that they had a common knowledge base or comfort with encountering texts, alone or in pairs. As I provided scaffolding for the less experienced students, it became clear that it could help the more experienced students as well.

I considered different forms of scaffolding and asked: What kinds of study guides and questions allow students to delve deeper into the text, and what study guides and questions send them off track or constrain them so much that they lose interest? What kind of instructions do I need to provide before they go off to study? How can I best facilitate discussions that follow their havruta work? I wondered about all of these things and more, experimenting with different approaches, crafting and recrafting questions both for havruta learning and for larger group discussion.

With many questions, I ultimately returned to graduate school to delve into them. In the hopes of beginning to untangle the transformative potential of studying religious texts with others, as well as how to constructively support this kind of learning and engagement, I began studying psychologist Robert Kegan's work about adult development. Kegan frames one of the purposes of education as leading us out (based on the Latin root *educere, to lead out*) of "one construction... of mind in favor of a larger one."[28] This conception frames the educational endeavor as something intentional, active, potentially transformative and enabling of new ways of thinking, seeing, and being. His particular understanding of adult development helps us understand some of the possibilities of the transformative potential of learning and the need for creating "holding environments," safe spaces that allow and constructively hold the tension involved in the growth process.[29] I began to think about the different kinds of holding environments that we as educators construct and what kind of holding environment allows for meaningful engagement and learning in havruta and larger groups, learning that is challenging yet supported. It was further into my research on havruta that I also began to think of the havruta unit itself as a kind of holding environment, a space to allow students to draw on their strengths and also push them beyond their perceived limits and cultivate certain attitudes and skills.

In graduate school, I had the privilege of studying with Eleanor Duckworth and being exposed to her understanding of Piaget's critical interview approach, transformed in Duckworth's hands into an approach called critical exploration, in which teachers select materials to engage students directly with subject matter and closely follow their thinking, sometimes asking probing questions along the way, in order to help the teacher decide how to proceed with the lesson. Duckworth's approach emphasized, among other things, the importance of closely following (and understanding) learning in order to inform teaching, the importance of creating space for student exploration of materials, and the role that a simple question asked by a teacher at the right moment can play in extending a student's thinking and learning. These ideas, coupled with my engagement with Vigotsky's work on the socially and culturally situated nature of learning, led me to engage in two pilot research projects on havruta. I chose havruta as a site for research because I thought havruta offered an unusual research opportunity to hear students' meaning-making process in

---

28   Robert Kegan, *In Over Our Heads, the Mental Demands of Modern Life* (Cambridge, MA: Harvard University Press, 1994), 164.

29   Ibid.; Robert Kegan, *The Evolving Self, Problem and Process in Human Development* (Cambridge, MA: Harvard University Press, 1982).

real time (not because I necessarily thought it was a be-all and end-all learning strategy).

In the first study, I videotaped one pair learning in havruta and used a framework called "skill theory" to try to identify some of the benefits of this learning context. In my second study, I audiotaped a pair over the course of multiple sessions and specifically focused on understanding the role of the teacher in designing the study tasks and asking questions, as well as how the material was physically displayed and shared and its impact on student learning.

Immersing myself in research on group learning, classroom discourse, literature, and literary theory, I closely studied a third pair as part of my work in the Beit Midrash Research Project. Influenced by my doctoral mentor Sharon Feiman-Nemser's work on teaching and co-planning, and Magdalene Lampert's work on the complexities of teaching and learning, I began to conceptualize what havruta learners were doing, specifically looking at the verbal moves they made in relation to the text and each other, and their modes of discussion. Influenced by sociocultural theories of knowledge and Lave and Wenger's idea of "learning as participation in the social world,"[30] I examined the important intersection between a havruta's social and intellectual work and how this impacted their study and relationships with each other and the text. I began to conceptualize havruta as a "Jewish interpretive social learning practice" with different modes of discourse.[31]

In a much larger subsequent study, which developed into my doctoral dissertation,[32] I analyzed more havrutot across learning sessions to analyze their meaning-making process and conceptualized core practices of havruta learning, three pairs in dynamic tension with one another: listening and articulating; wondering and focusing; and supporting and challenging. Using these practices as an analytic

---

[30]   Jean Lave and Etienne Wenger, *Situated Learning: Legitimate Peripheral Participation* (New York: Cambridge University Press, 1991), 43.

[31]   Orit Kent, "Interactive Text Study: A Case of *Hevruta* Learning," *Journal of Jewish Education* 72.3 (2006): 205–33.

[32]   Orit Kent, *Interactive Text Study and the Co-Construction of Meaning: Havruta in the Delet Beit Midrash* (Doctoral dissertation, Brandeis University, 2008). For a discussion of the six havruta practices, see also Orit Kent, "A Theory of Havruta Learning," *Journal of Jewish Education* 76.3 (2010): 215–45.

lens I examined different cases to see when and how havruta learning could be generative or go awry.

In my work in the Beit Midrash Research Project since 2007, I have continued to investigate the conditions and tools that support rich and meaningful text-based learning with others. In my teaching and writing,[33] I have explored what it means to teach core havruta practices to teachers to use in their teaching, and to students to use both in their havruta work and full classroom discussions. The work of Sarah Michaels and her colleagues on "accountable talk,"[34] as well as Sophie Haroutunian-Gordon's work on "interpretive discussion,"[35] has been influential in helping me pay attention to the specific kinds of talk that supports the generative use of these practices. I have been particularly interested in understanding how havruta practices are enacted by learners at different ages, ranging from young elementary school students to adults, and the ways in which their use can impact learners' relationships with each other, with Jewish texts, and with their larger Jewish community. More recently, my colleague Allison Cook and I have focused on the "live action" of teaching and learning in a variety of educational settings, investigating how teachers and learners usefully draw on frameworks and tools to support meaning-ful text-based conversations, and how "havruta-inspired pedagogy" can serve as a lever for deepening Jewish teaching and learning more broadly.[36]

---

[33]   For example, Orit Kent, "Teaching Havruta in Context," paper presented at the Network for Research in Jewish Education Annual Conference (New York, 2009) and Orit Kent and Allison Cook, "Images of the Possible in a Supplementary School: Text Study, Collaborative Learning and Meaning Making," paper presented at the Network for Research in Jewish Education Annual Conference (Toronto, 2011).

[34]   See, for example, Sarah Michaels, Catherine O'Connor, Megan Williams Hall, with Lauren Resnick, *Accountable Talk: Classroom Conversation that Works* (Pittsburgh: University of Pittsburgh, 2002), CD-ROM set.

[35]   See, for example, Sophie Haroutunian-Gordon, *Turning the Soul: Teaching through Conversations in the High School* (Chicago: University of Chicago Press, 1991).

[36]   Orit Kent and Allison Cook, "Havruta Inspired Pedagogy: Fostering an Ecology of Learning for Closely Studying Texts with Others," *Journal of Jewish Education* 78.3 (2012): 227–53; Allison Cook and Orit Kent, "Doing

In all of these contexts, I have been interested in exploring what learning texts with others requires of participants, the impact of different kinds of scaffolding, and the potential power of fostering rich engagement with different texts, ideas, and people as part of any Jewish learning process.

A Note About the Authors and Their Work

For a number of years, we worked together as the designers and teachers of the DeLeT Beit Midrash and as researchers on the Beit Midrash Research Project. We brought to this partnership a common love for deep Jewish learning, a desire to keep growing as teachers, and a belief in the great potential of havruta text study, along with our differing areas of emphasis and expertise. Elie brought his rich experience with Jewish learning and teaching, and a grounding in traditional and academic Jewish studies as well as in philosophical hermeneutics; this book conceptualizes havruta text study and its design through the lens of central principles from that philosophical tradition. Orit brought her own extensive experience in Jewish learning and teaching, as well as expertise in theories of learning, especially sociocultural theories of knowledge; her own scholarship conceptualizes text study in havruta and the design of ways to teach core skills and attitudes chiefly through the lens of learning theories.

The Beit Midrash Research Project

a. The Setting

The Beit Midrash for Teachers is an integral part of the DeLeT (Day School Leadership through Teaching) program at Brandeis University. At the time of our involvement, DeLeT was a 13-month, post-BA fellowship program designed to prepare teachers for elementary grades in Jewish day schools. It involved two summers of professional and

---

the Work: Interpretive Experience as the Fulcrum of Tanakh Education," *Hayidion* (Summer 2012): 58–60.

academic study and a mentored internship in a local day school during the intervening school year.

From 2003 through 2007, the beit midrash was a key component of DeLeT's summer curriculum, meeting twice a week over the course of five weeks. Meetings took place in a room set up for that purpose, allowing students to face each other during havruta study and sit in a circle when the entire class was addressed. The beit midrash was attended by both the new cohort of teacher candidates as well as by those nearing the completion of the program. Over the years, the numbers of participants ranged between sixteen and twenty. A standard beit midrash session lasted for three hours and consisted of three parts: a mini-lesson conducted by the instructors, a time slot for havruta text study, and a joint activity, drawing on what they had studied in havruta pairs.

A central characteristic of this setting was that many participants had limited previous havruta text study experience. We were faced with the challenge of developing a course of learning that would teach and induct participants into the practices of havruta text study and in becoming active and self-conscious learning members in a beit midrash environment.[37] We were very conscious of the fact that we were transplanting havruta text study from its traditional context (the yeshiva) and adapting it to an academic, professional setting that already offered many competing learning formats. Acknowledging that havruta learning entails activities that involve effort and skills (which require time to be learned), and that most of these student teachers had limited previous experience with havruta text study, if any, we asked ourselves: why engage student teachers in this type of learning activity? Are we promoting havruta learning for utilitarian values only (e. g., to gain a better understanding of a text) or also for some vocational value (e. g., it has the potential to cultivate specific humanistic qualities in future teachers)? We also took it upon ourselves to articulate the vision and practices of havruta text study that we wanted to teach.

---

[37]   This expectation of self-awareness (a form of meta-cognition) is a way to help students become independent, self-motivated learners. Together with Scheffler, we also believe it is a form of respect we owe them: "Teaching requires us to reveal our reasons to the student and, by so doing, to submit them to his evaluation and criticism," Israel Scheffler, *The Language of Education* (Springfield, IL: Charles C. Thomas, 1960), 57.

We experimented with and refined various teaching tools designed to help students learn core havruta text study practices.

We sought to cultivate in our beit midrash a learning environment conducive to havruta text study, paying attention to the physical setup of the room and to our own location as learners and teachers in the space. We especially wanted to ensure that the privacy of havruta pairs was respected, while at the same time signaling our availability to students should they have questions.

The Beit Midrash for Teachers had three goals. First, we sought to introduce students to ideas about teaching and learning reflected in classical Jewish texts that would relate to their future work as teachers in Jewish day schools. The texts we studied dealt with topics like teacher-student relationships and the value of learning with a partner.

Second, we wanted to have students explicitly explore "sound" havruta text study practices in the work of textual interpretation and the interpersonal work between havruta partners. We presented students with questions such as: "What do I bring as a reader and what does the text bring?" These questions helped them realize that the text has something to say and cannot merely serve as a projection of oneself.[38] Handouts invited questions about the characters' motivations as well as the nature of meaning in general. Integral to such textual interpretation is the interpersonal work of havruta text study, to which we also drew our students' direct attention, with questions like: How does one partner support or challenge the other's interpretation, and for what purpose would one do so?

Third, we wanted to create in the BMT a community of learners. We believe that havruta text study provides a powerful and compelling opportunity for people to experience and intentionally cultivate themselves as learners of texts, both in relationships with others, and with themselves. This is particularly relevant for teachers, who gain sensitivity to their students as learners by experiencing themselves as learners. In addition, the model of havruta text study that we developed has the potential to help prospective teachers cultivate dispositions vital to the kind of teaching promoted by the DeLeT program, dispositions such as intellectual openness, seeking evidence

---

38   Indeed, *eisegesis* (the [mis]interpretation of a text by introducing one's own presuppositions, biases, and agendas) is a phenomenon that is well known among scholars and teachers of texts, biblical texts in particular.

to support others' ideas and awareness of one's own preconceptions.[39] To become responsible for their own learning, to gain a sense of ownership of the interpretation of Jewish texts, and to experience collegial discussion about teaching and learning, are, in our view, all important elements of professional development for future Jewish teachers—and all products of quality havruta text study.[40]

Finally, while this was not an explicit or primary goal, at various times we imagined these prospective teachers in their future classrooms, as promoters and facilitators of havruta text study. While we did not presume to be training or otherwise preparing them to do so at a high level of practice, from the perspective of our joint belief in the power of well-crafted havruta learning experiences, we hoped that the BMT provided a positive and reflective initial experience that might serve as a foundation for future professional development and experimentation.

b. Research Context and Framework

With the creative, supportive, and inspirational leadership of Sharon Feiman-Nemser, the director of the Mandel Center, and her ongoing help and guidance, we turned our work in the BMT into the Beit Midrash Research Project. This research project offered a unique opportunity to simultaneously engage in the work of designing and teaching a beit midrash for teachers and study our practice and our students' learning.

---

[39]   Elie Holzer, "Ethical Dispositions in Text Study," *Journal of Moral Education* 36.1 (2007): 37–49.

[40]   For discussions on the impact of collaborative learning for the professional development of teachers see Brian Lord, "Teachers' Professional Development: Critical Colleagueship and the Role of Professional Communities," in *The Future of Education Perspectives on National Standards in America*, ed. Nina Cobb (New York: College Entrance Examination Board, 1994), 175–204. For the importance of professional communities on teaching, see Pamela Grossman et al., "Teaching Practice: A Cross-Professional Perspective," *Teachers College Record* 111.9 (2009): 2055–2100; Judith W. Little, "The Persistence of Privacy: Autonomy and Initiative in Teachers' Professional Relations," *Teachers College Record* 91.4 (1990): 509–36.

Our dual role as reflective teachers and teacher-researchers underlined the need to systematically theorize and document our work, starting with the formulation of a research agenda, which combined conceptual and empirical study. The questions that formed the basis of our initial research were:

1. How do we conceptualize good havruta text study and why?
   * What practices does good text interpretation entail?
   * What practices do good interpersonal learning relationships entail?
2. What disciplinary or theoretical perspectives help us conceptualize the intellectual and educational work in havruta text study?
3. What methods and learning experiences can be used to teach the skills and dispositions that are appropriate for this kind of havruta text study?

Our research stance and methodology draws on traditions of teacher research.[41] We experimented with a recursive cycle of four activities: conceptualizing the work ("what is good havruta text study?"); developing learning tasks and tools for teaching havruta text study; implementing our plans and tools in the BMT and subsequently revising and refining them; and finally, documenting our planning and teaching and our students' learning.

As we created instructional materials, designed learning experiences and collected data, we immersed ourselves in theoretical literature, ranging from philosophical hermeneutics, literary theory, and sociocultural theories of learning, as well as relevant Jewish sources, in an effort to make sense of our specific aims and practices. It was through this process, in which teaching practices and theoretical reflections continually informed one another, that we developed and refined our approach to teaching havruta text study.

---

[41] Donald Freeman, *Doing Teacher Research: From Inquiry to Understanding*, (Portsmouth, NH: Heinle & Heinle, 1998); Ruth Shagoury Hubbard and Brenda Miller Power, *Living the Questions: A Guide for Teacher-Researchers* (Portland, ME: Stenhouse Publishers, 1999); Marilyn Cochran-Smith and Susan L. Lytle, *Inquiry as Stance: Practitioner Research for the Next Generation* (New York: Teachers College Press, 2009).

c. Data Sources

Due to the cyclical nature of this research method, we cannot totally separate data collection and data analysis. The development of our thinking and our teaching has been an ongoing process of practice, interpretation, and revision providing multiple opportunities for adaptations, and at times returning back to earlier versions of our design.

We collected data of various kinds:

a. Instructional materials that we designed—e. g., graphic representations of concepts, written guidelines for havruta text study, the texts themselves, worksheets for specific learning tasks, the syllabus, and questions for reflection and evaluation.

b. Videotapes, audiotapes and transcripts of havruta pairs and BMT classes. Over the course of four summers, we videotaped our teaching sessions as well as individual havruta pairs. This included recordings of the mini-lessons which introduced each session, with special attention to our teaching narratives, our use of graphical representations, and students' comments.

c. Notes and memos. Reflective notes that included questions, thoughts and dilemmas that emerged in the planning stages of the Beit Midrash and in the wake of specific lessons; integrative notes and short memos in which, for example, we connected parts of our design and theoretical concepts in new ways; and notes that featured the experiential quality of specific sessions: e. g., surprises, impressions, overall feelings about what went well and what did not, and what participants might have said or done differently.

d. Field notes taken by colleagues. These notes recorded both our (the teacher educators') discourse and teaching practices, and the discourse and learning practices of the students.

e. Samples of students' work and evaluation. These included precourse assessment questionnaires meant to provide us with a baseline idea of students' knowledge, beliefs and expectations; midterm and final learning assignments; and written reflections and evaluations provided at the end of particular sessions as well as at the end of the course.

This book focuses on designs for the teaching of havruta text study, the thinking behind our practice and students' reflective comments regarding specific learning tasks. The teaching sessions described here draw examples from multiple summers, focusing on particular examples that we have found most compelling and illustrative of the above. All this practical work is explored through the lens of philosophical hermeneutics, which provides a critical foundation and justification for the work.

Sometimes we draw examples from our work in other settings, in particular, the Mandel Teacher Educators Institute (MTEI) and the Summer Teacher Institute organized by the Center for Studies in Jewish Education and Culture at the University of Cincinnati. At these sites, we continued to refine our theories and pedagogies, often working closely with colleagues such as Gail Dorph, Director of MTEI and Miriam Raider-Roth, director of the Center at the University of Cincinnati center.[42] Unless stated otherwise, however, the description of the sessions, as well as the quotes from our own teaching and from our students, originate in the data collected in the Beit Midrash Research Project. All other data sources are footnoted accordingly.

d. Sources of Inspiration

While this book is the first to offer a comprehensive conceptualization of the design and teaching of havruta text study through the lens of philosophical hermeneutics,[43] it stands in relation to other studies of collaborative learning, dialogical approaches to textual interpretation, and interpretive discussions. For example, in his books *Textual Power* and *Protocols of Reading*, Robert Scholes walks the reader

---

[42]   An additional site is Melamdim, a two-year post-bachelor teacher education program co-jointly based at the Hartman Institute in Jerusalem and Tel Aviv University, which prepares its participants to teach Judaic studies in US community day schools.

[43]   For an overview on the research that has been conducted on havruta learning, see Elie Holzer and Orit Kent, "Havruta Learning: 'What Do We Know and What Can We Hope to Learn?'" in *International Handbook on Jewish Education*, ed. Helena Miller, Lisa D. Grant, and Alex Pomson (New York: Springer, 2011), 407–18.

through his practice as a teacher of texts, focusing mainly on content and the importance of criticism in textual study.[44] In his book *The Practice of Reading*, Denis Donoghue discusses the nature and importance of literary interpretation, arguing that we must read texts closely and imaginatively, rather then theorizing about them.[45] He then demonstrates what this type of close and informed reading entails. Notwithstanding the special reading dynamic that happens in havruta learning, our work embraces a similar approach to text interpretation.

One major source of inspiration for our research is the work of philosopher of education Sophie Haroutunian-Gordon, who directs the teacher education program at Northwestern University. In *Turning the Soul*, Haroutunian-Gordon presents examples of interpretive discussions on literary texts that she documented in high school English classrooms. In *Learning to Teach through Discussion*, she analyzes how two fourth-grade teachers learn to lead interpretive discussions with special attention to the role played by questions.[46] Combining conceptual analysis with concrete descriptions of teaching strategies, Haroutunian-Gordon's work has, like ours, been influenced by the work of Hans-Georg Gadamer, as well as by her practical experience in teacher education and classroom teaching, thus providing us with a model to bring these different parts of our work into a fruitful interaction.

In this book, we hope to bring some of the fruits of our research to the larger community of educators and researchers interested in the educational potential of collaborative learning, text study in general, and/or the traditional practice of havruta text study in particular. We offer a model of havruta text study grounded in philosophical, literary, and learning theories, and formulated as a set of practices to be learned. We also offer tools and examples illustrating how teachers might design havruta learning environments, and in what contexts

---

44   Robert Scholes, *Textual Power: Literary Theory and the Teaching of English* (New Haven: Yale University Press, 1986); Robert Scholes, *Protocols of Reading* (New Haven: Yale University Press, 1991).

45   Denis Donoghue, *The Practice of Reading* (New Haven: Yale University Press, 1998).

46   Sophie Haroutunian-Gordon, *Turning the Soul*; Sophie Haroutunian-Gordon, *Learning to Teach Through Discussion: The Art of Turning the Soul* (New Haven: Yale University Press, 2009).

such practices can be taught and learned in the classroom. Finally, we discuss the educational value we perceive to be inherent in havruta text study when redesigned in contemporary settings according to this model.

Chapter Two explores the conceptual foundations for our approach to havruta text study, drawing on discussions in philosophical hermeneutics about the meaning of texts, the dialogical nature of understanding and learning, and the role of pre-knowledge in learning. We introduce two frameworks that organize our havruta research. The first framework distinguishes two phases of havruta text study: a first phase in which havruta partners aim to co-construct compelling textual interpretations through *interpretive* practices, and a second phase in which they engage in dialogue with the ideas presented by the text through *dialogical* practices. The second conceptual framework describes havruta text study as an interaction among a text and two havruta partners made up of three reciprocal relationships: between learner and text, between both learners, and between the learner and himself. We discuss the interpretive practices of havruta text study implied by these interactions in Chapter Two, and dialogical practices in Chapter Eight.

Moving from a conventional classroom environment to havruta text study requires learners to adapt to significant changes: learning in a physical setup that is different from the typical classroom, partnering with a learning colleague, and embracing new obligations for their own and their partner's learning. Chapter Three discusses how we deal with these changes by designing special lessons for the learning of havruta practices, setting up a supportive physical space, arranging havruta pairs, and raising learners' awareness of themselves and their havruta partner as learners.

The four chapters that follow focus on interpretive practices central to the first stage of havruta text study: questioning the text with open questions (Chapter Four); active listening for interpretation (Chapter Five); challenging and supporting textual interpretations (Chapter Six); and evaluating and discriminating between stronger and weaker interpretations (Chapter Seven). In each of these chapters, we present specific pedagogical practices and discuss their role in the development of textual interpretations, and some challenges they may pose to the havruta learner. We also present sample lessons designed to help students experiment with each practice, including samples of students' work and reflections on their learning.

Chapter Eight deals with the second stage of havruta text study. It includes a discussion of the type of dialogue that is called for between learner, text, and havruta partner, and a number of written learning tasks (such as adopting the text's perspective), that help enact this dialogue. Chapter Nine concludes with a philosophical evaluation of the transformative educational potential of the practices of havruta text study, cultivating such fundamental human capacities as intellectual openness, ethical sensitivity, critical thinking skills, self-awareness, and a responsibility for another's learning. These qualities are especially relevant in teaching and teacher development, but also reflect values inherent in humanist and Jewish learning traditions.

Each book project poses its own challenges to its author(s), especially in successfully framing the ways they would like to be understood. At a time when "learning in havruta" has become popular in a variety of contexts, we do not want readers to read into this volume as an automatic pedagogic preference for studying in pairs, for the use of havruta text study to the exclusion of other forms of teaching and learning, or for our particular approach as the only possible or best model of havruta text study. Like all teachers, we take a particular approach to teaching, and we take a particular approach to havruta text study specifically; this book is a presentation of that approach.[47]

---

[47] It is important to note here that, to date, most empirical studies on havruta text study have reflected more limited expectations of havruta learners or of their teachers, in comparison with the more comprehensive view of compelling, successful havruta text study articulated in this work. See for example: Shoshana Blum Kolka, Menahem Blondeim, and Gonen Hacohen, "Traditions of Disagreements: From Argumentative Conversations about Talmud Texts to Political Discourse in the Media," in *Coverage as Story: Perspectives on Discourse in Israeli Media. In honor of Itzhak Roeh*, ed. Motti Neiger, Menachem Blondeim, and Tamar Libes (Jerusalem: Magnes Press, 2008), 245–74; Dina Brawer, *Havruta and Talmud Study: Peer Interaction in Critical Thinking* (London: University of London, 2002); Steven M. Brown and Mitchel Malkus, "Havruta as a Form of Cooperative Learning," *Journal of Jewish Education* 73.3 (2007): 209–26; Baruch B. Schwarz, "Students' Havruta Learning in Lithuanian Yeshivot: The Case of Recurrent Learning," in *Education and Religion: Between Tradition and Innovation*, ed. Immanuel Etkes, Tamar Elor, and Baruch Schwartz (Jerusalem: Magnes Press, 2001), 279–308; Susan Tedmon, *Collaborative Acts of Literacy in Traditional Jewish Community* (Doctoral dissertation, University of Pennsylvania, 1991); Yair Gad et al., *Study of Learning Communities and Batei Midrash*, http://avichai. org/wp-content/uploads/2011/01/learning-summ-eng_0.pdf (2006); Aliza

We do not attempt to prove that havruta text study "works,"[48] to analyze it as it is enacted today in various settings, or to demonstrate the
long-term impact of our own teaching of havruta text study.

Instead, we invite the reader to actively and critically partake
in our elucidation of the kind of work that is involved in theorizing,
conceptualizing, designing, and enacting havruta text study, and of
the kinds of learning that it can make possible. Our main goals are
threefold. First and foremost, we want to raise practitioners' (that is,
teachers'/ teacher educators') consciousness about the need to conceptualize a comprehensive model of "havruta text study"—that is,
what it means generally and what we expect students to learn and do
when they are involved in it. Any such comprehensive model will,
in our view, ground the act of textual meaning-making in theories of
interpretation and provide a conceptual framework to understand the
various phases or layers of the learning that takes place in havruta text
study.

Second, our aim here is to demonstrate the need to curricularize
the teaching of havruta text study, articulating the specific practices
that students are to enact in the service of the particular model of
havruta text study, providing ways to help students learn those practices, and identifying what might be prevailing beliefs about and
approaches to text interpretation among students that could support
or conflict with that model.

Finally, we hope to convey here how our particular vision of
havruta text study reflects the transformative pedagogic potential of
dialogic exchange, and understands havruta learning not merely as
a means toward any given curricular ends, but as a "site" for the cultivation of ethical dispositions.

Segal, *Doing Talmud: An Ethnographic Study in a Religious High School in Israel*
(Doctoral dissertation, Jerusalem: The Hebrew University, 2011).

[48]   Teomim-Ben Menachem, *Women Study: Characterizing Conversation and
Learning in Women's Havrutot.* Chapter one shows that havruta learners
report on positive as well as negative outcomes of the havruta learning
format.

For the desire to read, like all the other desires which
distract our unhappy souls, is capable of analysis.
Virginia Woolf, "Sir Thomas Browne"

CHAPTER TWO:
THEORETICAL FOUNDATIONS

Philosophical hermeneutics and havruta text study

In his commentary on *Das Kapital*, Louis Althusser asks, "What is it to
read?" This may appear to be a simple question, but Althusser warns
us: "As there is no such thing as an innocent reading, we must say
what reading we are guilty of."[1] In the spirit of Althusser, the starting
point of our research is the awareness that reading cannot be confined
to a generic technique, given that any view of text interpretation is the
result of epistemological and cultural assumptions. Thus, neither text
study generally nor havruta text study specifically can be discussed
in absolute, objective terms. Indeed, people's attitudes toward working with texts implicitly reflect their deepest and most personal beliefs
about the nature of written language, interpretation and learning.

Years of observing, listening to, and talking with learners have
made us aware of a range of implicit beliefs they bring to what is called
"text study." Indeed, how a student engages with a text is informed
by a range of assumptions that are rarely articulated or discussed.
For example, some students hold an objectivist view of interpretation—that is, that a text holds only one true interpretation (identified
either with the author's intention or the understanding of the historical audience for whom the text was written), and it is their task, as
a reader, to retrieve it. Alternatively, some students take a radical relativist approach toward textual interpretation. These students maintain
that interpretation can be reduced to the values and beliefs that each
reader brings to the text. They reason that since people are different,
so are their interpretations: thus the phenomenon of multiple interpretations. These students often assume that all interpretations are

---

[1]   Louis Althusser and Étienne Balibar, *Reading Capital* (London: NLB, 1970).

equally valid, thus preventing any comparative or qualitative evaluation of the interpretations. We have also observed students relating to text study as something that resembles bibliotherapy, using the text as a starting point to talk about themselves, their beliefs, or their concerns. For these students, the task of text study is to find the anchor in the text that will enable that kind of talk.

While mostly unarticulated, these assumptions and beliefs, as well as others, determine to a great extent what people do and say in text study. They convey by their attitudes and behaviors their notions of what is involved in text study, the nature of "meaning" in a text, and even the very purpose of text study. Over the years of our work, we have come to conceptualize havruta text study primarily through the lens of philosophical hermeneutics.[2] While originating in an attempt to theorize the interpretation of texts, philosophical hermeneutics opens a broader scope, offering an epistemology grounded in an interpretive and dialogical view of both understanding and the self. Philosophical hermeneutics also raises literary questions regarding how vested interests of class, gender, or prior belief may influence how we read. It involves questions about types of texts and processes of reading:

---

[2]   Our work is based on an eclectic synthesis of key concepts of philosophical hermeneutics, especially those found in the works of Hans-Georg Gadamer and Paul Ricoeur. However, we do not pretend that our work fully reflects Gadamerian and/or Ricoeurian approaches. More recent literary and philosophical theories on the nature of reading and textual interpretation have enriched our understanding of the dynamics of text interpretation and have made our choices clearer (Mario J. Valdes, ed., *A Ricoeur Reader: Reflection and Imagination* [Toronto: University of Toronto Press, 1991]; Terry Eagleton, *After Theory* [New York: Basic Books, 2003]). Gadamer and Ricoeur address how interpretation is possible after the metaphysical shift away from the author and after the epistemological shift away from objectivity. For more on the connections between philosophical hermeneutics and literary theory, see Joel Weinsheimer, *Philosophical Hermeneutics and Literary Theory* (New Haven: Yale University Press, 1991); Mario J. Valdes, Phenomenological Hermeneutics and the Study of Literature (Toronto: University of Toronto Press, 1987); Denis Donoghue, *The Practice of Reading*. Over the last decades, the field of Jewish education has seen a rise in scholarship building on some of these theories: Jon A. Levisohn, "Openness and Commitment: Hans-Georg Gadamer and the Teaching of Jewish Texts," *Journal of Jewish Education* 67.1–2 (2001): 20–35; Deborah Kerdeman, "Some Thoughts about Hermeneutics and Jewish Religious Education," *Religious Education* 93.1 (1998): 29–43.

e. g., what is the meaning of a literary text? How relevant to this meaning is the author's intention? Is it possible to understand texts that are culturally and historically alien to us? Is "objective" understanding attainable, or rather relative to the readers' historical situations?

Philosophical hermeneutics provides us with central insights about the dialogical character of learning as well with elements of character education.[3] Thus, it informs not only the dynamic between a learner and the text but also the dynamic between havruta partners and within the learner herself. Our choice to call our subject "havruta *text* study" stems from our belief that the way we conceptualize the study of text determines, to a great extent, the interpersonal and intrapersonal dimensions of havruta learning.

Broadly speaking, philosophical hermeneutics sees history as a living dialogue between past, present and future, and seeks to ease the progress of this endless communication, in which texts play a central role. It is this perspective that makes philosophical hermeneutics appealing for application in Jewish education and particularly havruta text study, which is conceptualized as an enactment of such a living dialogue. Through this work, we lay out a model for a dialogic and intersubjective education that highlights the relationships among study partners and text, the latter being the major emphasis of the learning conversation. In our research, we have concentrated on the study of texts with a strongly evocative character (particularly narrative texts) that lend themselves to the kind of study in which philosophical hermeneutics is particularly relevant, by prompting questions about how we read, interpret, and interact with texts, especially those that originate in cultural and historical contexts other than our own.[4]

---

[3] See for example the role of the concept of *bildung* by Hans-Georg Gadamer, *Truth and Method* (New York: Continuum, 1996), which captures the centrality of learning and education as existential categories at the heart of philosophical hermeneutics. A seminal work that discusses learning and education from within philosophical hermeneutics is Shaun Gallagher, *Hermeneutics and Education* (Albany: State University of New York Press, 1992).

[4] While the foundations of philosophical hermeneutics are universal, some distinctions are in place according to various genres of texts. Also, modern hermeneutics is divided in sub-categories: literary hermeneutics (interpretation of literary and poetic texts), legal hermeneutics (interpreta-

We define havruta text study as a learning format in which two partners collaborate in establishing a text's meanings and engage in an open dialogue with the ideas of both the text and each other. Because its epistemology is grounded in an interpretive and dialogical view of both understanding and the self, philosophical hermeneutics offers a theoretical framework that, in the context of our practice-based research, helps us identify and articulate the different phases and various practices which might constitute havruta text study.

The Two Phases of (Havruta) Text Study

A first organizing framework of our work consists in identifying text study (and thus havruta text study) as a two-phase process: first to make sense of the text, and then to respond to the sense eventually made.

Havruta partners have the responsibility to "make the text speak," i. e., to generate together the best possible interpretations through which the text's ideas may be expressed.[5] It is in this spirit that we listen to the literary critic and novelist C. S. Lewis, who writes: "The first demand any work of art makes upon us is to surrender. Look. Listen. Receive"[6]; and "A true reader reads every work seriously in the sense that he reads it whole-heartedly, makes himself self-receptive as he can."[7] Havruta learners fulfill this task with a number of

---

tion of law), theological hermeneutics or exegesis (interpretation of sacred texts), historical hermeneutics (interpretation of testimonies and discourses about history), and *philosophical hermeneutics* (which offers an analysis of the foundations of interpretation in general).

[5]   The basis of such a metaphor resides in an extended philosophy of language and written language. See for example Gadamer, *Truth and Method*, 390–1, where reading a text is defined as transforming it back into language.

[6]   C. S. Lewis, *An Experiment in Criticism* (Cambridge: Cambridge University Press, 1992), 19.

[7]   Ibid., 11. Different literary theories adopt different positions on reading. For an example of a different, double-layered approach to text, see for example Rosenblatt's distinction between *aesthetic* reading, in which the reader's attention is concentrated on "what he is living through during the reading event," and *efferent* reading, in which "the reader's attention is focused on what he will take away from the transaction": Louise Rosenblatt, "On the Aesthetic as the Basic Model of the Reading Process," *Bucknell Review* 26.1

interpretive practices, designed to yield the best possible interpretations.

The first phase of havruta text study thus consists of resisting the urge to "use" the text for whatever purpose until compelling interpretations can be elicited. It should be emphasized that the reception Lewis refers to is not a synonym for passivity. The term "reception" acknowledges that the text has the right to have its own say first, even if this cannot be achieved without the active involvement of the learner's foreknowledge (as will be discussed further below).

In the second phase, students engage in personal dialogue with the ideas and claims of the text and with each other, taking them into consideration and responding to them, yielding new understandings. This is achieved through a number of dialogical practices designed to help each learner achieve "self-understanding," a concept that indicates that the student has come to understand himself in new ways in light of the dialogue.[8] As we further elaborate in chapters eight and

---

(1981): 17–32; Judith A. Langer, *Envisioning Literature, Literary Understanding and Literature Instruction* (New York: Teachers College Press, 1995), 21–2; 24–5.

[8] We recognize the fact that many of Gadamer's readers would oppose the distinction we make between first- and second-phase havruta text study, despite our own disclaimer in the next paragraph, and perceive it as identical to E. D. Hirsh's distinction between "meaning," that which the text is to represent, which does *not* change, and "significance" for a particular reader, which changes according to context (Eric D. Hirsh, *Validity in Interpretation* [New Haven: Yale University Press, 1967]; Eric D. Hirsh, *The Aims of Interpretation* [Chicago: University of Chicago Press, 1976]). Unlike Hirsh, we embrace the active contribution of the learner's horizon to the interpretive process, and thus hold that in some sense the texts themselves change also. Further, we believe that these two phases can be legitimately viewed as a pedagogical outgrowth of Ricoeur's distinction between explanation and understanding, which he discusses at length in his earlier work on hermeneutics. See Paul Ricoeur, "The Task of Hermeneutics," in *Hermeneutics and the Human Sciences*, ed. John B. Thompson (Cambridge: Cambridge University Press, 1981), 43–62; Ricoeur elaborates on what he calls "a productive notion of distanciation" in "The hermeneutical function of distanciation," in ibid., 131–44. In addition, see Paul Ricoeur, *Interpretation Theory: Discourse and the Surplus of Meaning* (Fort Worth: Texas Christian University Press, 1976), 71–88; Gregory J. Laughery, *Living Hermeneutics in Motion, an Analysis and Evaluation of Paul Ricoeur's Contribution to Biblical Hermeneutics* (Lanham, MD: University Press of America, 2002). See also

nine, it is this aspect of havruta text study that holds the potential for transformative learning. At this point it suffices to say that, following philosophical hermeneutics, learners should not be removed spectators but engaged participants in dialogue with one another and with what they seek to know. They look to what texts, works of art, and human co-conversants have to say to them, and to what they have to say to texts and other people. They also look to the part played in the conversation by their own and others' preconceptions.

It should be noted that while we use the term "phases" for didactic purposes, it should not be understood in a formal or linear sense, since the dynamic of havruta learning is open-ended and a great deal of overlap occurs. In reality, learners will engage back and forth with elements of each phase, as indicated in the cyclical graphic representation below. The two phases are sharply distinguished more in analysis than in reality; the distinction helps us indicate two different types of activities in working with a text, each with different purposes and specific practices, and each indispensable to the way we design the full scope of havruta text study.

Donoghue's use of "phases" of reading in *The Practice of Reading*, 81. Anthony Thiselton writes: "It remains helpful to distinguish hermeneutics as critical and theoretical reflection on these processes [of interpretation] from the actual work of interpreting and understanding as a first-order activity. Often writers speak loosely of someone's 'hermeneutic' when they discuss only how they go about the task rather then their reasons for doing so and their reflection on what is at issue in the process": Thiselton, *New Horizons in Hermeneutics: The Theory and Practice of Transforming Biblical Reading* (Michigan: Zondervan Publishing House, 1992), 1. Finally, it is worth quoting Walter Slatoff, who writes: "One feels a little foolish having to begin by insisting that works of literature exist, in part, at least, in order to be read, that we do in fact read them, and that it is worth thinking about what happens when we do. Put so blatantly, such statements seem too obvious to be worth making, for after all, no one directly denies that readers and reading do actually exist; even those who have most insisted on the autonomy of literary works and the irrelevance of the readers' responses, themselves do read books and respond to them. Equally obvious, perhaps, is the observation that works of literature are important and worthy of study essentially because they can be read and can engender responses in human beings": Slatoff, *With Respect to Readers: Dimensions of Literary Responses* (Ithaca, NY: Cornell University Press, 1970), 4.

The following diagram summarizes the two phases of text study on the basis of which we further design havruta learning:

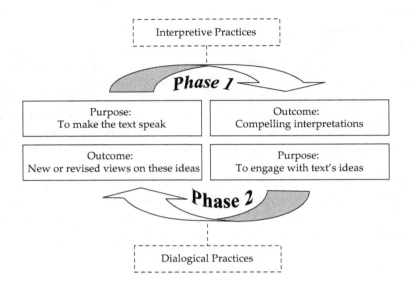

While havruta text study culminates in dialogue in the second phase, it is important to emphasize that the major axis of our design of havruta text study as discussed in this book pertains to the development of textual interpretations (in Phase 1). Havruta partners learn to become aware of the nature of this task, and learn the practices that are required to carry it out collaboratively. In so doing, they learn along the way how this task can potentially be altered or distorted by the inevitably active role of their own pre-existing preconceptions and projections. Our job is to help them acknowledge this by helping them become self-aware interpreters of text who adopt and enact certain practices, creating a space for the text's own ideas to emerge.

In the following section, we present a basic model of havruta text study, but we confine our analysis of its dynamics to its implications for the first phase of havruta text study. In chapter eight, we conduct a similar discussion regarding the second phase of havruta text study.

Havruta Text Study as Relationship: A Basic Model

Theorists like Paulo Freire, Ronald Arnett, and Malcolm Knowles emphasize the benefits of dialogue for the educational enterprise, such as the engagement of learners, the fostering of a sense of relevance, the building of character, and the development of community.[9] Hans-Georg Gadamer, who is perhaps singularly identified with philosophical hermeneutics, has contributed in a unique way to our understanding of the intersubjective nature of learning by proposing a dialogical mode of knowing through shared conversations on the interpretation of texts.[10] He characterizes the community that grows out of such conversations as one in which partners cooperate to establish a space in which they may or may not agree, and discusses how the relationship between learners affects the relationship they develop with the content of the text.

As researchers of havruta *text* study, we are also interested in what happens in the space where a learner meets a text. At its very core, philosophical hermeneutics accounts for this dynamic and reciprocal relationship between text and reader; it is our task to expand the implications of these insights to havruta learning and the reciprocal effects between *two* readers and a text. Thus, it is in the context of havruta text study that we have come to characterize philosophical hermeneutics as a relational epistemology in which learning depends not only on the content that is encountered but also on the nature of the encounter itself between text and learners.[11] We now discuss in what sense texts and learners affect each other during the first phase of havruta text study, in which both learners are involved in the development of textual interpretations.[12]

---

[9]   Paulo Freire, *Pedagogy of the Oppressed* (New York: The Seabury Press, 1972); Ronald C. Arnett, *Communication and Community: Implications of Martin Buber's Dialogue* (Carbondale: Southern Illinois University Press, 1986); Malcom Knowles, *Adult learning* (Houston: Gulf, 1990).

[10]   Hans-Georg Gadamer, *Truth and Method*.

[11]   Miriam Raider-Roth and Elie Holzer, "Learning to be Present: How Hevruta Learning Can Activate Teachers' Relationships to Self, Other and Text," *The Journal of Jewish Education* 75.3 (2009): 216–39. For a discussion of how these relationships play out in actual havruta encounters, see Orit Kent, *Interactive Text Study and the Co-Construction of Meaning: Havruta in the Delet Beit Midrash*.

[12]   As mentioned above, we elaborate on the second phase of havruta text study in Chapter Eight.

Relationship with Text

The primary concern of textual interpretation is with what is called the "worlds" that these texts open up. Paul Ricoeur distinguishes between the text's *work* and the text's *world*. By *work*, he refers to something that is crafted in terms of form, genre, and style and invites methodological examination. Yet, what a text refers to, its sense, is the *world* of the text. This world is the reference of the text; it is a perspective, a "way of looking at things."[13]

This concept applies to fiction, poetry, and literary texts, which address reality in a way that is rather indirect. Thus, interpreting the text does not necessarily consist of deciphering the author's intention, but rather of uncovering a view, a perspective that is projected in and through the text. Indeed, Gadamer's and Ricoeur's views agree with much of twentieth-century literary criticism, which refutes the intentional fallacy identifying the meaning of the text with the author's intention.[14] Instead, as soon as it is written, a text establishes its own form of discourse, offering something to the reader to be appropriated. This meaning is detached from the author's intention, since, once recorded, written discourse is both decontextualized from its historical setting and depsychchologized from its author.[15]

To interpret a text, Ricoeur asserts, is "to seek in the text itself, on the one hand, the internal dynamic that governs the structuring of

---

[13]   Paul Ricoeur, *Interpretation Theory: Discourse and the Surplus of Meaning*, 92. Central to our model of havruta text study is Ricoeur's emphasis that texts refer to reality, and not only to their internal structure as claimed by the New Criticism. What must be interpreted in a text is "a proposed world which I could inhabit and wherein I could project one of my ownmost possibilities," Paul Ricoeur, *Hermeneutics and the Human Sciences*, 142. His use of the term "world" of the text amplifies Gadamer's use of "the text's horizon," to which we refer further on.

[14]   See Leland Ryken, "Formalist and Archetypal Criticism," in *Contemporary Literary Theory: A Christian Appraisal*, ed. Clarence Walhout and Leland Ryken (Grand Rapids, MI: Eerdmans Publishing Co., 1991), 6.

[15]   Following Ricoeur, this does not imply an incoherent notion of an authorless text. The tie with the author is not abolished "but distended and complicated" (Paul Ricoeur *Hermeneutics and the Human Sciences*, 201). Ricoeur's assertion about written language and meaning is rooted in philosophical traditions. See for example Paul Ricoeur, *Interpretation Theory: Discourse and the Surplus of Meaning*; Hans-Georg Gadamer, *Truth and Method*.

the work and, on the other hand, the power that the work possesses to project itself outside itself and to give birth to a world that would truly be the 'thing' referred to by the text."[16] In other words, the task of textual interpretation is to have the world of the text—its meaning—emerge through the work of the text. This corresponds with our first phase of havruta text study, whose purpose is to "make the text speak" by generating sound textual interpretations.

To generate such an interpretation is not as straightforward as it may seem. Does the text shape interpretation or does interpretation shape the text? Philosophical hermeneutics rejects this either/or approach, instead viewing meaning as the result of a two-way encounter between text and reader. This idea is conveyed by the term "the hermeneutical circle," in which both reader and text participate.

Indeed, the meeting between the reader and the text is always affected by the reader's cultural context, prior history, and everyday embodied experience, what Heidegger calls "fore-knowledge,"[17] and Gadamer calls the "fore-meaning" or "preconceptions" of the learner, of which the learner is never fully aware.[18] Far from being a detached observer, the learner occupies a standpoint that limits and conditions what can be known. We borrow Gadamer's broader term of "horizon" to help us capture the dynamic that takes place in the interpretive process between the learner and the text.[19] This term refers to these cultural, linguistic, biographical, and philosophical worlds in which the learner operates, the limits beyond which one cannot see. It is linked to one's habits of looking at things in a particular way. Texts also have a horizon, for they also reflect the preconceptions of their historical situations.

---

[16]   Paul Ricoeur, *Hermeneutics and the Human Sciences,* 17–18.

[17]   Martin Heidegger, *Being and Time* (New York: Harper Perennial, 1962).

[18]   Gadamer, *Truth and Method.* It should be emphasized that "preconceptions" are a fundamental constitution of human beings: "Long before we understand ourselves through the process of self-examination, we understand ourselves in a self-evident way in the family, society and state in which we live. The focus of subjectivity is a distorting mirror. The self-awareness of the individual is only a flickering in the closed circuits of historical life. That is why the prejudices of the individual, far more than his judgments, constitute the historical reality of this being" (Gadamer, *Truth and Method,* 278).

[19]   Gadamer defines "horizon" as "the range of vision that includes everything that can be seen from a particular vantage point" (*Truth and Method,* 302).

Interpreting a text implies a reciprocal movement that takes place between the anticipatory movement of the interpreter's horizon and the horizon he or she encounters in the text.[20] The learner projects onto the text from his horizon, and the text offers to the interpreter something whose meaning may differ from what he, the interpreter, initially thought the text to mean and to say.

This reciprocity is conveyed by the arrow in the following diagram:

Text

Learner

This movement continues until some consensus, a "fusion of horizons," is achieved in the mind of the interpreter and understanding is attained. In this context, consensus is not a synonym for the interpreter's agreement with the claim of the text. Rather, understanding is a form of temporary consensus between what the interpreter believes the text to say and what is reasonable to claim that the text is saying. Interpretation is thus, first and foremost, about trying to understand what is being said and why, which is different from agreeing or disagreeing with what is said in the text. Meaning, therefore, does not reside "in" the text but is the result of interpretive fusion.

---

[20]   Heidegger and Gadamer distinguish between the first hermeneutical circle, which reflects the dynamic of parts and whole as data gradually provided by the text to the reader, and the second hermeneutical circle, which refers to the dynamic that takes place between the reader and the text's horizon, leading to a fusion of horizons. We do not expand here on the difference between these two circles as we imply elements of each at various phases of our discussions of the interpretive process.

Another kind of movement is discussed by literary theorist Wolfgang Iser, who expands on Gadamer's work, emphasizing the intersubjective relationship between reader and text.[21] For Iser, reading is a performative activity guided by the text and processed by the reader. In this view, the text-reader relationship is predicated on the text's "gaps," (or "blanks"), those places left open by the text because of its inherent inability to fully describe everything. It is this indeterminacy that activates the interpretive process, as the reader fills these blanks in with inferences and projections originating in his or her own horizon and temporary understanding of the text.[22]

At the same time, through the dialectic of presence/absence of words and through its structure, the text regulates what are or are not acceptable inferences. This is why, according to Iser, reading "provokes continually changing views in the reader."[23] Iser summarizes this movement as

> a process set in motion and regulated not by a given code but by a mutually restrictive and magnifying interaction between the explicit and the implicit, between revelation and concealment. What is concealed spurs the reader into action, but this action

---

[21]   Wolfgang Iser, *The Act of Reading: A Theory of Aesthetic Response* (Baltimore: Johns Hopkins University Press, 1978).

[22]   The view that understanding involves the active participation of the learner's pre-existing knowledge is also found in theories of cognitive and socio-cultural psychology as well as in constructivist approaches to learning. See for example John D. Bransford, Ann Brown, and Rodney Cocking, *How People Learn: Brain, Mind, Experience and School* (Washington D. C.: National Academy Press, 2000). See also Ann Brown, "Communities of Learning and Thinking, or a Context by Any Other Name," in *Developmental Perspectives on Teaching and Learning Thinking Skills*, ed. Deanna Kuhn (New York: Karger, 1990); Jean Lave, "The Practice of Learning," in *Understanding Practice: Perspectives on Activity and Context*, ed. Seth Chalkin and Sean Lave, (Cambridge: Cambridge University Press, 1993); Louise Rosenblatt, *The Reader, the Text, the Poem, the Transactional Theory of the Literary Work* (Carbondale: Southern Illinois University Press, 1978). For a discussion of these theories in direct relation to havruta text study, see Orit Kent, *Interactive Text Study and the Co-Construction of Meaning.*

[23]   Wolfgang Iser, *The Act of Reading,* 167.

is also controlled by what is revealed; the explicit in its turn is transformed when the implicit has been brought to light.[24]

While no understanding is possible without the activation of pre-knowledge, Gadamer emphasizes that we must not stick blindly to our fore-meaning if we want to truly understand the text. In practical terms, this means that while we read and listen through the filter of our fore-meaning, we are also called upon to remain open to the work of the text and the meaning that it may convey. It is important to note that these fore-meanings or preconceptions may hinder the development of sound textual interpretations in two ways. First, by assuming s/he has already grasped the meaning of the text, the reader may overlook cues in the text that may lead to a different, more coherent and grounded interpretation. Second, values and beliefs about the topic addressed in the text may close off the learner's ability to see that the text reflects an alternative, if not contradictory, view to his own beliefs. It is with this in mind that C. S. Lewis challenged all readers of texts: "The necessary condition of all good reading is to get ourselves out of the way."[25]

Gadamer articulates similar ideas when he advocates that one who studies text must be, from the start, sensitive to the text's alterity.[26] This kind of sensitivity involves neither "neutrality" with respect to content nor the extinction of one's self. Rather, what is expected from the reader is a growing sensitivity to the reciprocal effects of text and learner on each other and the learner's awareness of his own bias.

The fact that meaning is impacted by a reader's fore-knowledge, as well as by his "filling in" of the text's blanks, offers one explanation as to how the same text can generate several interpretations. A second explanation lies in the very polysemic nature of written language, which opens up more possibilities of meaning than the author may

---

[24]   Ibid., 168–9.

[25]   C. S. Lewis, *An Experiment in Criticism*, 93.

[26]   Notwithstanding this assertion, Levinas critiques Gadamer for not going far enough to establish the alterity of the other as such. For a discussion on this topic and a fruitful attempt to reconcile both philosophies, see Jeff Warren, "Toward an Ethical-Hermeneutics," *European Journal of Psychology, Counseling and Health* 1–2.7 (2005): 17–28.

have intended, as we have explained earlier.[27] Still, according to Gadamer, "within this multiplicity… not everything is possible," and thus, learners of texts will have to evaluate what makes some interpretations more coherent, compelling, or robust than others.

Text as Partner

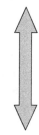

Learner as Partner

The dynamics described so far underline the active involvement of the text in the interpretive process, which we reflect by labeling it above as a *partner*. It should be noted that we are not using the word "individual," but rather "partner," a word that exalts the uniqueness of the subject but also stresses relationship and interconnectedness. We also label the text as partner given that it plays a central role in introducing the topic of the dialogue with which the learner will engage in the second phase of havruta text study. More than simply a metaphor, labeling a text as a partner is grounded in philosophical traditions of language that have attended to the locutionary quality of written language.[28] In that regard, it is interesting to note that for Gadamer, tradition "expresses itself like a 'Thou.'"[29] And yet, he also writes that "a text does not speak to us in the same way as does a 'Thou.'"[30] This

[27]   See for example Paul Ricoeur, *Interpretation Theory: Discourse and the Surplus of Meaning* and Hans-Georg Gadamer, *Truth and Method*.

[28]   See also Steven Kepnes' work grounded in the philosophy of Martin Buber and his use of the term "Thou" to indicate the text: Steven Kepnes, *The Text as Thou: Martin Buber's Dialogical Hermeneutics and Narrative Theology* (Bloomington, IN: Indiana University Press, 1992).

[29]   Gadamer, *Truth and Method*, 358.

[30]   Ibid., 377.

reminds us that unlike in human conversation, it is the interpreter's task to make the text speak.[31]

The textual partner has, indeed, a paradoxical nature. While it is multi-vocal in the sense that it lends itself to more than one interpretation, it has no actual voice to make itself heard. A text is mute, and therefore vulnerable to readers' misreading or manipulation. It is on this basis we emphasize havruta learners' responsibility toward the text, and the challenges they face in first making it "speak" on its own terms.[32]

Responsibility toward the text requires first and foremost accountability to the text, and the first responsibility is to respect the aim of the text as a communicative act. It is the attempt to understand the text as well as possible, for what it is rather than what the learner thinks it ought to be. This signals the role of interpretive practices such as repeated readings, paraphrasing, and questioning the text, as will be further discussed.

It bears mention that a philosophical hermeneutical approach to textual study forecloses the option of self-effacement that we find in some religious traditions (self-effacement in front of the authoritative text or teacher) and in classical positivist historical orientations (self-effacement in the presence of scientific method). It also challenges views that consider text learning a passive activity, and those that are focused on outcome in the form of "the correct" interpretation of a given text. From a broader epistemological perspective, the relational dynamic that takes place between the learner and the text

---

[31]   Robert Bernasconi, "'You Don't Know What I'm Talking About': Alterity and the Hermeneutic Ideal," in *The Specter of Relativism: Truth, Dialogue, and Phronesis in Philosophical Hermeneutics*, ed. Lawrence K. Schmidt (Evanston, IL: Northwestern University Press, 1995), 183. In later writings, Gadamer distanced himself from terms like I and Thou when talking about intersubjectivity. See Hans-Georg Gadamer, "Subjectivity and Intersubjectivity: Subject and Person," *Continental Philosophy Review* 33.3 (2000): 275–87.

[32]   Some philosophers go so far as to speak about an ethical responsibility toward the text in the reader's effort to make it speak. See for example Emmanuel Levinas, *Beyond the Verse: Talmudic Readings and Lectures* (New York: Continuum, 2007); James Risser, *Hermeneutics and the Voice of the Other: Re-reading Gadamer's Philosophical Hermeneutics* (New York: State University of New York Press, 1997); Olivier Abel, "Du Sujet Lecteur au Sujet Ethique," *Revue Internationale de Philosophie* 225 (2003): 369–85.

challenges popular conceptions of text study as an isolated, lonely, and non-dialogical endeavor.

Relationship with Partner

The relational characteristics of text study are even more pronounced in the havruta format. Just as havruta text study is predicated on having a relationship with the text, it is equally based on the human relationship with one's partner.

Havruta Partner  Havruta Partner

During the first phase of havruta text study, both partners work together to construct compelling textual interpretations, sometimes disagreeing about which is more convincing. They draw on their mutual knowledge, articulating their respective understandings, and using them to further develop their own. Again, they engage in this process within their horizons, that is, from their specific cultural and biographical contexts. According to Gadamer, the interaction between learner and text provides the clue to unraveling the understanding and interpretation that take place in the conversation between two people.[33] Similar to the interaction that takes place between learner and text, each havruta partner is involved in a reciprocal movement of projection and reception. What one havruta partner says, comments

---

[33] And vice versa. Gadamer writes: "I moved the idea of conversation to the very center of hermeneutics" (Richard Palmer, ed., *Gadamer in Conversation* [New Haven: Yale University Press, 2001], 39). Following Ricoeur, we note that there are differences between the interaction of two learning partners and the interaction between an interpreter and a text. For example, in a live conversation, there are more opportunities for a speaker to clarify his or her intentions. The discourse between the learners is not "fixed" by writing. It therefore reflects not only "a world" but also the speaker's intention. Ricoeur also makes the reading of a text the paradigm for interpreting actions and events (Paul Ricoeur, *Hermeneutics and the Human Sciences: Essays on Language, Action and Interpretation*, 131–44).

upon, or asks in his attempt to interpret the text impacts the other partner's interaction with the text. Likewise, the process of co-constructing textual interpretations can be characterized as a consensus-seeking dialogue. This means that while they help and influence each other, both havruta learners aim to achieve textual interpretations that they will both recognize to be compelling, even if they contradict each other.

In this sense, havruta learning can be seen as a social achievement—an encounter with difference, with alternative possibilities. These views are echoed in various sociocultural theories of knowledge and learning. While these theories rest on different epistemological assumptions than those undergirding most of this book (e. g. the role of horizons or the ontological primacy of language), they have nevertheless provided us with additional language for describing certain aspects of our work, particularly the interpersonal dimension of havruta text study. For example, Lev Vigotsky has enhanced our understanding of the role played by social interaction in creating conditions for the co-construction of knowledge.[34] The co-construction of textual interpretations is a central feature of havruta learning.[35] Carl Rogers discusses the qualities of interpersonal relationships that facilitate learning.[36] And in a broader perspective, education theorists have added to our understanding of how intersubjectivity enhances pedagogy by impacting intrinsic motivation, enhanced self-esteem and caring.[37]

Likewise, certain pedagogical theories identify the contribution of "constructive controversy to peer learning."[38] In two studies,

---

[34] Lev Vigotsky, *Mind in Society* (Cambridge, MA: Harvard University Press, 1978).

[35] For an elaborated discussion of this idea as well as additional concepts of socio-cultural theories of learning in their contribution to havruta text study, see Orit Kent, *Interactive Text Study and the Co-Construction of Meaning*, particularly page 14, and Orit Kent "A Theory of Havruta Learning."

[36] Carl R. Rogers, "The Interpersonal Relationship: The Core of Guidance," in *Person to Person: The Problem of Being Human; A New Trend in Psychology,* ed. Carl Rogers et al. (Lafayette, CA: Real People Press, 1967), 85–101. We elaborate on Rogers in Chapter Three.

[37] Charles Bingham and Alexander M. Sidorkin, *No Education Without Relation* (New York: Peter Lang, 2004).

[38] David Johnson and Roger Johnson, *Learning Together and Alone: Cooperation, Competition, and Individualization* (Englewood Cliffs, NJ: Prentice-Hall, 1975; reprinted Boston: Alyn and Bacon, 1999).

Hacohen and Blum-Kulka, Blindheim, and Hacohen identified disagreement as a major characteristic of havruta text study, but one
that does not jeopardize constructive relationship.[39] These different
concepts of interaction between learners inform the ways we seek to
cultivate various interpersonal dynamics among havruta learners.[40]

Relationship with Self

Havruta Partner

A third, less visible, but no less important, relational aspect of
havruta text study is that which exists between the learner and herself.
By definition, this is a self-reflective interaction, in which the learner
must come face to face with her own beliefs, prejudices, assumptions,
and projections. During the first phase of havruta text study, this
confrontation with oneself is an inherent part of the reciprocal relationships with text and havruta partner as discussed.[41] The learner's
awareness of her own prejudices helps her avoid unhelpful projections

---

[39]   Gonen Dori-Hacohen, "Integrating and Divisive Discourses: The
       Discourse in Interactions with Non-Jewish Callers on Israeli Radio Phone-
       in-Programs," *Israel Studies in Language and Society* 3.2 (2011): 146–65;
       Shoshana Blum-Kulka, Menahem Blondeim, Gonen Hacohen, "Traditions
       of Disagreements: From Argumentative Conversations about Talmud Texts
       to Political Discourse in the Media." Similar views are echoed in talmu-
       dic literature: e. g. Tractate Shabbat 63a; Tractate Kiddushin 30b. See also
       Elie Holzer, "'Either a Havruta Partner or Death': A Critical View on the
       Interpersonal Dimensions of Havruta Learning," *The Journal of Jewish
       Education* 75 (2009): 130–49.

[40]   See Appendix 2: "Written guidelines for havruta text study."

[41]   We also note that the psychological process of self-reflection entails inter-
       subjectivity. See Alex Gillespie, "The Social Basis of Self-Reflection," in *The
       Cambridge Handbook of Sociocultural Psychology*, ed. Jaan Valsiner and Alberto
       Rosa (Cambridge: Cambridge University Press, 2007), 678–91.

onto the text, or allows her to make sense of her havruta partner's explanations as she attempts to develop a coherent and sound interpretation of the text.[42]

Thus, in the interpretive process, learners should permit the text to surprise, intrigue, or even confuse them. To do so requires a self-consciousness that is not present naturally, but which the learner can develop by becoming aware of changes taking place within his consciousness throughout the interpretive process.[43]

To summarize, in the first phase of havruta learning, both learners join forces in one major task, making the text speak by developing one or more compelling interpretations. The two learners are not expected to hold the same interpretations, but to reach a consensus about which interpretations they consider coherent or sound. To become artful havruta participants, each learns to monitor and become self-aware of the reciprocal dynamic that takes place between himself and the text, between himself and his havruta partner, and inside himself.

The Havruta Learning Triangle

We now integrate these three types of interactions into what serves as our second organizing framework, as illustrated in the diagram below. The conceptualization of a havruta learning triangle draws on the work of David Hawkins. In his article, "I, Thou, and It," Hawkins conceptualizes the respective roles of teacher, learner, and subject matter

---

[42]   Cultivating the learner's attention to this aspect of havruta text study through careful listening will be addressed in Chapter Four.

[43]   Cultivating a self-consciousness toward the interpretive process is well described by W. Iser: "If interpretation has set itself the task of conveying meaning of a literary text, obviously the text itself cannot have already formulated that meaning. How can the meaning possibly be experienced if—as is always assumed by the classical norm of interpretation—it is already there, merely waiting for a referential exposition? As meaning arises out of the process of actualization, the interpreter should pay more attention to the process than to the product" (*The Act of Reading*, 18).

as a triangular formulation, with each dependent on and influenced by the others.[44]

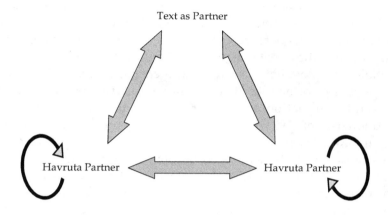

Hawkins argues for the active role of the subject matter (It): "The third corner of the triangle affects the relations between the other two corners, how the It enters into the pattern of mutual interest and exchange between the teacher and the child."[45] In the havruta relational triangle, we replace the subject matter (It) with the text, which

---

[44]   David Hawkins, "I, Thou, and It," in *The Informed Vision: Essays on Learning and Human Nature*, ed. David Hawkins (New York: Agathon Press, 2002), 48–62. Teacher educators and researchers have labeled Hawkins' triangle as the *instructional* triangle. For its use in teacher education, see for example David K. Cohen, Stephen W. Raudenbush, and Deborah L. Ball, "Resources, Instruction, and Research," *Educational Evaluation and Policy Analysis* 25.2 (2002): 1–24. It is a central framework in the Mandel Teacher Educator Institute (MTEI), which prepares teacher educators for Jewish education, and also in the DeLeT program where it helps teacher candidates organize their evolving understandings of classroom teaching. In reference to havruta text study, Raider-Roth and Holzer, in "Learning to be Present: How Hevruta Learning Can Activate Teachers' Relationships to Self, Other and Text," have come to use the term *relational* triangle. For a related discussion of this triangle and Hawkins' understanding of the role of engagement and engrossment in learning relationships, see also Orit Kent, *Interactive Text Study and the Co-Construction of Meaning.*

[45]   David Hawkins, "I, Thou, and It," 50.

becomes a partner ("Thou"), and we add circular arrows to indicate the relationship with oneself that occurs within each learner.

Learning how to become a havruta learner means learning how to navigate these exchanges with full self-awareness and sensitivity to the dynamic of the interactions. In the spirit of Hawkins, we maintain that when students become consciously aware of the various interactions in which they are engaged, they become more intellectually and psychologically available to the text, their partner, and themselves.[46] Following the principles of philosophical hermeneutics, acquiring skills and information about a praxis does not alone make a good practitioner—yet one will not be able to become a good practitioner without acquiring that information and those skills. Exposure to practical experiences enables one to become a good practitioner. Thus, as part of what it takes to learn havruta text study, we include the transformation of students' awareness and attitudes that will hopefully occur as a result of engaging with the practices of havruta text study.[47]

The Identification of Havruta Text Study Practices

We use the term "practices" in this book to indicate a frequently repeated skill-based action that is performed consciously, accompanied by an individual's understanding of its underlying rationale. In the context of havruta text study, we identify three categories of practices that activate the three interactions discussed so far:

Textual practices, which focus on the interaction between learner and text.

Interpersonal practices, which concentrate on the interaction between the student and her havruta partner.

---

[46]   Miriam Raider-Roth and Elie Holzer, "Learning to be Present: How Hevruta Learning Can Activate Teachers' Relationships to Self, Other and Text."

[47]   Knowing how to navigate these aspects of learning and being open to the challenges that transformation may pose is for Gadamer what makes a person "gebildet." Bildung is a rich and complex term that encompasses what it means "to be educated." We adopt a similar view when we think about the educated havruta learner.

Intrapersonal practices,[48] which concern the student's active engagement with his own preconceptions, values, and beliefs as they are activated during havruta text study.

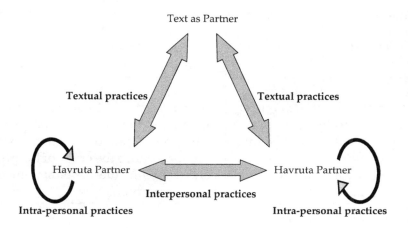

In three subsequent chapters, we discuss interpretive practices in each category that are instrumental in fostering sound textual interpretations: for example, questioning the text serves as a textual practice (Chapter Four); listening to one's own preconceptions in the interpretive process serves as an intra-personal interpretive practice (Chapter Five) and challenging the havruta partner's interpretation serves as an interpersonal interpretive practice (Chapter Six).

The following table offers a more comprehensive view of this idea with examples of the interpretive practices divided into the three categories:

---

[48]   We owe the use of the term "intrapersonal" to describe this aspect of havruta text study to Miriam Raider-Roth: Miriam Raider-Roth and Elie Holzer, "Learning to be Present: How Hevruta Learning Can Activate Teachers' Relationships to Self, Other and Text."

Interpretive Practices of Havruta Text Study

Textual practices Practices that focus on the interaction between learner and text	The learner performs multiple readings, reads the text aloud, paraphrases the text, analyzes its structure, asks open questions, and evaluates different interpretations.
Intrapersonal practices Practices that are characterized by the learner's active engagement with his own preconceptions, values, and beliefs as they are activated during havruta text study.	The learner listens to the text's information and to his havruta partner's comments about the text in ways that may reduce the effect of his preconceptions in the development of textual interpretations.
Interpersonal practices Practices that concentrate on the interaction between the learner and her havruta partner	The learner listens to, comments on, and questions her havruta partner's comments during the interpretive process; She challenges and supports her partner's interpretations of the text.

As we have noted, these practices mainly grow out of a theoretical and conceptual view of the interpretive process. In a related set of studies, Kent lays out another, overlapping framework that identifies six havruta practices stemming from empirical analysis of what learners do and say when studying texts with a havruta partner.[49] Despite their differing points of origin and the differences in the way they categorize and identify practices, they share many assumptions and values, as well as a commitment to parsing (and fostering) the practices that characterize rich havruta text study.

---

[49]   Orit Kent, *Interactive Text Study and the Co-Construction of Meaning*; Orit Kent, "A Theory of Havruta Learning."

We would be remiss if we did not, in this chapter on theoretical foundations, at least briefly identify the resonances of our work with several other important theories of learning and teaching.

Our approach to the teaching of havruta text study is consistent with John Dewey's theory that in order for people to learn, they must engage in educative experiences that allow them to actively build knowledge, not just absorb it.[50] As will be further elaborated in this volume, we see our task as teachers as one of designing learning experiences to help facilitate the learning of havruta text study practices. The design of these experiences echoes Bandura's basic principles of social learning that concern the cultivation of new practices and attitudes; they include the need for extensive experimentation, the need to label and discuss new skills and attitudes in order to learn how to recognize them, and the need for practice opportunities.[51]

As will be evident in subsequent chapters, our framework is rooted in a self-reflective approach, in which students are provided with a language and ample opportunity to engage and experiment with the practices we analyze in this volume and discuss their own experiences of the learning process.[52] The premise that reflecting on one's performance in order to revise it is an inherent part of good learning draws on a long tradition, starting, again, with Dewey. Donald Schon's concepts of reflection-in-action and reflection-on-action have enriched the discourse of practitioners and find resonances in our work.[53] Scholars like Zeichner and Liston emphasize how reflection is enhanced by communication and dialogue with others, a process inherent in the model of havruta presented here.[54]

---

[50] John Dewey, *Experience and Education* (New York: Collier Books, 1963).

[51] Albert Bandura, *Principles of Behavior Modification* (New York: Holt, Rinehart & Winston, 1969); Albert Bandura, *Social Learning Theory* (New Jersey: Prentice Hall, 1977).

[52] It goes without saying that it is only over time that students can integrate these practices into their learning, see Burbules and Bruce, (2001).

[53] Donald Schon, *The Reflective Practitioner: How Professionals Think in Action* (London: Temple Smith, 1983); Donald Schon, *Educating the Reflective Practitioner* (San Francisco: Jossey-Bass, 1987).

[54] Kenneth M. Zeichner and Daniel P. Liston, *Reflective Teaching: An Introduction* (Mahwah, NJ: Lawrence Erlbaum Associates, 1996).

These theorists of reflection are interested in learners' growing awareness of what they do, know, and do not know in any given
context, as well as their ability to think about their own thinking and
activity processes. This heightened awareness is an important element
in the ability of students to evaluate and thus continually improve
their work of havruta text study; indeed, we see a self-reflective stance
as inherent to the art of havruta learning. Reflection, in this case, is
similar to the Greek concept of *phronesis*, translated as practical intelligence.[55] In an educational context, Kessels and Korthagen link this
term to the understanding of specific concrete cases and complex or
ambiguous situations accompanied by an understanding of how to
operate in these situations. It is this kind of self-conscious practical
knowledge that our model seeks to cultivate among havruta learners.[56]

Before we turn to the practical discussion of our model of
havruta text study in the coming chapters, we must include a note
regarding the open-ended character of havruta text study, even as we
are committed to its skillful structuring and curricularization. The outcome of a given havruta conversation cannot be known ahead of time,
even for people who are familiar with the textual material; neither
teachers nor students know exactly what they are going to say or see,
as the ideas and insights that emerge in each interactive study experience are largely unpredictable. Our view of havruta text study invites
the participants' personalities and even their strongly held opinions,
asking each participant to bring to the table a fundamental interest
in generating interpretations, an openness to dealing with competing
interpretations, and a willingness to engage in the sometimes uncomfortable, even confrontational aspects of this conversation.

Warnke's description of conversation in the work of Gadamer
echoes this view in its ideal form:

> Just as the conclusion of a genuine conversation is not the sole
> property of either one of the dialogue partners, the outcome
> of Verstehen (understanding) is neither our own property, the
> result of the dominance of our prejudices, or the property of the

---

55   Aristotle, *Nicomachean Ethics*, trans. Terence Irwin (Indianapolis: Hackett
Publishing Company, Inc., 1999).

56   Jos Kessels and Fred Korthagen, "The Relationship between Theory and
Practice: Back to the Classics," *Educational Researcher* 25 (1996): 17–22.

tradition, the result of its dominance. Instead, just as in conversation, the result is a unity or argument that goes beyond the original position of the various participants; indeed the consensus that emerges in understanding represents a new view and hence a new phase of the tradition.[57]

---

[57]   Georgia Warnke, *Gadamer, Hermeneutics, Tradition and Reason* (Cambridge: Polity Press, 1987), 104.

Torah is only acquired in community.
Talmud Berakhot 63b

"Well, now that we have seen each other," said the Unicorn,
"If you'll believe in me, I'll believe in you. Is that a bargain?"
Lewis Carroll, Through the Looking-Glass, Chapter Seven

CHAPTER THREE:
SETTING THE STAGE FOR HAVRUTA LEARNING

Like collaborative and groupwork-based learning, havruta text study challenges habits and norms of the traditional classroom. The physical setup of the classroom students are familiar with may not be the most conducive to this new type of learning. Havruta learners are expected to learn new interpersonal and interpretive skills. Instead of being tempted to remain unengaged, the havruta learner is confronted with the need to be actively involved in the dynamic of peer learning. Instead of only being concerned with what the teacher is saying, he is confronted by the need to learn with a fellow student. And instead of only paying attention to her own accomplishments, the havruta learner is expected to take into account her partner's success as well.

It would be a mistake to assume that students of all ages easily adapt to these changes—that they soon know, for example, how to work with each other in a constructive, collegial fashion. Chances are good that they have not had similar (and successful) previous successful experiences. Some may have had collaborative experiences in, say, sports, but unlike the disorganized and open-ended nature of havruta text study, roles in sports are closely guided by the rules of the game, the coach, and the referee. Teaching students to become havruta learners thus implies not only providing them with opportunities to learn key practices of havruta text study, but doing so in ways that help them cope with these changes.

In our vision, becoming a havruta learner also requires opening oneself to new foci of attention, developing new attitudes, and learning new behaviors in regard to two major aspects of havruta learning. First, students must become self-reflectively and critically concerned with their own learning; second, they must learn that the scope of their concern does not only include the instrumental (that is, the student's personal learning), but also the ethical-relational aspect of havruta text study (the student's concern for, and ability to contribute to, his havruta partner's learning).

As reflected by the circular arrow in the diagram below, reflective attention to oneself as a learner is a defining element of intra-personal practices, as it engages the student with different aspects of his personality and his identity as a learner. Similarly, the ethical responsibility for one's partner's learning constitutes one of the foundations of interpersonal practices. For example, among the practices we teach, students learn to challenge their partner's textual interpretation, even when they agree, in order to help their partner refine and improve the quality of the interpretation.

These two aspects are new to all of our students, even for the ones with some prior experience in havruta learning, because they are not addressed in traditional settings of havruta text study (at least not explicitly). It is therefore useful to address them when beginning to teach havruta text study, especially since they constitute the basis for further learning of havruta text study practices.

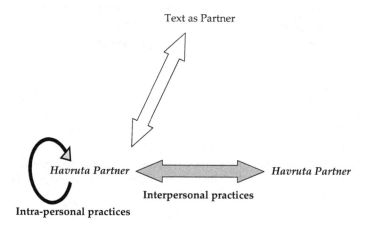

In this chapter, we explain our thinking about, and provide examples of how we deal with, these changes and foundational aspects of havruta text study. We begin by delineating the more phys-ical aspects of facilitating the learning of havruta study: how we go about setting up the physical space in which havruta learning is to take place, in order to facilitate the differences in havruta text study, and go on to describe the design of what we call "havruta lessons," which are designed to help students learn the practices of havruta text study. Following that, we discuss a set of three learning experiences designed to help raise the student's consciousness of himself and his havruta partner as learners. Finally, we conclude the chapter by discussing what we have learned and how we go about pairing up students.[1]

Setting Up the Beit Midrash Space

In principle, havruta text study can happen in any place where two people decide to study a text together, though traditionally speaking, havruta text study is associated with the beit midrash, a space filled with tables and books (e. g., a study hall in a yeshivah or synagogue) in which multiple havruta pairs engage in simultaneous study.[2] Designing a beit midrash is best thought of as not just the procurement of furniture and a library, but as a complex and multifaceted endeavor, one that deserves our attention as educators and researchers.[3] We will identify here the features of a beit midrash space that we believe help to create a supportive environment for havruta learning.[4] In doing so, we operate on the assumption that the beit midrash should be a purposeful and intentionally designed learning environ-

---

[1]   For a discussion of physical set up and pairing among young learners, as well as other set-up factors that affect havruta learning, see also Orit Kent and Allison Cook, "Havruta Inspired Pedagogy: Fostering an Ecology of Learning for Closely Studying Texts with Others."

[2]   Readers may recall the movie *Yentl* in which Barbara Streisand plays a woman eager to study Talmud. One of the scenes provides a vivid image of a beit midrash in Eastern Europe at the beginning of the twentieth century.

[3]   For an initial discussion of this topic in the context of DeLeT's Beit Midrash, see Sharon Feiman-Nemser, "Beit Midrash for Teachers: An Experiment in Teacher Preparation."

[4]   We understand that classroom teachers will often be unable to dedicate a special space and will have to use their regular classrooms. In such cases, most of the elements we discuss in the context of DeLeT's Beit Midrash can be adapted to the traditional classroom as well.

ment, one that reflects the host institution's core values and supports a dialectic exchange among individuals and groups.

We begin by arranging for each havruta pair to sit face to face at a separate table. While the table may be perceived as an unnecessary and cumbersome physical divide that may (symbolically) keep partners at a distance, we believe that it serves several important purposes related to fostering a successful havruta learning dynamic. The table allows additional relevant study materials to be available to the students. It also makes it easier for them to write as they learn. By no means unimportant, by having the text on a table havruta partners are able to freely use their hands during the learning conversation. In general, having havruta partners face one another allows for maximal use of body language, facilitating interpersonal communication that builds on both facial and hand expressions.

Ideally, there should be space between each table, affording individual havruta pairs a sense of privacy. At the same time, we make sure to arrange the tables close enough to enable verbal exchanges among different havruta pairs. Indeed, we encourage students to freely ask for help or support from their peers in the beit midrash and to view them as resources, thus purposefully helping to decentralize the role of the teacher as the sole source of knowledge. The setup of the separate-yet-connected tables is designed to embed a particular dialectic of the student's participation in a beit midrash, involving a back and forth movement between two roles: that of a havruta partner and that of a participant in a broader learning community.

The setup of the space also reflects something about the teacher-student relationship. A beit midrash environment should break the standard "teacher in the front, students in the rows" divide. The where and how of the teacher's position in the beit midrash space, a seemingly minor point, brings us to the larger question of the teacher's role in the beit midrash during periods of havruta learning. There are, of course, several ways to answer this question.[5] Ours is based on our belief that the teacher's physical location and behavior during the time allocated to havruta study should reflect and project three important

---

[5] A systematic reflection on the activities and the challenges of teachers in havruta learning environments is discussed in Orit Kent and Allison Cook, "Havruta Inspired Pedagogy: Fostering an Ecology of Learning for Closely Studying Texts with Others."

values: availability to students, attentiveness to their learning process, and proving a role model of exemplary (havruta) learning.

First and foremost, the teacher should be available to students who have questions or need help. This means that the table where she sits should be accessible from all sides of the room. Second, she must be able to supervise interactions between and among the havruta pairs. This is, of course, relevant in the case of younger students who may have the tendency to use the time for havruta learning as a break, but we believe it is equally relevant for more mature students, who also have the need to feel that someone is interested in their learning process—especially when the havruta learning dynamic is not proceeding smoothly. It is important that students sense that the teacher cares about what is going on between havruta partners and even encourages students themselves to raise questions about the havruta dynamic. At times, this may require that the teacher makes decisions about if, how, and when to intervene in a havruta pair's learning. For example, a teacher may present new tasks to a havruta pair that claims to be "done" with their learning of a given text. The teacher may also test their interpretations of the text or decide to check in when she senses a havruta pair is engaged in endeavors other than study.

Third, we believe the teacher should, as much as possible without compromising his availability, be involved in his own study during havruta learning time. Ideally, this should take place with a havruta partner (e. g., a fellow teacher), but if that is not possible, it is still worthwhile for the teacher to engage in study alongside his students. Overall, through his behavior, the teacher contributes to the modeling and building of "beit midrash character" that is committed to and focused on text study, by demonstrating an obvious seriousness about the learning that students are nevertheless able to conceive of as within their grasp.[6] This helps to create a sense of a community where learning is valued by everyone, irrespective of their formal roles in the classroom or institutional hierarchy (i. e., teacher, student). With this in mind, when designing a beit midrash space, we typically set a table apart for the teacher to engage in her personal study. Ideally,

6   Adapted from Magdalene Lampert's notion of "academic character" where she talks about the teacher's impact in a classroom where students study collaboratively, Magdalene Lampert, *Teaching Problems and the Problems of Teaching* (New Haven: Yale University Press, 2001), 327.

however, this should not be a formal "teacher's desk," but one table among others.

Once in a while, students ask to hold their havruta learning in a separate room. The most common reason for this request is the level of noise in the beit midrash which some students find disturbing, preventing them from giving either their havruta partner or the text their full attention. We usually take this opportunity to acknowledge that the noise level created in a beit midrash runs counter to prevailing cultural norms about reading and learning. In Western societies, reading is very often both a solitary and silent pursuit; in contrast, in a beit midrash people read aloud to each other, which requires a fair amount of voice projection, and then talk—often passionately—about the text. The noise created by the study of havruta pairs is closer to the one created by various working groups in a classroom—and even this comparison does not do justice to the noise in a beit midrash, since (e. g.) four groups of six students each (when not everyone speaks at the same time) does not compare with the noise level of twenty-four people talking and reading aloud at the same time in one space. Over the years, we have found that among those who raise this concern, many simply need some time to adapt to this new learning environment. We therefore encourage students to try the shared beit midrash space for a couple of days. We share with them our views on the importance of creating a common learning community and our understanding that this might pose a challenge for them, and we invite them to re-discuss this matter with us after a couple of days.[7]

As for the setting up of the room itself, it is important to make additional learning resources available to students within the beit midrash space. The Jewish literary tradition is multilayered and intertextual in the sense that texts address, allude to, and interpret other texts across time and space. Thus, for example, talmudic texts interpret biblical sources and other texts that have not been incorporated into the talmudic canon. Biblical texts are typically accompanied by a half a dozen commentaries or more, going back thousands of years. As part of havruta text study, students are encouraged to consult those source texts in their original contexts, and we try to ensure that

---

[7]   In our experience, the vast majority of students seem to adapt to the noisy beit midrash space. For those for whom this remains a challenge, we seek alternative solutions such as studying in a separate room.

relevant classical works are available to students in the beit midrash. This includes reference work such as dictionaries, a biblical concordance, and relevant encyclopedias. In those institutions whose core values of Jewish learning include an ongoing conversation with literature and arts from other cultures and civilizations, teachers may want to make relevant resources accessible for student use in the beit midrash as well, to offer them options for broadening the scope of the topic discussed by locating their learning in a cultural comparative and historical approach.

In recent years, we have had to confront the role of laptops in the beit midrash. Not only do students increasingly use their laptops to take notes and write up summaries, but laptops also serve to access online textual resources that might be relevant to their studies. On the whole, our experience has shown that laptops can interfere with the quality of engagement we hope to cultivate in the havruta pair (and not only because they offer an ongoing temptation for students to check their e-mail). We have found that the laptop ends up occupying the role of a fourth "player" in the havruta dynamic, attracting the learners' gaze and ultimately preventing students from being fully accessible to their havruta partner or to the text. We have found the best solution to be having a few laptops available to all in a corner of the beit midrash, giving students the opportunity to access additional information or resources without having a disruptive effect on the havruta learning dynamic. Teachers can also set aside some time toward the end of the havruta learning period for students to write their summary notes on their laptop.

The Design of Havruta Lessons

Essentially, we integrate a havruta text study approach into a range of text-based thematic lessons, merging two different but complementary curricular strands (that is, the learning of havruta skills and the encounter with texts on subjects chosen for a given set of learners). In the course we designed for student teachers at DeLeT, participants were asked to engage in havruta with the theme of teaching and learning as reflected in texts from the Jewish tradition. In the larger class discussions that follow havruta learning, students discuss and reflect, as a group, on the themes of teaching and learning they encountered in the texts and that they find relevant to their work as emerging teachers.

In addition to these thematic lessons, we schedule a number of lessons specifically oriented around the teaching of skills for havruta. Their goal is to introduce students to particular practices of havruta text study and for them to experiment with these practices in a direct and reflective way. These lessons follow their own curricular sequence, and have their own structure. They begin with mini-lessons in which students are introduced to havruta text study practices; they then engage in special (havruta learning-based) activities designed to develop their experiences with each practice. Each lesson ends with a discussion and/or reflection with the aim of helping students consider how to cultivate and integrate a given practice going forward.

Even in more thematically-oriented lessons, written guidelines used in both the "havruta" and "regular" lessons call students' attention to their engagement in various practices and cover the full scope of both phases of havruta text study.[8] Integration between the thematic and the havruta curricular strands is further promoted by the fact that in the havruta lessons, students utilize texts from the thematic curriculum, and in the "regular" lessons, they continue to experiment with and cultivate the practices of havruta text study.[9]

Helping the Student Become a Reflective and Responsible Havruta Learner

As mentioned earlier, one of the hallmarks of our approach to havruta text study is raising each student's attentiveness to their own learning

---

[8]   An annotated template of the accompanying guidelines is further discussed in Appendix 2.

[9]   The goal of developing a richer connection between the educational themes of Jewish texts and the learning of havruta practices has guided us in planning our classes. For example, we have often asked students to experiment with the role of questions in text study while studying a narrative text in which the plot puts forward the role of questions in the teacher-learner relationship. For these types of connections and the use of Jewish texts in professional development, see Elie Holzer, "Conceptions of the Study of Jewish Texts in Teachers' Professional Development"; Elie Holzer, "Teachers' Learning and the Investigation of Practice," *Mekhkarei Morashtenu* 2.3 (2004): 291–302; Elie Holzer, "Choosing to Put Ourselves 'at Risk' in the Face of Ancient Texts: Ethical Education through the Hermeneutical Encounter." See Appendix 1 for further elaboration on our selection of texts for havruta lessons.

trajectory, learning style, and potential strengths and limitations within the context of havruta text study. To this end, we have designed a personal written assignment, to be completed before the lesson and both emailed to the teacher and brought to class in hard copy. The assignment asks the student to reflect upon herself as a learner, and also has her imagine and anticipate herself in her role as a havruta partner for another learner.

As will presently become clear, the written assignment serves three complementary purposes: it helps the student reflect and learn about himself as a learner; it helps the student tell the havruta partner something about himself as a learner; and it provides us, the instructors, with important information about the students, which we use as we establish havruta pairs. The first goal is further reinforced by a second exercise in the form of a lesson in which students begin to explore what havruta learning might contribute to their personal learning experience and in what practical ways this could be concretized. Finally, students are introduced to the ethical-relational dimension of havruta learning through an exchange that builds on the personal written assignment.

The Assignment: Myself as a Havruta Learner[10]

In this assignment, we provide an individual written assignment as a tool to foster self-reflection. The assignment's introduction provides the student with an initial description of his role during havruta text study, and introduces the three dimensions of havruta learning, without calling them by their formal names:

> A practice that requires people to listen closely to and engage with their own ideas, their partners' ideas, and the ideas in the text, and to be open to revising their initial interpretations.

---

[10]   In discussing the purposes that are served by this assignment, we refer the reader to Appendix 3 for a copy of the document.

This is helpful not only for the student with no prior experience but also for the more experienced student, as it is likely the first time that what is expected of him during havruta study has even been explicitly discussed. This is reinforced by a list of "features of good havruta text study," which offers the student a list of useful concrete strategies and behaviors and helps her form an idea of what she will actually be expect to learn to do over time.

The actual assignment is designed around seven questions that we have revisited and refined over the years. Of special importance are those questions in which the student is asked to reflect on his weaknesses or vulnerabilities as a learner, and on what he anticipates in his role as havruta learner:

> Think of yourself as a *learner*: describe two elements that make learning satisfying for you.
>
> Think of yourself as a *learner*: describe two elements that make learning challenging for you.

Straightforward questions such as these signal to the students that despite the centrality of the social interaction that takes place in havruta learning, to grow into a havruta learner implies entering an environment that values heightened, self-reflective attention towards their own study.

An additional question has students similarly consider the specific framework of havruta text study, and is formulated so that it can engage new and more experienced havruta learners alike:

> What 2–3 things in the list of "Good Features of Havruta Study" do you perceive as being most challenging for you to perform? Explain why.

Inviting students to be mindful about themselves as havruta learners is accompanied by encouraging them to develop a mindfulness of their havruta partner's learning as well, thus addressing the interpersonal dimension of havruta learning. The ability to assist one another's learning depends, of course, on the other person's needs, but also on what students feel they can contribute. A clearer sense of the latter may increase the student's self-confidence about drawing on these abilities in havruta learning. Another of the questions of the assignment is meant to help raise this awareness:

> Think of yourself as *teacher*: Based on the list "Good Features of Havruta Study," describe 2–3 things that you believe you will be able to bring to havruta study that will be helpful for your partner's learning.

A note on our use of the word "teacher" to indicate the role that the student takes in supporting his havruta partner's learning: in the context of DeLeT, it made sense to use the word "teacher" because we wanted students to begin to identify with the practice-based care for someone else's learning. In that regard, indeed, the intensity of the havruta learning format provides student teachers with a powerful first-hand experience of the value of dispositions such as openness and attentiveness, also necessary for good teaching.[11] Even when havruta learning is not taught to teachers *per se*, the use of the terms "teacher" and "learner" can still be useful because they indicate the double role of each participant in a havruta learning relationship. We use that language to help students expand their understanding of havruta learning to include this deep commitment to another's learning.

The last questions invite direct expression of any concerns the student may have in this double role of learner and teacher, which provides us, the instructors, with important information about each student in particular:

> Think of yourself as a *learner* and a *teacher*: What do you do when circumstances cause you to "shut down?" When something in a text or with a learning partner offends or distances you, how do you usually react? How do you reconnect after such moments?
>
> Please share two questions and/or concerns you have about havruta text study.

---

[11]   Elie Holzer, "What Connects 'Good' Teaching, Text Study and Havruta Learning? A Conceptual Argument."

This question having the student reflect on his reactions when he "shuts down" during learning did not appear in the initial years when the assignment was introduced, but is the outcome of later research that has been conducted on havruta learning in which participants had describe how they "shut down" on several occasions and for different reasons.[12] By indicating that either a text or a learning partner might cause one to disconnect, this question adds a new dimension to the student's awareness of himself as a learner. It addresses a deep layer of the intrapersonal dimension of havruta text study—that moment when the learner's values, beliefs, and/or sensitivities are challenged, potentially provoking a negative reaction.

The formulation of this question provides the student with language for and a lens through which to view this subtle yet important aspect of havruta learning. It makes this potential experience visible, and suggests the possibility of turning it into an experience from which one can learn and grow. In this case, the student is asked to think about how she reconnects after such moments, inviting her to focus on the constructive aspect of such unpleasant experiences.

Students are asked to send their assignments to the instructors before class and also to bring a copy to share with their havruta partner. Knowing that what he writes will be read by both the instructors and his havruta partner can sometimes inhibit the student, preventing free and fully honest self-reflection. Nevertheless, this assignment begins to set the norm that serious learning involves frequent and honest self-reflection, and that havruta learning involves dealing with those more vulnerable sides of oneself and of one's havruta partner, in a supportive and collaborative environment.

A Session: The Instrumental Aspect of Havruta Learning

We have found that the above assignment often raise excitement and expectations in regard to havruta text study, especially by students who have little or no previous experience with this learning format—

---

[12]   Miriam Raider-Roth, Vicky Stieha, and Billy Hensley, "Rupture and Repair: Episodes of Resistance and Resilience in Teachers' Learning," *Teaching and Teacher Education* 28 (2012): 493–502.

but it can also raise some concerns and anxieties. Students wonder who they are going to be paired up with, how this will feel, etc. In this session, we attempt to address these concerns, mainly by beginning to make students aware of the fact that successful havruta text study is not a natural gift. Rather, it is something that will have to be learned and cultivated over time by each of them, through ongoing practice, self-awareness, and the full collaboration of their havruta partner.

We write on the board the header: "The Instrumental Aspect of Havruta Text Study: What and How Can It Contribute to Our Learning?" We explain that our long-term goal is for them to become successful and effective havruta learners of Jewish texts. What will help them get there are the many opportunities to study and discuss Jewish texts in a havruta format, and special learning activities designed to help us learn and experiment with specific practices of havruta text study. One central element for growth into havruta learners is developing an understanding of what havruta text study can contribute to one's individual learning experience—that is, to attend to the instrumental aspect of havruta learning and what concrete practices might be conducive to that end.

We invite students to explore through discussion and a short text study a few examples of what "improvement" or "learning better" could mean in the context of havruta learning.[13] The first task begins with the student's own ideas. We ask everyone to take a couple of minutes to think about what they know about havruta learning (based on previous experiences and/or based on what they read in the assignment) and to write what they think the adjective "better" might refer to by answering the first question:

In what sense can havruta learning contribute to "better" learning?

Students are then directed to the second question on the worksheet that asks them to offer an example of a practice that might help them to achieve the contribution they described above:

What do you believe to be one important practice (that is, something you or both of you could do) that could promote this/these contribution(s)? Explain your choice.

---

[13]   For the study tasks discussed in this section, see also Appendix 4.

By juxtaposing these two questions, we intend to signal at the outset that to state lofty goals for havruta learning is not enough if we do not explore how to enact those goals in practice.

Havruta pairs then share their responses with one another and sometimes with the larger group as well. In most cases, students present a wide variety of responses. For example, a student may cite the ways in which havruta partners can each contribute their particular strengths, such as a strong Hebrew background or a special gift for summarizing complex discussions. An approach that would build on the former would be to call upon the partner's knowledge of Hebrew without both partners having to formally translate the text; one way of capitalizing on the latter is to allot time to the havruta partner to offer a summary of the discussion before the pair proceeds to a new topic.

We then proceed to the second task with the goal of eliciting deeper thinking through a rich metaphor provided by a text. We note that talmudic literature offers reflections on the potential advantages of studying with a partner. We explain that this is not surprising, since the Talmud reflects a culture that values study in general and text study in particular, often in partnership. However, it is important to acknowledge that the kinds of reflections that appear in talmudic literature are not expressed in what we would recognize as a modern literary genre, written with an expansive narrative voice and expressing an introspective and self-reflective style. Rather, as in the text students will shortly examine, the rabbis' reflection is expressed through the use of metaphor, which invites the reader to explore its possible meanings. Rich metaphors allow for a variety of potential interpretations, and thus we encourage students to come up with more than one suggestion.

At this point, we orient the students toward the next section of the worksheet, which provides them with basic information about the text they are about to study. They engage in reading the following text:

> Rabbi Hama son of Hanina said: What is the meaning of the verse "Iron sharpens iron" (Proverbs 27:17)? This is to teach you that as in the case of one iron sharpens the other, so also do two scholars sharpen each other's mind by halakhah (Babylonian Talmud, Tractate Ta'anit 7a).

They then use the following question as a guideline for discussion:

> Following this interpretation, what might be important effects of studying together that are conveyed by the metaphor of "iron sharpens iron"? (E.g., *This metaphor seems to suggest that learning together is important because...*).

Students are then asked to suggest possible practices that would help achieve the ideal described by Rabbi Hama son of Hanina.

These two tasks reinforce that the answer to how havruta text study might help us learn is not completely sealed in our speculative thoughts or in self-reflective texts. Rather, it is through experimenting with havruta text study, and reflecting on our own insights and experiences, as well as those expressed in texts, that we can hope to fulfill the learning potential of this format.

We usually end this part of the session by inviting students to share their thoughts with other havruta pairs in the larger beit midrash or to write some of their ideas up and distribute them to the class at our next meeting. We intentionally employ language that fosters a learning environment in which different point of views are valued. Thus, for example, we might say, "We invite you to share your thoughts so that we can all learn from and take advantage of multiple perspectives."

Sometimes students question whether the havruta format is indeed so instrumental for learning. We reinforce this question, as it encourages students not only to reflectively attend to havruta text study, but also to examine critically when and whether havruta text study can be instrumental for one's learning.[14]

---

[14]   In interviewing female Israeli havruta pairs, Esty Teomim-Ben Menachem has gathered a number of insights as to the negative effects of havruta text study on their learning; see Teomim-Ben Menachem, *Women Study: Characterizing Conversation and Learning in Women's Havrutot.*

*A Learning Exchange: The Ethical-Relational Aspect
of Havruta Learning*

In our vision, havruta learning, as a particular form of collaborative learning, should do more than serve instrumental purposes. Rather, it should also help to nurture and cultivate the student's awareness and ability to care about, empathize with, and assist another person in her or his own learning process. When the student perceives the scope of his responsibility to include a genuine care for the learning of his partner, and when this deep concern translates itself into concrete solicitousness and effective assistance, the student is said to enact the ethical-relational dimension of havruta text study.[15]

To frame this view in a broader cultural perspective, this cooperative spirit among learning partners is an intentional attempt to transcend what often prevails as the everyday, conventional "being with" each other in the classroom.[16] Indeed, educators have written about alienation as a key factor in educational failure: "The low expectations, breakdown of social order, and academic failure are only symptoms of the much deeper problem of alienation."[17]

---

[15]   The concept of the ethical-relational dimension of havruta text study has developed in the course of our work and research. Deeply inspired by the works of Emmanuel Levinas and Hans-Georg Gadamer (despite their different views on this topic) we first addressed this aspect of havruta text study in Elie Holzer, "What Connects "Good" Teaching, Text Study and Havruta Learning? A Conceptual Argument," *Journal of Jewish Education* 72 (2006): 183–204. For the ethical traits that can be cultivated by the learner in his relationship with the text, see Elie Holzer, "Ethical dispositions in Text Study." For a further development of the concept of ethical dimension in direct relationship to the havruta partner as it appears in rabbinic literature see Elie Holzer, "'Either a Havruta Partner of Death': A Critical view on the Interpersonal Dimensions of Havruta Learning."

[16]   The types of relationships expressed as *being with* and *being for* are to be found in Zygmunt Bauman, *Life in Fragments: Essays in Postmodern Morality* (Oxford: Blackwell Publishers, 1995), 51–2. Translated into the havruta learning relationship, one of the major differences between these two modes of relationship is that *being for* may challenge social established convention — for example, that it is improper to challenge someone else's interpretation of a text. See our discussion in Chapter Six for the role of challenging.

[17]   Charles Bingham and Alexander M. Sidorkin, *No Education Without Relation*, 6. In Gadamer's vision of a hermeneutic community, partners must cooperate to establish a mutual world in which they may not

In contrast, the ethical-relational aspect of havruta text study aims to have each student cultivate a learning relationship, a mode of being together which is *for* and *to* the benefit of his havruta partner's learning and growth. This ethical dimension of havruta learning should ideally characterize the interpersonal relationships between havruta learners in both the first and the second phase of havruta text study.

We now proceed to discuss an example of a lesson[18] that we designed with the goal of introducing students to the ethical-relational aspect of havruta text study. Before we discuss the pedagogical aspects of this endeavor, we offer a disclaimer. We believe that what counts as ethical responsibility in the havruta context cannot be encapsulated by a prescribed list of rule-governed behaviors, ethical codes or precepts. Rather, this kind of ethical responsibility lies within the very ambiguity of the communication that takes place between two havruta partners. The ambiguity does not originate in a lack of understanding but rather from the fact that being actively present for one's havruta partner's learning cannot be contained only in one's cognitive grasp.[19] Rather, it mobilizes a sense of mutual empathy to be cultivated over time.

Our goal is to help each student begin to mobilize his personal empathy for the learner that resides in his havruta partner. In our work with older participants, we begin by calling their attention to the fact that havruta learning can be perceived as one particular instance of human dialogue. Here is the assignment we provide them with:

---

agree. What is important is how partners coordinate to establish meaning between themselves; see Barnett W. Pearce and Kimberly A. Pearce, "Taking a Communicative Perspective on Dialogue," in *Dialogue: Theorizing Difference in Communication Studies,* ed. Rob Anderson, Leslie A. Baxter, and Kenneth N. Cissna (Thousand Oaks, CA: Sage Publications, 2004), 39–56.

18   Parts of this lesson have been designed in the context of the Summer Teacher Institute, organized by the Center for Studies in Jewish Education and Culture at the University of Cincinnati.

19   For an important article on presence of teaching, see Carol Rodgers and Miriam Raider-Roth, "Presence in Teaching," *Teachers and Teaching: Theory and Practice* 12.3 (2006): 265–87.

Poets, philosophers and theoreticians of various fields have called people's attention to different aspects of human conversation. In that perspective, Martin Buber has provided us with a little description of one central aspect of dialogue. Please read it for yourself first and then explain to your havruta partner in your own words what you understand the main idea of this text to be:

In genuine dialogue the turning to the partner takes place in all truth, that is, it is a turning of the being. Every speaker "means" the partner or partners to whom he turns as this personal existence. To "mean" someone in this connection is at the same time to exercise that degree of making present which is possible to the speaker at that moment. The experiencing senses and the imagining of the real which completes the findings of the senses work together to make the other present as a whole and as a unique being, as the person that he is. But the speaker does not merely perceive the one who is present to him in this way; he receives him as his partner, and that means that he confirms this other being, so far as it is for him to confirm. The true turning of this person to the other includes this confirmation, this acceptance. Of course such an acceptance does not mean approval; but no matter in what way I am against the other, by accepting him as my partner in genuine dialogue I have affirmed him as a person.[20]

We use this text because it orients the reader to one major dimension of dialogue that is often not addressed explicitly in educational settings: the intentional work of the participant to make the learning partner present to oneself, to affirm his unique existence to oneself.

We then tell the students that we hope to help them open themselves to this central aspect of havruta learning. We explain that we believe that as an intense and somewhat intimate learning format, havruta learning offers them an opportunity to learn to cultivate a different way of being in conversation with another person. At the same

---

[20]   Martin Buber, "Elements of the Interhuman," in *Martin Buber: The Knowledge of Man- Selected Essays*, ed. Maurice Friedman (Baltimore: Humanities Press, 1966), 75–6.

time, this is a limited form of intimacy: in our setting, we are first and foremost interested in getting to know our havruta partner's personality as a learner, not necessarily everything about his private life. This is what we mean by interpersonal relationships in the context of havruta text study. The goal is to explore how we can be helpful to our havruta partner's growth and learning. Still, it is natural that during this first encounter with a havruta partner, students take some time to get to know each other a little.

Through this exercise students come to share some of their vulnerabilities and/or concerns about themselves as learners, particularly as havruta learners. It is also important that each student let her havruta partner know some concrete things that he might do or at least be aware of during the havruta learning. In other words, rather than assuming that the student will find out on his own how he might help his havruta partner, we prefer him to be attuned to his havruta partner's own suggestions for what might be most helpful. To help facilitate this encounter, we allow for student's reciprocal sharing of the individual assignments they completed about themselves as learners in the "becoming a havruta learner" assignment. The various parts of this learning activity are an outcome of our thinking in our goal to heighten students' awareness to each other as learners.

First, we have each student concentrate on reading her partner's description, because we believe that silent reading can help create a refined attention. Second, we encourage the asking of clarification questions. This is meant to help students cultivate a basic inquiry stance toward their partner. Third, participants are explicitly asked to share what they believe might help them learn better. Our experience has taught us that participants seem to avoid talking about this unless we insist on it. Finally, students conclude this learning session by writing up what they have learned about their havruta partner as a learner, and what specific aspects of havruta text study they will proactively address during the upcoming havruta sessions, with the goal of facilitating both their own learning as well as that of their partner:

Over time, we have seen a wide variety of answers to this question. Some students provide concrete reflections, like the student who had become aware that his havruta partner considers herself a "visual learner." He therefore committed himself to using visual representations to explain his ideas whenever possible and allow time for his havruta partner to do the same. Other students offer broader reflections, such as one student's commitment to "fully and respectfully listen to my havruta partner's ideas before interrupting him."

> Reflecting about what you have learned about yourself and about your havruta partner as learners, what are two things you hope to work on over the next 3–4 havruta text study sessions? Please be as specific as possible as to what you might do to contribute to your havruta partner's learning as well as your own (for example, some people might want to work on their listening skills, specifically learning to listen to their partner's entire comments before responding; some people might want to work on being clear in articulating their own ideas; etc.)

This final personal written summary is important because it gives students a chance to translate what they learned from this experience into practical commitments. It is through this writing activity that each havruta partner creates his or her own parallel and personal "curriculum" of havruta text study. This written summary will be used throughout the course, as we ask students to go back to this document and share their progress on their practical commitments, give each other feedback, and make adjustments as necessary. Indeed, we believe that formalized roles and responsibilities are not in conflict with the open-ended character of havruta text study, and we encourage students not only to share but also to negotiate how they want to develop the various aspects of their learning relationship.[21]

From a broader perspective, these three learning experiences are meant to cultivate basic attitudes towards a learning relationship that were articulated by Carl Rogers.[22] Rogers attempted to conceptualize

---

[21] This book does not include the discussion of such subsequent activities but we underline their central role in the curriculum meant to help students become good havruta learners. Omitting explicit refinement of this aspect of the interpersonal dimension of havruta text study would leave this opening session as a stand-alone activity without further impact.

[22] Carl R. Rogers, "The Interpersonal Relationship: The Core of Guidance," in *Person to Person: The Problem of Being Human, a New Trend in Psychology*, ed. Carl Rogers et al. (Lafayette, CA: Real People Press, 1967), 85–101.

what he had learned to be central to healthy and effective interpersonal relationships in the helping professions (psychotherapist, religious worker, guidance counselor, social worker, clinical psychologist), and in facilitating learning in particular.[23] He indicates three fundamental qualities or attitudes that are particularly important in facilitating learning: congruence, acceptance and empathic understanding. Rogers talks about these as they regard the teacher, as qualities that contribute to a climate of self-initiated experiential learning. The learning experiences described above exemplify how two of these qualities are addressed.

The need to impress others, often expressed in the effort to present oneself as knowledgeable, is a common characteristic in formal learning environments and may thus also characterize havruta partners. Rogers' insistence on *congruence* refers to the individual's effort to reduce, as much as possible, the front or façade that he puts on in the relationship. This means that the feelings that students experience are available to them—to their own awareness—and that they are able to live with these feelings and to communicate them. We encourage this attitude by having the students write and share some of their vulnerabilities and/or concerns as learners in general and as havruta learners in particular. The second of Rogers' attributes which is directly relevant to havruta learning is *empathic understanding*, which refers to the ability of students to understand each other's reactions from the inside and have a sensitive awareness of the way in which the learning process occurs in the other. Again, we hope to lay the groundwork for the cultivation of this attitude by having students read and listen to each other's descriptions as learners and havruta learners, and by having each tell in what practical ways their havruta partner might help them in the learning process.

Composing Havruta Pairs

Should teachers match students up in havruta pairs, or should this be left to the students themselves? Certainly, one could argue that adult students have the life experience and discretion to choose a part-

---

23   Carl R. Rogers, "The Interpersonal Relationship in the Facilitation of Learning," in *The Carl Rogers Reader*, ed. Howard Kirshenbaum and Valerie L. Henderson (London: Constable, 1990), 304–11.

ner that will make for a good havruta learning experience. On the other hand, allowing students of any age to choose their havruta partners may leave out certain people, especially those who might be less socially accepted. Also, we have found that students often tend to choose someone they feel comfortable with or someone they already know well, thus depriving them of the potential opportunity to engage with others different from themselves, including those with different learning styles.[24]

This challenge of pairing up havruta partners is all the greater for teachers like us who are interested in helping students consciously attend to and develop their havruta practices and relationships over time. What criteria, then, might we consider in thinking about the pairing of havruta partners?

While the learning dynamic that develops between havruta partners is dependent on many unpredictable elements, we nevertheless try to use some key criteria as we pair up havruta partners.[25] For example, whenever possible, we find it preferable to pair up students who do not know each other. This choice connects directly to our view of the ethical-relational dimension of havruta text study: we expect each student to cultivate a sense of responsibility for helping his havruta partner with his own learning. We believe the havruta learning experience is enhanced when students are asked to engage in the process of having to "learn" someone else as a person and as a learner, beginning from scratch, as it were.

---

[24]   From an historical perspective, it is worthwhile to mention that at times, either the head of the talmudic academy (the yeshiva) or some kind of students' union took the responsibility of pairing up students for havruta. See Mordechai Breuer, *Ohale Torah: Hayeshiva Tavnita veToldoteha* (Jerusalem: Merkaz Zalman Shazar Publication, 2004), 248.

[25]   Teomim-Ben Menachem provides interesting data showing that women attribute success in havruta text study first and foremost to some kind of undefined "chemistry" that takes place between learners and, broadly speaking, place much more emphasis on the quality of the personal relationship then on subject matter knowledge or skills. We do not possess enough parallel data collected by male havruta pairs to comment on the possibility of a gender-based explanation. It should also be noticed that Teomim-Ben Menachem's findings relate to women who study in havruta over an extended period of time, five days a week for a minimum of one year (see *Women Study: Characterizing Conversation and Learning in Women's Havrutot*).

As we pair students up, our aim is to create balanced and lively matches. Towards that end, we have discovered four criteria which contribute to the quality of the havruta learning dynamic:

a. *Pre-knowledge*: First, we evaluate both partners' background knowledge. This is particularly important in Jewish education, where we sometimes encounter major differences among students' Jewish knowledge and Hebrew language skills. As a general rule, we want to avoid a dynamic in which one havruta learner will be perceived as the sole holder of knowledge. We therefore prefer to pair up students who seem to share a similar level of Jewish background or whom we can imagine complementing each other in other areas of knowledge.

b. *Experience*: As teachers, we must remember that some students may have already had previous havruta learning experiences. Again, because we want to avoid a scenario in which one havruta partner dominates the entire learning dynamic, pairing someone who perceives himself as knowing what it takes to study in havruta with a student for whom this is the very first experience might turn out to be a destabilizing choice. We have found that havruta relationships work best when partners have comparable previous experience, enabling them to explore it together for the first time or, conversely, to revisit and revise their previously held conceptions.

c. *Gender and culture*: Over the course of our research, we have at times found ourselves asking to what extent gender plays a role in the havruta dynamic and how gender differences contribute to and/or hinder the havruta learning dynamic. Feminist epistemological and psychological theories present different and new ideas about the connections between knowledge, learning, and relationships that might have practical implications for havruta learning in general and pairing havruta pairs up in particular. For example, according to Carol Gilligan, Jennifer Coates, and Amy Sheldon, women tend to silence their personal views and prefer a consensus when engaging with people with different views.[26] One empiri-

---

26   Carol Gilligan, *In a Different Voice: Psychological Theory and Women's Development* (Cambridge, MA: Harvard University Press, 1982); Jennifer

cal study conducted on adults who have been introduced to havruta text study seems to indicate interesting tensions between women's perceptions of their role in society and the requirement to challenge one's partner in havruta learning.[27] While we have not observed significant differences between men and women as havruta learners and participants in our own teaching—our experience suggests that types of previous career training and whether participants are North American or Israeli are more relevant for a havruta's dynamics—this is an area that could benefit from further research

d. *Character/Personality*: Finally, specific personality traits are sometimes significant. For example, it would not necessarily be a good idea to pair up a student we know to be very shy with a student who is particularly outgoing. To the extent that we have had some prior encounters with our students and have begun to develop some basic ideas about their personality, we allow ourselves to rely on our intuition in terms of who might constitute a fitting havruta pair. Of course, this does not always guarantee success, but at the same time, we do not believe this element should be ignored or neutralized.

It is important to reiterate that while pairing up havruta partners, we try to keep a sense of flexibility and a clear awareness that pairing up people for this kind of intensive learning is not a simple or straightforward skill. Our responsibility as teachers is to make students feel that we expect them to engage in what might not be an immediately intimate learning relationship, while at the same time signaling that we are available to help them, and in the more extreme cases, to suggest an alternative arrangement.

Over time, we came to appreciate how the information provided in the *"Myself as a Havruta Learner"* assignment could help us, the

---

Coates, *Women Talk: Conversation Between Women Friends* (Oxford: Blackwell Publishers, 1996); Amy Sheldon, "Conflict Talk: Sociolinguistic Challenges to Self-assertion and How Young Girls Meet Them," *Merrill-Palmer Quarterly* 38.1 (1992): 95–117; Amy Sheldon, "Talking Power: Girls, Gender Enculturation and Discourse," in *Gender and Discourse*, ed. Ruth Wodak (London: Sage Publications, 1997), 225–44.

[27] Miriam Raider-Roth and Elie Holzer, "Learning to be Present: How Hevruta Learning Can Activate Teachers' Relationships to Self, Other and Text."

instructors, pair up students in havruta pairs.[28] A careful reading of students' responses often reveals what they anticipate to be challenging for them, what they see themselves contributing to the havruta learning dynamic or other bits of information about themselves as students and as people. For example, a student named Renee writes:

> Another thing on the list that I find difficult is challenging my havruta about his/her interpretation and/or statement of the text. I am not a confrontational person and therefore I usually tend not to challenge people's thoughts or ideas. I usually go with the flow and try not to cause disagreements so it is hard for me to challenge people, especially about their own ideas and opinions.

Another student, Rebekah, writes:

> Another challenging feature from the list is taking risks by challenging my hevruta partner. I do not like confrontation and do not want to appear as though I don't respect my hevruta partner's point of view.

Since learning to challenge another's interpretation plays a central role in our curriculum, we pay special attention to this information provided by Rebekah and Renee. In the case that most of the other criteria seem to indicate Renee and Rebekah would be a good match, the information provided here might lead us in one of two directions.

One option is to pair up Rebekah and Renee. Because both have concerns about challenging another's opinion, they might feel less inhibited to experiment together with this practice, partnering into a kind of common exploration while knowing that their partner also feels vulnerable.

Of course, a different line of reasoning might lead us to a different conclusion. In the same class, a student named Michael wrote in his assignment:

---

28   This assignment has been used in this way for the first time in the context of the Summer Teachers Institute, University of Cincinnati, 2007.

What would be most helpful for my own learning is to have a partner who is willing to listen to my ideas while at the same time questioning them. I need to be challenged away from my comfort zone and encouraged to try and look at things from a different perspective.

It may well be that for Renee or Rebekah, a havruta partner like Michael, who welcomes and is interested in being challenged, provides an opportunity to experiment with challenging in a safe way. And yet, we can also take Michael's information and consider pairing him up with Josh, who wrote: "I hope that we will enable one another to be challenged and leave our comfort zone."

In this example, the multiple options can become complex. Yet, sometimes, the havruta matching process is relatively straightforward. For example, from Lisa we learn the following:

I anticipate that the strengths I will bring to Hevruta study will include my ability to articulate interpretations of the text and effectively "probing" different interpretations and statements. One of the major strengths that I feel I bring to this study is my experience with and interest in detailed text study, both over the past year and as an English literature major in college.

Similarly, we hear from Judith:

My ability to articulate my interpretation of the texts at hand will be a strength of mine. I am unsure if this belief is a result of my Jewish texts study background, my previous experience with Beit Midrash for Teachers, or because of my personality (striving to be logical).

Clearly, these are two students who feel confident generating textual interpretations. Although it remains to be seen how their evaluations will translate into havruta learning, we do learn that both have a background in text study (English literature for Lisa and havruta learning for Judith). It would therefore probably not be a good idea to pair one of them up with a student who has no real prior experience with text study, which would likely lead to an unbalanced learning relationship. For example, it would not be a good idea to pair Lisa or

Judith up with Suzi, who wrote in her assignment: "I'm nervous that I won't be able to bring much to the interpretation table."

Sometimes students reveal in the assignment something about their personalities or psyches that we may factor in as we pair them up. Chava, for example, writes about herself as a learner:

> Being more of an internal person, it is often hard for me to express how I am feeling, and the same goes when I am trying to explain my interpretation of text.

And Claire writes that

> Sometimes I have a tendency to look at everything in black and white, right or wrong, and I miss out on all the in-betweens. I would like to be able to be more open-minded, taking risks with my interpretations, and exploring the gray areas.

Chava's and Claire's responses were generated by the following question:

> Think of yourself as a learner and a teacher: What do you do when circumstances cause you to "shut down?" When something in a text or with a learning partner either offends you or distances you, how do you usually react? How do you reconnect after such moments?

Again, this question was added only in later years, as a direct outcome of research that was conducted on students who had previously partaken in a havruta text study curriculum.[29] The participants

---

29 The research examined participants' "shutting down," moments of disconnection from the learning relationships and ways, strategies they use to help themselves reconnect with both learning partners and texts. Based on those findings, Miriam Raider-Roth and Elie Holzer introduced this question in the pre-course assignment of a havruta text study course, that took place under the auspices of the University of Cincinnati's Center for Studies in Jewish Education and Culture. For the research in question see, Miriam Raider-Roth, Vicky Stieha, and Billy Hensley, "Rupture and Repair: Episodes of Resistance and Resilience in Teachers' Learning"; Vicki

were all experienced teachers, which may explain the level of sophisti-
cation that we found in the responses. Consider, for example, how the
following responses shed light on the personality of the participants,
as we, teachers, consider how to pair them up. John, a young man in
his early twenties, writes:

> When something offends me, my first thoughts are usually
> angry. Depending on the topic, for example, if the offense was
> targeted towards my family, religion, or something else that
> I hold very dear, my mouth might start to water, I might clench
> my teeth and I might have the impulse to yell or take some other
> confrontational action. However, I can count on one hand the
> amount of times that this happened to me. I am actually extraor-
> dinarily difficult to offend, embarrass, or cause to shut down.
> I do not believe that it is worth burning bridges or embarrass-
> ing yourself over a petty remark or line of text. During the rare
> occasions where I do think about flying off the handle, I think
> of my father, who has always told me to think before I act, and
> of my mother, who has always told me that two wrongs never
> make a right. As a result of these life lessons, I know that yelling
> at someone, pounding a desk, or attempting to hurt someone
> with my words will not help the situation. Therefore, if I am
> offended, I usually opt to calmly ask the offender to talk with
> me one on one, so that we can sort out our differences.

Sarah, a mid-career teacher, writes:

> As a learner and a teacher, I "shut down" when I feel that my
> ideas or thoughts have no weight or significance to others, the
> audience (or classroom) is unreceptive or unwilling to partici-
> pate or engage in exploration of ideas or concepts. My reaction
> to offensive text or a learning partner that distances me: If
> I'm aware, I try to be silent but sometimes I will disagree ver-
> bally before I can stop myself. I try to analyze why I'm taking

---

Stieha and Miriam Raider-Roth, "Disrupting Relationships: A Catalyst
for Growth," in *Disrupting Pedagogies and Teaching the Knowledge Society:
Countering Conservative Norms with Creative Approaches*, ed. Jullie Faulkner
(Hershey, PA: IGI Global, 2011).

personal offense before I interact with [the] offender. Sometimes
I will make graphic organizers to sort out my thinking. My preference would be to engage cognitively rather than emotionally.
… [A] way to reconnect with learning partner: Change my
viewpoint to see if I can understand the historical or experiential perspective of author or learning partner; search for areas
of agreement; gather more information to try to make sense of
their position; meet privately to state clearly the offense without emotion, repeat for clarification; build consensus to "agree
to disagree." If this is a persistent situation that becomes emotionally charged, then change learning partner otherwise there
will be little learning.

Both John and Sarah seem to have developed self-awareness,
infused by cognitive distinctions, to help themselves handle situations
in which they feel shut down or offended. Particularly important is the
fact they each seem to also have developed practical steps designed to
straighten things out with their partner. This is an important piece of
information while considering pairing up students like John and Sarah
together with students who come from significant different cultural or
religious backgrounds. Indeed, we have witnessed instances in which
traditional Jewish texts addressed sensitive issues like Jews' and
Christians' relationships, or religiously committed vs. not religiously
committed Jews.[30] These texts led students of particular cultural or
religious backgrounds to express personal opinions, not realizing how
offensive they were for their havruta partner. While this kind of situation is inherent in what might happen during havruta learning, it is
helpful, while pairing up havruta partners, to know about students
like John or Sarah who bring constructive ways to deal with such situations (as reflected in their transcripts).

In conclusion: The different realms in which we intervene as
teachers at the designing stage (setting the physical space up, pairing
up havruta partners, and having students establish how they will help

---

[30]   The former case refers to an incident which took place at the Summer
Teacher Institute organized by the Center for Studies in Jewish Education
and Culture at the University of Cincinnati. The latter refers to an incident
which took place in the context of the *Melamdim* teacher education program
at the Hartman Institute in Jerusalem.

each other in the learning process) could reflect a desire for micro-management on our part, one that could turn out to be detrimental to the creative and open dynamic of havruta learning.

Indeed, the constant examination of the fine line between establishing structures and norms, and allowing for creative and dynamic experiences, is a major characteristic of what it means to design and teach havruta text study. It is therefore important to reiterate that beyond the specific examples developed and discussed in this chapter, these various aspects of havruta learning require continuous examination and adaptation. For instance, over time, we design additional opportunities for students to reflect on their own learning and to both share and discuss with their havruta partner in what practical ways they could support each other's learning. This is done in more or less formal ways, ranging from written classroom reflections and personal diaries to informal conversations. We also continue to inquire (through observations and conversations) about the relationships between havruta partners and, whenever needed, we do not hesitate to intervene and eventually make changes in the pairs. Finally, as students accumulate experience in havruta learning, we like to ask for their suggestions as to what changes in the beit midrash space might contribute to making it more supportive of havruta learning.

To understand a question means to ask it.
To understand meaning is to understand it
as the answer to a question.

Hans-Georg Gadamer

A wise person… does not hasten to answer.
His questions are on the subject
and his answers to the point.

Ethics of the Fathers, Chapter 5

Deciding the question is the path to knowledge.

Hans-Georg Gadamer

Chapter Four:
Questioning for Interpretation

Since Socrates, the art of asking questions has been seen as an indispensable skill of teaching and of learning. Through thoughtful questioning, teachers can not only extract factual information, but help learners to connect concepts, draw inferences, cultivate creative thought, and engage in the process of critical thinking. Educational literature mainly emphasizes the teacher's use of questions to promote learning among students, rather than students questioning each other.[1] In contrast, one of the characteristics of havruta text study is that the teacher is not at the core of the learning dynamic as it unfolds with its give-and-take of questions and answers.

---

[1]   This is even the case in research on text-based learning and on the use of interpretive questioning (i. e., a question for which there is more than one answer possible). For the use of questions, only by teachers, in interpretive discussion, see Sophie Haroutunian-Gordon, *Turning the Soul*, 6–7, 54; Sophie Haroutunian-Gordon, *Learning to Teach Through Discussion: The Art of Turning the Soul*, 91–118. For an example of a scholarly work that is directly oriented to the teaching of questioning to students, see Isabel L. Beck, Margaret G. McKeown, Rebecca L. Hamilton, and Linda Kugan, *Questioning the Author: An Approach for Enhancing Student Engagement with Text* (Delaware: International Reading Association, 1997).

Questions fuel the exchanges between text and havruta partners and between both havruta partners, and as such constitute a central element in the activation of the interpersonal, intrapersonal, and textual dimensions of havruta text study. Thus, to become independent, mindful havruta learners, students should be given opportunities to consider in greater depth the function and impact of questions, and to acquire the skills necessary to ask good questions on their own.

In this chapter, we discuss the role of questioning as an interpretive textual practice. We begin with the role that questions asked about the text play in the development of interpretations. We then examine the unique impact of "open" questions: the openness that is referred to consists of the choices the question creates between alternative interpretations. We then proceed to discuss a sample lesson designed to help students cultivate a mindful use of open questions and understanding of their impact on the development of alternative textual interpretations.

This focused attention on open questions also creates an opportunity for students to reflect upon the preconceptions by which they interpret the text. When students question and examine these preconceptions, they use questioning as an interpretive intrapersonal practice. In the last section of the chapter, we discuss an example of this type of questioning as a self-reflective practice.

Questioning as a Textual Practice

As in most tasks involving collaborative examination, questions will naturally and spontaneously be asked in the havruta learning interaction. For example, havruta learners might ask each other for the meaning of a term in the text. Yet, there are other, more complex kinds of questions, which require intentionality and guided learning, as they are less likely to occur spontaneously.

A first reading of a text yields an holistic grasp of its meaning, but this first impression amounts more to a first "guess" or "wager" about the meaning.[2] The text may contain subtle details that do not show up on the readers' radar at first. Moreover, that initial understanding may itself "blind" the student to important features of the text. A second, more attuned and open-minded engagement with the

---

[2]   Paul Ricoeur, *Hermeneutics and the Human Sciences*, 209.

text is therefore called for, the purpose of which is to examine, validate, refine or revise this initial understanding. This can be achieved by the use of analytical and critical methodologies.[3] In Ricoeur's words: "To explain more is to understand better."[4] For that purpose, we ask students to adopt strategies like reading aloud, performing multiple readings, paraphrasing the text, breaking it into parts, and raising questions about the text.[5]

Indeed, the meaning of a text is revealed in the interplay of questions and answers.[6] More broadly, not only formal questions but also other strategies all represent variations of what it means to question the text, in the sense that they activate what Paul Ricoeur calls a "productive notion of distanciation,"[7]—that is, a scrutinizing perspective that helps the learner pay closer attention to the structure and

---

[3]   This reflects Ricoeur's concept of "explanation," see Chapter Two. These methodologies include, for example, structural and historical analysis of the text.

[4]   Paul Ricoeur, *Time and Narrative Vol. 1* (Chicago: University of Chicago Press, 1984), x.

[5]   Re-reading is a common technique used in close reading. See for example David Galef, *Second Thoughts: A Focus on Rereading* (Detroit: Wayne State University Press, 1998). Galef examined how re-reading changes the reader's perspective after the first reading. Re-reading enables the revelation of hitherto unnoticed connections and insights, and thus illustrates the creative dimensions of the reading act. See also Wolfgang Iser, "The Reading Process: A Phenomenological Approach," *New Literary History* 3.2 (1972): 279–99. Ricoeur connects the need for multiple readings to the polysemic nature of a text in *From Text to Action: Essays in Hermeneutics II; Studies in Phenomenology and Existential Philosophy* (Evanston, IL: Northwestern University Press, 1991), 32.

[6]   Hans-Georg Gadamer, *Truth and Method*, 362–80.

[7]   Paul Ricoeur, *Hermeneutics and the Human Sciences*, 131–44. On the inherent importance of questioning for understanding, Gadamer writes: "The close relation between questioning and understanding is what gives the hermeneutic experience its true dimension... that is why we cannot understand the questionableness of something without asking real questions, though we can understand a meaning without meaning it. To understand the questionableness of something is already to be questioning. There can be no tentative or potential attitude to questioning, for questioning is not the positing but the testing of possibilities... A person who thinks must ask himself questions" (Gadamer, *Truth and Method*, 376).

those details of the story that may provide clues about its meaning, and helps the learner to revisit his initial understandings of the text.[8]

In that process, we must determine which type of questions may specifically contribute to a fuller interpretation. Let us begin by acknowledging that texts themselves have an effect on the reader's questions, and that different texts set different boundaries for what constitutes appropriate questions. For example, according to Wayne Booth, readers ask three kinds of questions of text: "those that the object seems to invite one to ask; those that it will tolerate or respond to, even though perhaps reluctantly, and those that violate its interests or effort to be a kind of thing in the world."[9]

In this context, we adopt Gadamer's distinction between open, pedagogical and rhetorical questions. An *open* question creates a choice between alternative interpretations or the "considering of opposites."[10] In fact, the very essence of questioning is to open possibilities and keep them open, at least for a while. Without this openness, a question is merely a device. It is by looking at the text from the perspective of a particular question that an open question paves the way toward alternative interpretations.[11]

And yet, open questions are not the questions many of our students are used to asking or are exposed to in a traditional class-room environment, where pedagogical and rhetorical questions seem

---

[8]   "The matter of the text is not what a naïve reading of the text reveals, but what the formal arrangement of the text mediates" (Paul Ricoeur, *Hermeneutics and the Human Sciences*, 93). Generally, we do not design special havruta lessons to help students experiment with and learn these other strategies like reading aloud, performing multiple readings, paraphrasing the text, and breaking it into parts. We have found them to be less complex, and have observed that students do not encounter special difficulties integrating them as part of their learning. However, we do discuss with students the role of these strategies and explain in what sense they support the act of "distanciation" that is so important at this stage of their initial reading. We also periodically remind them to practice these strategies—for example, as part of written guidelines for havruta learning. See Appendix 2 for an illustration.

[9]   Wayne C. Booth, *The Company We Keep: An Ethics of Fiction* (Berkeley: University of California Press, 1989), 90.

[10]   Hans-Georg Gadamer, *Truth and Method*, 365.

[11]   "Questioning opens up possibilities of meaning, and thus what is meaningful passes into one's own thinking on the subject" (ibid., 375).

to prevail. A *pedagogical* question is not open because the answer is already known to the questioner. There is no openness in the questioning, and in fact there is no questioner, only a "teacher" who knows the answer and wants a "student" to reproduce it. An oral examination, for instance, is not an example of true dialogic questioning because teacher and student do not attempt to reach an agreement about the subject, and excludes the possibility of a given standpoint being challenged. Similarly, a *rhetorical* question gives its own answer, so that there is really no question at all, only an implicit assertion.

In fact, asking open questions is more difficult than answering them.[12] Gadamer warns us that asking questions is not actually a method of knowing.[13] For him, questioning consists in remaining open during reading so that questions can occur. We, however, as instructors, believe that students can become aware of and develop their ability to ask open questions, but we also keep in mind that our challenge lies in helping students learn to discern the *questionability* of the text, not merely teaching questioning as a technique.[14]

Here is an example of a lesson that is designed to introduce students to questioning, with the goal of helping them "problematize" and deepen their initial understanding of the text, become aware of the variety of questions that can be instrumental in text study (especially open questions), and begin to realize how those questions may impact their interpretations.

---

[12]   "In order to be able to ask, one must want to know, and that means knowing that one does not know" (ibid., 363).

[13]   Ibid., 365.

[14]   See Orit Kent, *Interactive Text Study and the Co-Construction of Meaning*, for a case of a havruta pair that helps illustrate the importance of this point. In this case (#3), the pair asks open questions, but see them as something to get through; they utilize questioning as a technique and not as a stance toward the text. Kent has identified a related practice, which she terms "wondering," a central activity of which is the asking of questions. Wondering can play both an interpretive role as well as an interpersonal role and is often motivated by gaps in the text and in the conversation, ibid.; Orit Kent, "A Theory of Havruta Learning."

Learning to Question the Text for Interpretation

This lesson begins with a mini-lesson in which we introduce the importance of questioning as an interpretive textual practice. Next, students engage in havruta text study, during which they practice questioning and explore its role in the development of compelling interpretations. Finally, students are given time to analyze and reflect on their learning experiences.

The Mini-Lesson

The mini lesson serves two major purposes: it introduces students to their responsibility to try to "make the text speak" and to the role of the practice of questioning in this process.

We start the lesson by situating the function of questions within the broader picture of the interpretive process. We discuss how, as we know from daily experience, speaking does not guarantee that what is meant by one person will be accurately understood by another. Sometimes more is meant than the words convey; sometimes the person who speaks assumes that the listener already knows certain things and sometimes, instead of listening, the addressee may just project his own thoughts and beliefs onto what is said by his conversational partner.

We then ask students to reflect upon their own previous personal experiences in serious conversation, and the techniques they have used to ensure that they are well understood and also understand well. In the ensuing discussion, we introduce the idea that questioning is a central strategy in helping us better understand and reduce subjective projections onto what has been said. We then introduce the Havruta Learning Triangle (see Chapter Two), which portrays the text as one of three partners in the havruta study interaction.

We trace a parallel between listening to a partner in a conversation and approaching the text as a partner in havruta learning. Often in human conversation, the speaker uses various techniques to make himself understood and the listener uses questions as a means of understanding. In our discussion, we ask students to comment on what might be the text's "vulnerability," given its inability to speak for itself. We also ask them to think, as readers, about the practical implications of this vulnerability. Students may mention the need to listen carefully, and the need to revise and make sure that the interpretation they offer is grounded in the text. Some students comment on the danger of mis-using the text when readers are driven by what they want it to say.

We then invite them to comment on two statements from the novelist and writer Steven C. Scheer:

> "Good readers are what they read. Bad readers read what they are."

> "Good reading is an act of love, bad reading is an act of self-love."

If it has not been articulated by the students, we underline that among other things, Scheer tries to make us aware of the fact that we are free, and thus responsible for shaping our interactions with a text in different ways; some readers are cognizant of the fact that the text is a separate entity deserving of respect as such, but others tend to read themselves into the text, instead of attempting to first listen to it. In this context, we introduce the rationale behind strategies that are part of the overall practice of questioning, such as reading aloud, performing multiple readings, paraphrasing the text, breaking it into parts, and raising direct questions. We emphasize how questioning as a central textual practice can help us reduce our own projections and preconceptions about what the text says and revisit our primary understanding. It can also increase our attention to what is found in the text as well as what is missing from the text, and help us make sense of it. Indeed, upon close and open reading, we often find either apparent inconsistency or at least ambiguity in a text, both of which open up interpretive possibilities.

We then situate questioning in the Havruta Learning Triangle diagram, identifying its role in the triadic relationship:

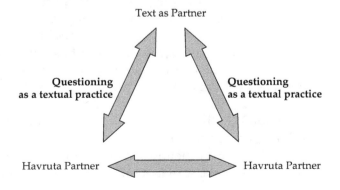

Text as Partner

Questioning
as a textual practice

Questioning
as a textual practice

Havruta Partner

Havruta Partner

Finally, while we encourage students to ask all kinds of questions, we want to introduce them to the central role of *open* questions, emphasizing that these questions can be answered in more than one way. We also emphasize that while it is natural for students to immediately offer answers to questions their partners raise, it is the formulation of questions *per se* that is most essential in the first phase of text study.

We often introduce them to this quote from Gadamer: "To ask a question means to bring into the open."[15] This is precisely what we ask our students to do as learners of text: to re-open the text to fresh possible meanings through the use of open questions that cultivate a sense of indeterminacy.[16]

The Practice: Questioning and Generating Interpretations

We point to the fact that we have selected a narrative text from rabbinic literature, an aggadah, which by its very nature invites open questions. For example, such narrative texts typically describe the literary characters' words and actions, but not their feelings, thoughts or motivations, inviting questions that are critical to the interpretive process.[17] Additional questions may pertain to missing information or

---

[15]   Hans-Georg Gadamer, *Truth and Method*, 363.

[16]   Maurice Blanchot beautifully describes this fundamental role of questioning in words which we often share with adult learners: "The question, if it is incomplete speech, rests upon incompleteness. It is not incomplete as a question: on the contrary, it is speech that is accomplished by having declared itself incomplete. The question places the full affirmation back into the void, and enriches it with this initial void. Through the question we give ourselves the thing and we give ourselves the void that permits us not to have it yet, or to have it as desire. The question is the desire of thought" (Maurice Blanchot, *The Infinite Conversation: Theory and History of Literature, Vol. 82* [Minneapolis: University of Minnesota Press, 1993], 12).

[17]   See Appendix 1 for our discussion on the selection of texts and Appendix 2 for what kind of relevant textual background information we provide.

potential alternatives to the meaning of key words, etc. The following is an example of a text we may use for this lesson:[18]

1. Rabbi Shimi bar Ashi used to attend (the classes) of R. Papa	1. רב שימי בר אשי הוה שכיח קמיה דרב פפא
2. and used to ask him many questions (*Alternative translation*: many difficult questions).	2. הוה מקשי ליה טובא
3. One day he observed that Rabbi Papa fell on his face [in prayer] and he heard him saying, "May God preserve me from the embarrassment caused by Shimi" (*Alternative translation*: from the insolence of Shimi.).	3. יומא חד חזייה דנפל על אפיה. שמעיה דאמר: רחמנא ליצלן מכיסופא דשימי.
4. The latter thereupon vowed silence and questioned him no more.[19]	4. קביל עליה שתיקותא ותו לא אקשי ליה.

As mentioned above, we first have students engage in several strategies that are instrumental in helping students "question" their initial understandings of the text. We walk them through guidelines like those that follow, and share their underlying rationale:

> - Please take turns reading the text aloud.
> - Help each other paraphrase the text.
> - Discuss the possible parts of the story.
> - Read the text again. You may notice new details.[20]

---

[18] Instead of providing students with a copy of the text in its original Talmudic context, we distribute an annotated version of the text with numbered line sequence. This graphic layout invites greater attention to the text's literary elements, such as omission, structure, dialogue, and narration. Numbered lines help the students refer to specific parts of the text in havruta and in larger group discussions.

[19] Talmud, Tractate Ta'anit, 9b.

[20] It should be noticed that in principle, these four tasks could be performed by any solitary reader who would seek to create the necessary distance from the text so that his initial understanding can be re-examined. Even in a havruta pair, each learner could examine the text on his own using

Students begin by reading the text aloud and paraphrasing it to each other. While typical of traditional havruta learning, this is not a common practice in many contemporary settings of Jewish learning. We explain to our students that we insist on this practice because it draws in both partners to a joint task and also establishes the presence of the text as a partner in the exchange. As each reader lends her own voice to the "voice" of the text, she makes it audible in the havruta exchange and she and her partner can become attuned to its details.[21] Paraphrasing the text as well as discussing its possible parts are often more challenging that they initially seem to be, but these activities help both partners concentrate on their joint effort to make the text speak, checking their understanding with their partner and avoiding rushing to a hasty personal conclusion about what they have read.

After students perform these initial tasks, we introduce the concept of open questions, as discussed above.[22] Students are then asked to articulate with their havruta partner a number of open questions, and then write on a flipchart that is visible to the other havruta pairs what they feel are the three most compelling open questions.

Here are several examples of students' questions:

- The text labels Shimi as a rabbi. Was he already a rabbi when he attended Rabbi Papa's classes? If so, might this have been an extra cause for some kind of pressure or apprehension on Rabbi Papa's behalf, since he not only had students but also a colleague in the classroom?
- Why did Rabbi Shimi actually ask all these questions, and what kind of questions were these? Didn't he understand what Rabbi Papa said, in contrast to the other students ("many questions")?

---

these questions. In designing these tasks, however, we apply some of the insights from social learning theories, such as the contribution of conversation to understanding, and have havruta partners perform these tasks by addressing one another. We further elaborate on this aspect of our design of havruta learning in Appendix 2.

[21]   A discussion on the culture of reading aloud in the context of being read to can be found by Alberto Manguel, *A History of Reading* (New York: Penguin Books, 1996), 109–23. For further discussions of traditions of silent and aloud reading, see Guglielmo Cavallo and Roger Chartier, *Histoire de la Lecture dans le Monde Occidental* (Paris: Seuil, 1997).

[22]   See Appendix 6 for an alternative version of this part of the session.

- If Shimi asked challenging questions, what made these questions challenging?
- Didn't Rabbi Papa have the knowledge to answer the questions? Did the questions require him to engage in a certain type of thinking he wasn't ready for?
- Did the questions challenge Rabbi Papa's knowledge or perhaps his authority?
- Why did Rav Papa choose to handle this awkward teaching situation through prayer?

By focusing the entire class on these questions, by making them visible to all and by allocating these questions a critical amount of time as part of havruta learning, we reinforce the centrality of questioning as a practice and help students expand the scope of the questions they ask. This strategy also helps sensitize students, at the very outset of the learning process, to the great variety of open questions that some texts can elicit.

Once the top questions are all visible, we ask the havruta pairs to examine them and try to categorize them into different types of questions (e. g., questions pertaining to the characters' motivations, questions about missing information, etc.). Students identify and name the categories of questions, and provide examples. We record these categories and make them available for students to work with in subsequent classes.[23]

We often also distribute a copy of open questions raised about the same text by students from previous classes. In addition to serving the above goals, this practice of sharing the questions of a "previous generation" of students exemplifies a central ideal of Jewish text study, namely that there can be something generative when such study is conducted not only through synchronic but also through diachronic exchanges. Making these questions visible at this stage of the lesson can further impact the students' interpretive process by providing them with new venues for interpretations.

The students then regroup into havruta pairs and discuss which of the questions they find most promising and generative. They provide an explanation for their choices and proceed to articulate potential

---

23   This practice enacts Bandura's principles of learning new practices as discussed in Chapter Two.

textual interpretations. The articulation of a comprehensive textual interpretation is not a simple matter, as such an interpretation would be constituted by more than by the sum of its separate parts, the details and questions that have been discussed in connection to the text. We help students take this next step toward the articulation of a larger textual interpretation by providing them with guidance questions like "What do you understand the text to be about?" and "What do you think the text is saying?" These questions help formulate not only the "issue" or "topic" that is raised by the text, but also what the textual partner is actually saying to us, the reader.[24] One practical way to help students answer these questions is to have them complete the following two sentences:

> I believe this story to be about ....
>
> and it is saying that ....

Here are two examples of interpretations that we collected from students who used these prompts to make a clear distinction between a descriptive conceptualization of the text's topic and the view it addresses to the reader:

- I believe this story to be about the importance of being aware of the inexplicit norms of interaction between teacher and student in the classroom. This story is saying that students like Shimi are not aware of boundaries they cross when constantly putting their teacher in embarrassing situations which reveal his limitations. The story suggests not only that this might elicit strong negative feelings from the teacher, but also that when things deteriorate, the insensitive student may also end up losing his ability to ask even those questions that would *not* embarrass the teacher.
- I believe this story to be about communication and expectations in relationships between teachers and students. This particular story says that when communication fails (especially the teacher's communication that seeks a heavenly solution rather than

---

[24]   In Chapter Eight, we further elaborate on the conceptual basis for the making of such assertions about a text.

communicating with his student) then relationships fail and the student's learning is hurt.

In this final part of the lesson, students are asked to reflect back on the interpretive process and, if relevant, make connections between the open questions they asked or were exposed to, and the interpretations of the text they have elicited. This reflection raises the students' awareness of this connection between open questions and possibilities for interpretation. To that end, we sometimes provide them with an individual written assignment, articulated as follows:

> Write as specifically as possible what in the text led you to this interpretation (or these interpretations) and, specifically, if any of the questions you've raised or were exposed to played a role in helping you develop a particularly compelling interpretation.
>
> Please be ready to share your interpretation (s) and your thoughts with the larger group.

When possible, we use the framework of individual writing to allow for a stronger personal and more self-aware experience in retracing possible connections between questions and interpretations. This task also requires students to be accountable for the textual evidence that supports their interpretation. Thus, students learn to see how open questions, as well as the cues and textual proof they find in the text, are significant contributors to their textual interpretations.

The final discussion in the larger group of both the interpretations and the open questions that led to them is usually a lively and enlightening experience for all participants, bringing diverse and at times competing interpretations to light. What makes this particular text so compelling in this particular context is that it concerns one of the roles that questions play in the teacher-learner relationship. It introduces possibilities for thinking about the many dimensions of questions in learning settings, dimensions that go far beyond merely asking for information. For example, we have seen students consider Rabbi Shimi's asking of "many and/or difficult questions" as an opportunity to discuss the social impact of questioning (i. e., the question draws the teacher's attention to the student and too many questions may not allow enough time for other students to question). Other students have talked about questioning as a practice that can not only nurture but also disrupt relationships between student and teacher.

Personal Reflection: Questioning as an Intrapersonal Practice

"I never thought the Talmud would criticize the behavior of a leading rabbi." This reflection from Mike, a young student teacher in his early twenties, reflects similar comments we have heard from students who have experimented with open questions and their potential impact on textual interpretations.[25] As we inquired about what he meant, Mike said that he came to realize that his initial understanding of the text was driven by a clear assumption that whatever the meaning of the text was, Rabbi Papa had to be perceived as the victim of Rabbi Shimi's misconduct. "Because it could not be," he said, "that the Talmud would criticize Rabbi Papa's behavior, a prominent Talmud scholar." To our question about why he made such an assumption, Mike spontaneously replied that all he had been taught or had read so far which pertained to talmudic stories had been clearly tainted by a similar moralistic pattern: the rabbi is the holy character of the story, a character who does not fail, in contrast to other people around him who do not maintain his moral standards. Mike said that it was only when he was trying to come up with open questions together with his havruta partner, and actively sought out what he called "unconventional" insights, that he came to realize that perhaps his assumption about Rabbi Papa's moral perfection might not be appropriate to this text. How do we account for Mike's realization and what does it tell us about learning opportunities that occur in the interpretive process?

We saw that meaning can only be constructed via the active involvement of the learner's pre-knowledge or preconceptions. Mike's preconceptions about rabbis in talmudic stories is not a typical instance of Wolfgang Iser's concept of "filling the gaps," where the reader inserts new data into the text.[26] Rather, it is a pre-textual

---

25   This data was collected in the year 2010, at *Melamdim,* a two-year post-bachelor teacher education program co-jointly based at the Hartman Institute in Jerusalem and Tel-Aviv University.

26   Wolfgang Iser, *The Act of Reading.*

assumption about the literary corpus (in Mike's case, a belief about "rabbis in the talmudic literature"), which the learner brings and which predetermines his interpretation of this particular text before the actual reading. It is in the differential space between Mike's initial interpretation and the new, radically different interpretation that he and his partner elicited that Mike had an opportunity to become aware of this preliminary character of his understanding. Realizing such preconceptions is invaluable for the student's understanding of himself and central to any future open approach to text study.

Given that students report having significantly changed their initial interpretation during the lesson, we ask them to analyze and articulate together with their havruta partner what might have been preliminary assumptions that they brought to their first interpretation. Once they articulate these assumptions, we ask students to question them, examining where they come from, and considering in what sense this reflection may illuminate the personal preconceptions they hold more generally.

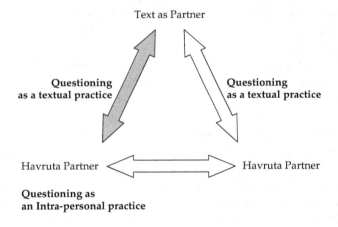

Text as Partner

Questioning
as a textual practice

Questioning
as a textual practice

Havruta Partner

Havruta Partner

Questioning as
an Intra-personal practice

Applied in this way, questioning becomes an interpretive intrapersonal practice, performed toward the end of the interpretive process, as illustrated in the diagram. Not only does it offer the student an opportunity to learn something about himself, it may also raise his consciousness of the benefits of proactively seeking to uncover some of his preconceptions during havruta text study.

In conclusion, questioning the text is a rich practice that is indispensable to the development of textual interpretation. It is a major tool that helps the learner avoid locking himself too easily into what might only consist of a first impression of the text's meaning. "Making the text speak" indeed requires a certain dialectic process, constituted by openness to the idea that the text might say something different than originally assumed, and that the cultivation of a certain distance with the text is necessary so that it can be examined from a new perspective. Practices like repeated readings, reading aloud, paraphrasing, and above all asking open questions are central tools in that regard.

By making havruta learners conscious of the role of open questions in their ability to develop alternative interpretations, we aim to help them cultivate an increasing ability to seek and perceive what is question-worthy in a text. We aim to help students see that "problematizing" an initial understanding of a text can yield new and rich insights, not only about what the text might be saying, but about some of the learner's own preconceptions.

Torah is acquired with forty-eight qualities:
...listening and illuminating...

Ethics of the Fathers, Chapter 6

Man has learned much since morning/
For we are a conversation and we can listen/
To one another.

Holderlin, from *Celebration of Peace*

CHAPTER FIVE:
LISTENING FOR INTERPRETATION

In our work facilitating havruta learning for students, we have consistently emphasized and structured the practice of good listening—not only to one's human partner, but to the text as well. With any text, it is important to "hear" it on its own terms, rather than rushing and projecting our prior assumptions onto it or making it fit our expectations. At the same time, interpreting a text always involves some amount of projection both because of the subjective nature of understanding and because the text by its very nature invites readers to fill in gaps.[1] Consequently, learning to develop sound textual interpretations consists of learning to consciously and intentionally manage this dual nature of the interpretive process. In Chapter Four, we discussed the role of questioning in the service of that process; here, in a similar vein, we will investigate another central practice, that of listening.

As an interpretive practice, listening plays a complementary role in the process of textual interpretation. While questioning is clearly pro-active and verbal, listening has a more receptive, non-verbal quality—though it also requires active and at times audible engagement.

---

[1]   Hans-Georg Gadamer, *Truth and Method*; Wolfgang Iser, *The Act of Reading*; Paul Ricoeur calls readers' attention to the need to examine the ways in which they read with a healthy measure of suspicion, knowing well how easy it is to be seduced into convenient or self-affirming interpretations, in *Freud and Philosophy* (New Haven: Yale University Press, 1970).

This chapter addresses the need for the havruta learner to cultivate a way of listening that does not merely respect but actively considers what the text and the havruta partner say, in a way that will contribute positively to the meaning he attributes to the text. In that regard, focusing on listening and on its specific contextual aspects means considering the particular role that listening plays in the dynamic of textual interpretation—that is, how the learner listens to the text and how he listens to the text when mediated by the havruta partner's comments. In addition, listening operates as an expansive activity by allowing the learner to perceive and revise more directly the preconceptions he projects in this dynamic.[2]

In this chapter, we begin by addressing how these aspects of listening operate in havruta text study and discuss what may make it challenging for havruta learners. We then proceed to review an instructional strategy designed to help havruta learners cultivate these different aspects of listening during the interpretive process.

Listening as an Interpretive Practice

Listening is central to learning, yet it is only recently that researchers have recognized the more complex and challenging aspects of listening in the context of teaching and learning.[3] Beyond its common understanding, close to that of "hearing"—that is, receiving and taking in sound or meaning—good listening is much more complex. It involves intentionally focused attention, and an openness toward

---

[2]   For an analysis of how this plays out in an actual havruta session, see Orit Kent, *Interactive Text Study and the Co-Construction of Meaning*; Orit Kent, "A Theory of Havruta Learning." Kent discusses four kinds of listening, and considers how they reflect the listeners' different intentions and in turn how these affect modes of listening to people and texts.

[3]   Kathy Shultz, *Listening: A Framework for Teaching Across Differences* (New York and London: Teacher College Press, 2003); Michael Welton, "Listening, Conflict and Citizenship: Towards a Pedagogy of Civil Society," *International Journal of Lifelong Education* 21 (2002): 197–208; Clark Thomas, "Sharing the Importance of Attentive Listening Skills," *Journal of Management Education* 23 (1999): 216–23; Vivian G. Palley, "On Listening to What Children Say," *Harvard Educational Review* 56 (1986): 122–31; more recently, Teacher College Record has dedicated a special issue to listening in the context of teaching and learning: *Teachers College Record* 112.11 (2010).

something that may not be easily grasped because of its elusiveness and complexity.

The concept of the "fusion of horizons" that we discussed in Chapter Two shows how interpretation involves the learner in a process that is simultaneously proactive and receptive, a progressive process of meaning making that occurs when two horizons meet each other and emerges from that interaction. In that fusion, a circular movement takes place between the anticipatory movement of the learner's horizon on one hand and what he encounters in the text on the other. While reading, the learner sheds assumptions, makes inferences and anticipates what is to come next. New sentences may confirm or undermine our anticipation, so we read backwards and forwards, predicting and negating, a process which Gadamer describes as the "interplay" between two movements.[4] The receptive aspects of interpretation occur when the learner lets information provided by the text conflict with his previous understanding, disrupting his preconceptions and projections and making him revise the meaning he attributes to the text—and yet, the learner can only understand what the text is saying by activating and projecting his prior knowledge and preconceptions.[5] While inevitable, and even indispensable to understanding, the proactive projection in all interpretive activity can block the learner's ability to engage equally in the receptive mode, and hinder the give-and-take that leads to textual understanding.

Since havruta text study happens in a triadic dynamic, for the individual havruta learner, new information is both provided directly from the text and conveyed to him by the comments, questions and assertions of his havruta partner. In that regard, listening in the interpretive process entails paying attention both to what is said by the text

---

[4]   Hans-Georg Gadamer, *Truth and Method*, 293.

[5]   On various aspects of the receptive mode in text study, see Elie Holzer, "Ethical Dispositions in Text Study"; for a similar aspect of text reading, this time from the perspective of literary theory, see the concept of the delay of information, as discussed by Meir Sternberg, *The Poetics of Biblical Narrative: Ideological Literature and the Drama of Reading* (Bloomington, IN: Indiana University Press, 1985). For a pedagogical strategy implying the development of moral imagination, see Elie Holzer, "Allowing the Text to Do Its Pedagogical Work: Connecting Moral Education and Interpretive Activity," *Journal of Moral Education* 36.4 (2007): 497–514; Elie Holzer, "Educational Aspects of Hermeneutical Activity in Text Study."

and/or by the havruta partner, and to what he, the learner himself, *does* with what he heard. Thus, conceptually listening in interpretation functions as a textual practice (in the interaction between learner and text), an interpersonal practice (in the interaction between havruta partners as they comment on the text to each other), and as an intrapersonal practice (in the listening one does to one's own thinking, enabling the uncovering, examination, and revision of preconceptions)[6].

The following diagram illustrates these three aspects of listening from the point of view of the individual havruta learner. The one-way arrows indicate the sources of information to which he is exposed and in relation to which he is to cultivate listening.

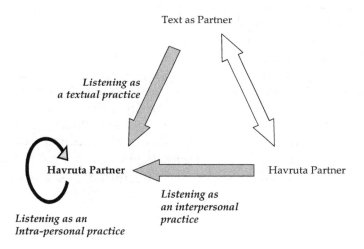

Text as Partner

Listening as a textual practice

Havruta Partner   Havruta Partner

Listening as an interpersonal practice

Listening as an Intra-personal practice

---

[6] We also elaborate on this last aspect of text study in Chapter Eight. In contrast to philosophical traditions in which the subject pretends to know itself by immediate intuition or by introspection, philosophical hermeneutics assumes that we understand ourselves only by the hermeneutic engagement with the signs of humanity deposited in cultural works (Paul Ricoeur, *From Text to Action: Essays in Hermeneutics II*). In this view, a person remains unaware of some parts of his own self, in the form of preconceptions he holds. Focusing on and listening to one's own preconceptions during the hermeneutical encounter with a text can also present an opportunity to become more aware and learn something about oneself in relation to the subject matter that is addressed. From this perspective, during the interpretive process some of one's own preconceptions appear as an "Other" to oneself. In Chapter Eight, we discuss the educational implications of this view.

Gadamer brings our attention to "the incapacity for listening" that we often manifest, which he identifies with ignoring what the other says, mishearing, not hearing the other's silence, and stubbornness. He attributes this incapacity chiefly to his observation that most people merely listen to themselves.[7] It is precisely because listening as a practice is neither "natural" nor habitual for most learners that cultivating the above mentioned types of listening is often challenging. This is the case for several particular reasons. First, students are not accustomed to being engaged in this type of conscious listening during the interpretive process, as it is rarely addressed in the classroom. Second, although teachers frequently address the importance of listening to each other in classroom discussion, this is often enacted by tuning out—simply not engaging—when other students speak. A discussion that is based on listening, however, is quite different from, say, a successive series of comments that no one interrupts but are not necessarily related—in essence, a pseudo-conversation.[8] Even when the importance of listening to fellow students is meaningfully addressed by classroom teachers, this is rarely true regarding listening to a text. The intimate and intense learning exchange that occurs in havruta text study provides a valuable opportunity to cultivate a more genuine type of listening, to the text as well as one's learning partner. Our instructional strategy helps students begin to experiment with and develop aspects of the practice of listening during havruta text study.

---

[7]   Hans-Georg Gadamer, "The Incapacity for Conversation," *Continental Philosophy Review* 39.4 (2006): 358.

[8]   From a broader cultural perspective, Charles Derber talks about "conversational narcissism" to describe the ways "conversationalists act to turn the topics of ordinary conversations to themselves without showing sustained interest in others' topics" (*The Pursuit of Attention: Power and Individualism in Everyday Life* [Oxford: Oxford University Press, 1979], 5). Applied without the implication of individual or cultural pathology, this observation gives us additional language for framing the benignly self-focused types of listening (or non-listening) we at times see in beginning learners in havruta text study.

Learning to Listen in Interpretation

Instructional Strategy

Our instructional strategy addresses three aspects of the challenge of cultivating learning in havruta text study.

a) *The invisible nature of interpretation:* One major characteristic of the interpretive process is that it remains largely invisible. It takes place inside the learner and is not expressed. This invisibility not only makes the interpretive process difficult for students to perceive, but is also hard for teachers to address. For these reasons, our goal is to find ways to help make this process more visible.

b) *The complexity of the interpretive process:* Attending to the havruta partner's comments and to the text itself as well as to one's own preconceptions about the text makes listening particularly challenging. In our instructional method, we therefore suggest separating these foci of listening for didactic purposes, to allow students to learn something about each of them.[9]

c) *The swift pace of the interpretive process:* In havruta text study, interpretation can take place very quickly. This makes it particularly difficult for the learner to derive the maximum benefit from the effects of the interpretive process, when information that originates in the text challenges his preconceptions and all the more so, to engage in listening.

Our instructional strategy is characterized overall by slowing down the reading and the interpretive process that is performed by the havruta pair. In this way, students will have an opportunity to record some of the pointed moments of their listening, and to become aware of how this kind of proactive listening may contribute to the unfolding process of interpretation.

---

[9]   For an analysis of listening in havruta learning which provides empirical evidence for this challenge, see Orit Kent, *Interactive Text Study and the Co-Construction of Meaning.*

The Mini-Lesson

The session begins with a mini-lesson in which students are introduced to the aspects of listening discussed above, followed by a hands-on experience and students' reflections. Students are first re-acquainted with the havruta learning triangle. We ask them to comment on their understanding of what the two-way arrow between havruta learner and text represents. The students usually comment on the fact that text study is a two-way process in which they, as learners, bring something to the text (e. g., their interest, knowledge they have), while the text provides them with information.

We then draw their attention to what goes on inside themselves as they engage in the give-and-take of textual interpretation in a havruta learning format. To make this kind of mental activity a little more visible, we often use the example of what happens to people when they engage in a conversation with someone they have been introduced to for the first time. At the outset, they make assumptions about that person, based on how he or she dresses, his or her name, or what they have been told about that person. As the conversation progresses, they are steadily taking in new information (e. g., information that the person provides as well as non-verbal cues), and either prior assumptions are reinforced or, on the contrary, are altered in light of the new information. To be sure, without the projection of some prior knowledge and assumptions, the conversation would not have taken place, but an unwillingness to revise those assumptions regardless of new information would lead to serious misjudgments. As with all conversations, being aware of our own listening processes during havruta text study involves more than the mere application of techniques for understanding (in the case of text study, for reading and learning). Rather, it orients us to a fundamental stance toward textual interpretation—one that can and should be cultivated over time.

We elaborate our point with the following figure:

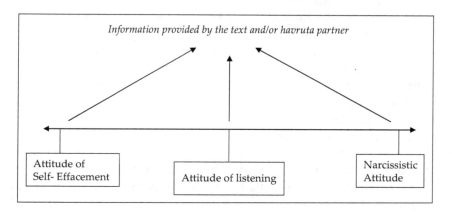

An attitude of self-effacement is one in which the learner takes in what is said by the text and/or the havruta partner and adopts the latter *prima facie,* that is, without actively examining how it impacts his own understanding of the text. At the other end, a narcissistic attitude characterizes the learner who neutralizes his receptive mode, preferring to stick to the meaning that he has made up so far about the text, not ready to revise the latter even in the light of new information (which is automatically integrated into his prior reading and assumptions). Between these two extreme attitudes, listening requires moments of genuine receptiveness and processing of what has been heard.

The Line-by-Line Havruta Learning

Students sit in havruta pairs facing each other. We distribute a copy of the text that we have edited into separate lines. The text is covered by a thick sheet of paper. Students are told that they will only be allowed to uncover and read specific lines when we tell them to do so. This procedure is meant to slow down the interpretive process and help them listen to what they will hear from the text and their havruta partner.

At each line, students are invited to comment on what they have read in their havruta pairs, to ask questions or to make a comment about the characters' motivations, to say what they expect to happen next, or more generally, what they understand the meaning of the story to be.[10] We stress that there are no right or wrong questions or comments, and that they may not be capable of answering all of the questions. What matters is to hold on to possible and potential meanings, scenarios of what is going on in the text, up to the point where new information may compel them to revise, reinforce, or drop some of these meanings and scenarios. We stress that this process will most probably generate some competing interpretations, which should remain on the table until someone at any point feels that his or her interpretation is no longer relevant.

Among various texts we have used with this instructional strategy, we have found the story of Rabbi Hama son of Bissa (described below) to be especially conducive to this listening exercise. It has an unfolding plot at its heart, and it is long enough to enable an unfolding interpretive process, but not so long that it cannot be completed in one session. Thematically, it is possible (although not indispensable) to connect central ideas of the story with the sophisticated aspects of listening that are addressed as a practice in this session. Like many short talmudic stories, it has enough gaps in describing the motivations and feelings of the characters to generate the process of gap-filling.[11] Finally, it is a text that does not require much prior knowledge, thus enabling the full participation of students with both more and less background in rabbinic literature.

To best be understood, study of this text should be preceded by encountering another short text that provides the background story for our text (see Appendix 7). We usually read this background text together with all the participants, as it helps put all of them on the same page before engaging in the line-by-line study that follows.

We uncover the first line and read it together. It says: "Rabbi Hama son of Bissa went away and spent 12 years at the house of

---

[10]   This move is a pedagogical application of Wolfgang Iser's description: "Each sentence correlate contains what one might call a hollow section, which looks forward to the next correlate, and a retrospective section, which answers the expectations of the preceding sentence… Thus every moment of reading is a dialectic of protension and retention, conveying a future horizon yet to be occupied, along with a past (and continually fading) horizon already filled" (*The Act of Reading*, 112).

[11]   For the concept of textual gaps, see our discussion in Chapter Two.

study." The floor is then open for people to share their comments and questions with their havruta partner. We often first take the lead and model the kind of questions that can be asked:

> "Why did he leave his place?"
>
> "Wasn't there a local house of study?"
>
> "Was the other house of study more prestigious?"
>
> "Was Rabbi Hama married? Did he have children? If he did, did he leave to pursue his studies, regardless of his duties and obligations at home?"

We then uncover the second line: "When he came back he said: 'I will not do what the son of Hakhinai did.'"[12] Students begin to wonder aloud and to make inferences, they say for example:

> "How long has he been away?"
>
> "Based on the comparison with the son of Hakhinai, we infer that R. Hama had a family as well. Has he been in touch with his family during his absence?"
>
> "Unlike in the story of the son of Hakhinia, the text does not say here why R. Hama is returning home. Does he think that he achieved his studies?"
>
> "In what way precisely isn't R. Hama going to imitate the son of Hakhinai?"

The reading process continues like this, line-by-line.[13] Most often, the more the process progresses, the more confident students feel to actively participate. Some lines generate a high number of comments, questions, and conjectures. During the process, students experience the need to re-read previous lines in order to make sense of the new information. At times they have to drop or revise a hypothetical

---

[12]   The "son of Hakhinai" refers to the preceding short text. See Appendix 7.

[13]   The full version of this text is to be found in Appendix 8.

interpretation, thus experiencing something of the hermeneutical circle by which a reader processes the dialectic between parts and whole of the story. For example, the third line reads: "He therefore entered the (local) house of study and sent a message to his house."

At this point, students often revisit their assumption that R. Hama left his local town because he had no place to study. "What then," they wonder, "could have been his motivation to leave?" The various hypotheses offered at this point play a projecting role as they come to interpret subsequent developments in the narrative.

Our role as instructors consists of pacing the speed of study by having everyone move on to a new line at the same time. While we listen to the various havruta pairs, we monitor the time that we allow for the exchanges in pairs for each different line of the text. We also model generic questions, for example, "So, what is going on at this point?" This directs the students toward the articulation of a temporary synthesis. Another question might be "Where do you think this is going and why?"; in answer, they project what they think is going to happen.[14] At times, we encourage havruta partners to probe each other's comments in order to have them articulate what has prompted them to say what they said.

To heighten the students' attention to the impact of what they listen to during their unfolding interpretation of the story, we provide several "Reflection Pauses" during which they are asked to reflect and complete the following chart.

---

14   Projecting one's expectations as to where the plot of a narrative is leading next is inherent in the interpretive process of generating meaning, thus the importance of this question. Ricoeur discusses at length how anticipation is always at work as we interpret a narrative text. See Paul Ricoeur, *Time and Narrative Vol 1*.

Reflection Pause #1

Please reflect on what happened during your text study and fill in the following chart:

At this point of our study, what do I tentatively think this story is about?	What is one thing I've heard from my havruta partner that has contributed to this tentative interpretation of mine?	What is one thing I've heard from the text that has contributed to my tentative interpretation?

The chart is meant to help students capture vivid and tangible moments of their listening experience in the elusive flow of the interpretive process, and establish explicit connections that might have occurred between what they listened to and the unfolding shape of the meaning they take from the story.

Comments by students that we have collected over the years show that not only does the line-by-line method turn text study into a playful experience, it also helps them listen attentively; they often experience shifts and changes in the unfolding meaning of the story they have been processing during this study session. The experience compels students to pay attention not only to details provided by each line, it also makes them more alert to the unfolding dynamic of the plot. The reflective pauses have them think about the *temporary* meaning they make of the story at different stages of the interpretive process.

Our goal is to help students begin to realize the connection between the various moments of listening and their textual interpretations. However, due to this heightened attention to the process they undergo, students still need time to pull things together and articulate one or several overall interpretations of the text. A first step consists, therefore, in having students articulate one or several integrative interpretations of the text. For that purpose, we provide them with guiding questions, using similar language to that used in the session on questioning:

Articulate a compelling interpretation:

Based on your line-by-line examination of the text, discuss with your *havruta* partner what you believe to be a good interpretation of this story. Make sure to support your interpretation with textual evidence.

Write your interpretation (of course, you may each have your own):

I /We believe that this story is about ....
....

And it says that ....

A second step consists in having students attend to the potential contribution to their final interpretation of the text of the insights they have gleaned or "captured" from the text and/or havruta partner. Students are given time to work on this step by answering the following question:

Between listening and developing interpretation:

Please examine the second and third columns in your table. Do you have any insights as to how this information may have helped you develop your final interpretation? Please share these thoughts with your havruta partner.

Last, but not least, we invite students to examine some of their preconceptions:

Listen to and identify your own preconceptions:

We learned that text interpretation develops in a process during which we also project prior knowledge, pre-conceptions, beliefs and assumptions that we bring to the text.

Think again about your experience in studying the text line-by-line.

a. Try to retrace one of those moments when you discussed "what is going to happen next," what you anticipated and how it compared to what actually happened next.

b. Try to retrace one of those moments when you had to take back something you were assuming about one of the characters and/or the plot.

Take the time to examine your projections and assumptions. Can they tell you anything about pre-conceptions or beliefs you hold in general and which were elicited in studying this particular text? Please discuss your findings with your havruta partner.

Insights from Students' Reflections

What is important is that the written reflections provide students with an opportunity to explore how listening may have contributed to their ongoing understanding of the text and of themselves.

We have used this instructional strategy in various educational settings where people learned havruta text study. Based on the feedback from students and our own experience, we have two general observations to offer: Very often, when presented with a text, students focus their discussion and engage in learning by paying most attention to the "bottom line" of the text. Due to the nature of the line-by-line method and the emphasis on listening, students begin to appreciate how significant learning can take place at various stages of the reading process, not just once the text is read through.

Second, reading the story through completely before engaging in its analysis and interpretation can obscure some literary aspects of the narrative. Having readers attend, listen and process one line at a time without having access to what is going to follow underscores how crucial plot is to reading.[15] Students report that being plunged, temporarily, into an incomplete sense of the unfolding meaning provided by the narrative, (and the time allocated to dwell on that while trying to figure it out), awakens in them a deep sense of excitement and identification with the existential situation that they perceive in the text.[16]

Most important for the purpose of this learning experience are ways by which the slowing down of the reading/interpretive process that takes place in the havruta pair helps students experience first-hand with various aspects of listening, as described above. Following are a few illustrations of what participants have said as they were reflecting on what this learning experience elicited for them in that regard.[17]

Mark, a mid-career social science teacher, reported that focusing attentively in order to listen made him aware of

> how much I myself usually focus on the content. This makes me more aware of "how" I learn and of the importance of what makes for the learning process to work.

Through the focus on listening, Mark has broadened his awareness to the learning/interpretive process as such. His statement "what makes for the learning process to work" seems to point to the three foci of listening that have been attended to in this learning experience.

---

[15]   Paul Ricoeur, *Time and Narrative Vol. 3.*

[16]   Ricoeur discusses at length the role of imagination in entering the world of the text and opening oneself up to the existential power of the narrative to re-describe reality (Paul Ricoeur, *Hermeneutics and the Human Sciences*). It is interesting to note that we have had students who have asked to participate two or three times in this kind of line-by-line study session despite the fact that they had already studied the actual text. They reported that this instructional strategy helped them to re-experience the tension created by the line-by-line method, to open themselves to renewed, attentive listening and thus to come up with new insights. More important, the fact they were already familiar with the text it made it easier for them to focus on and to further improve their listening ability in its three different orientations.

[17]   The following reflections were collected in 2011, among teacher students of *Melamdim*, a two-year post-bachelor teacher education program co-jointly based at the Hartman Institute in Jerusalem and Tel-Aviv University.

Similarly, Joel a teacher in his late twenties, reports that this helped him become aware of the dynamic by which interpretation gets constructed. He says:

> It helps you very clearly identify your evidence. It makes it easy
> to see where your interpretation is making a transition.

Here, purposeful listening impacted the student's heightened awareness of two aspects of the interpretive process: the text as an "other" than himself (Joel's need to clearly identify textual evidence), and specific changes in understanding that occur in this process.

Of particular interest is this reflection from Jordan, a 22 year student:

> There was a particular moment in the process when I realized I was carrying a strong pre-conception through my interpretation. It happened when we moved from line 7 ("he became distressed") to line 8 ("Had I been here," he said, "I would have had a son like this")[18]. After our reading of line 8, my havruta partner commented: "what is going on with this guy? He is so full of himself that he can't even imagine that the young man in front of him is his son." So far, I was seeking to make sense of the story on the assumption that having studied for a long time, R. Hama would somewhat serve as a role model through his behavior. This is usually how I am used to interpreting stories about rabbis in the Talmud. It now occurred to me that this text may actually be showing us just the opposite: that there is a connection between R. Hama's being away and study and his disturbing disconnect from reality.

Jordan's reflection exemplifies one of the purposes of slowing down the reading process while having students focus on listening and become aware of the hermeneutical circle. He allowed the text (mediated by his havruta partner's comment) to uncover a pre-conception he brought to the interpretive process. He then activated the new information and allowed it to alter his understanding, and to disrupt his preconception.

---

[18]   The full text is to be found in Appendix 8.

Finally, Steven, a teacher in his late twenties, points out that cultivating attentive listening to both text and havruta partner can help learners become better human beings in general, far more capable of listening to others.

As we further discuss in Chapter Nine, some practices of havruta text study are more than learning tools. They are best conceptualized as dispositions, a term which captures simultaneously the skill as well as a long-standing formative effect of that skill on the learner, way beyond the confines of havruta text study. Through his experience of the intricacies of listening to text and havruta partner, Steven seems to already intuit this broader potential impact. He comes to realize that listening is an expansive activity, one that provides a way to perceive more directly the ways people participate in the world around them.

In conclusion, while listening is essential in any conversation, it takes on a particular importance in the context of havruta text study, which involves the student in a triadic relationship captured in the dialectic movements described by the hermeneutical circle. In the particular line-to-line strategy, students are invited into the experience of careful collaborative listening to the text. Listening is thus enacted in the web of relationships that constitutes havruta text study. In that regard, listening constitutes a core relational practice as it invites the student to intentionally attend, both in a receptive and in an active mode, to some of the more subtle intricacies that constitute the interpretive process taking place between text, havruta partner, and oneself. To that end, we introduce students to a new terminology ("slow reading," "pre-conceptions," "foci of listening") and to different attitudes toward text and partner ("self-effacement," "narcissistic attitude").

By making havruta learners conscious of the effects of listening on their ability to develop textual interpretations, we aim to help them cultivate an increasing ability to seek and perceive what there is to listen to in a text and by a havruta partner, beyond initial impressions. However, following the hermeneutical circle, we teach them that preconceptions and assumptions do not have to be eliminated in order to engage in a productive interpretation. Rather, as much as possible, they need to be consciously managed. It is in this sense that listening is an intended choice and a practice to be cultivated, refining a process that begins with assumptions.

Rabbi Hiyya b. Abba said: Even father and son,
master and disciple, who study Torah at the same gate [in the same subject]
become enemies of each other; yet they do
not stir from there until they come to love each other
Talmud, Tractate Kiddushin 30b

Iron sharpens iron
Talmud, Tractate Ta'anit 7a

CHAPTER SIX:
SUPPORTING AND CHALLENGING[1]

Introduction

Supporting and challenging are central practices in havruta text study, and build on the work that the havruta pair does when they listen deeply to each other and the text, and when they question the text in order to develop ideas about it. The practices of supporting and challenging can help havruta partners build up their ideas into more compelling interpretations, as well as help them reconsider and reconstruct weak ideas and even put them aside when necessary. In addition to helping havruta learners further develop and refine their interpretations, these practices can also help the havruta partners develop and support their working relationship by indicating to each person that her partner takes her ideas seriously and is willing to work on them with her. In that sense, these practices function as both interpersonal and interpretive practices.

In this chapter, we explore the role of supporting and challenging in havruta work, including an analysis of students' oral and written reflections, and reconstruct and discuss a lesson designed to foster students' awareness of and facility with this pair of practices, identifying and discussing the different parts of the lesson and their distinct purposes.

---

[1]   This chapter was written by Orit Kent.

Why Supporting and Challenging?[2]

Supporting and challenging, when used together, can enable *havrutot* to work collaboratively, drawing on their full range of intelligences to strengthen their joint and individual interpretations and their interpersonal capacities as a *havruta* pair.

The focus of supporting and challenging behavior is one's partner's ideas. When one is supporting, one is trying to help make her partner's idea as strong as possible by noticing additional evidence or details in text that can strengthen the interpretation on the table. In this way, supporting the ideas of one's *havruta* is disconnected from how one might feel personally about one's partner and whether or not one agrees with one's partner's idea. The goal of supporting is to help one's partner develop as compelling an interpretation as possible. Even if one does not agree with one's partner, one can still support him or her in making her ideas stronger. As a secondary effect, in the process of doing so each partner may gain insight into her partner's ideas, or even her own.

Barnes and Todd identified supportive behaviors as an important aspect of learning: "The support implicit in attending seriously to another's opinion may in educational contexts be a form of support most likely to influence learning."[3] They explain that "when one replies to another person's remarks in careful detail, one is assigning significance and validity to it."[4] In this way, it helps the partners develop a sense of trust in each other, a sense that their conversation is a joint exploration. This lays the groundwork for productive challenging, since it reinforces the notions that this havruta is not about winning or losing but helping each other in different ways to explore and build stronger ideas together.

Similarly, challenging in this context does not require disagreement with one's havruta. When one is challenging, one is helping one's

---

[2]   Some parts of this chapter are adapted from Orit Kent, *Interactive Text Study and the Co-Construction of Meaning* and Orit Kent, "Teaching Havruta in Context."

[3]   Douglas Barnes and Frankie Todd, *Communication and Learning Revisited, Making Meaning through Talk* (Portsmouth, NH: Heinemann 1995), 47.

[4]   Ibid., 47. They define supportive behaviors a bit differently than we do but their observations about its impact are still applicable.

partner strengthen her interpretation of the text, by pointing to weaknesses in a particular idea and/or making space for her to come up with more compelling ideas. Challenging gives *havruta* partners the opportunity to step back and rethink their ideas: Are the ideas supported by the text? Do the ideas really offer a compelling interpretation of what the text is trying to teach? What are the limitations of this idea? How does this interpretation stand in the face of an alternative interpretation?[5] When effective, challenging can help a partner come up with a better-articulated version of her interpretation, an interpretation that accounts for more of the text, or a new idea altogether.

Research on learning points to the importance of constructive conflict in developing and retaining ideas and intellectual skills, among other things.[6] Johnson and Johnson write that "intellectual conflict could be one of the most powerful problem-solving, decision making, and instructional procedures available." They note that "[w]ithin controversy the critical issue is how issues become transformed through interaction." They specifically distinguish intentionally "structured controversies," which seek to "develop, clarify, expand, and elaborate one's thinking about the issues" and in which "disagreement leads to a transformation of the issue..." from debate, a forum in which two or more individuals argue positions that are incompatible and one person wins based on having presented his position

---

[5] Eleanor Duckworth calls our attention to the role of such questions in slowing down "rapid assumptions of understanding" and pushing ideas to "their limits, to see where (they) hold up and where (they) do not hold up" (*The Having of Wonderful Ideas* [New York: Teachers College Press, 1996], 78).

[6] David Johnson and Roger Johnson discuss some of the benefits of conflict or controversy in *Cooperation and Competition, Theory and Research* (Edina, MN: Interaction Book Company, 1989). See also David Johnson, Roger Johnson, and Karl Smith, "Academic Controversy: Enriching College Instruction through Intellectual Conflict," *ASHE-ERIC Higher Education Report* 25.3 (Washington, DC: The George Washington University, Graduate School of Education and Human Development: 1997) and David Johnson and Roger Johnson, ""Energizing Learning: The Instructional Power of Conflict," *Educational Researcher* 38.1 (2009): 49. In their numerous publications, they describe what they call "constructive controversy," a pedagogical approach that takes advantage of the constructive features of engaging in conflict. This approach asks participants to explore the advantages and disadvantages of particular ideas with the aim of reaching a new synthesis. In our context, we do not posit that the goal is always synthesis.

most effectively.[7] Johnson and Johnson explain the theory underlying their ideas: "[C]onflict among ideas, theories, or conclusions leads to uncertainty about correctness of one's views, which leads to epistemic curiosity and the active search for additional information and perspectives, which, in turn, leads to reconceptualized and refined conclusions."[8]

To succeed at this, learners need to be willing to embrace disequilibrium.[9] Internal disequilibrium is something that occurs when we are faced with conflicting ideas. By being challenged with alternatives, our own views and cognitive structures can be rendered unstable. In order to re-establish a sense of stability and find a resolution, we may be moved to think and try out new ideas and discard old ideas and ways of thinking. Disequilibrium, and in turn challenging, can be unsettling since it requires us to move beyond the comfortable confines of familiar ideas and behaviors into unknown territory in order to find better solutions. At the same time, disequilibrium is at the heart of our capacity to transform our knowledge and ways of thinking.

The practice of challenging in havruta text study is very similar to the work of "intellectual conflict," and we too have found that students need help to prepare for what this work entails and structure to constructively engage in it. Without help, the partners avoiding the risk of possible tension between conflicting ideas by jettisoning their prior ideas without analysis, rejecting new ideas out of hand, or simply conflating the differences between ideas.

---

[7]　　　David Johnson and Roger Johnson, *Cooperation and Competition, Theory and Research, 87.*

[8]　　　David Johnson and Roger Johnson, ""Energizing Learning: The Instructional Power of Conflict," 49.

[9]　　　For discussions of disequilibrium, see Jean Piaget, *The Psychology of Intelligence* (New York: Harcourt, 1950). For discussions of this subject rooted in Piaget's work and related ideas such as "cognitive conflict," see for example David Johnson, Roger Johnson, and Karl Smith, *"Academic Controversy: Enriching College Instruction through Intellectual Conflict,"* 89; Robert Kegan, *The Evolving Self, Problem and Process in Human Development;* Barbara Rogoff, *Apprenticeship in Thinking* (New York: Oxford University Press, 1990), 141, and Laurent Daloz, *Mentor, Guiding the Journey of Adult Learners* (San Francisco: Jossey-Bass, 1999), 216.

The constructive use of the practice of supporting also needs to be scaffolded. Our anecdotal observations in a number of contexts over several years, as well as analysis of videos of havruta learning in the DeLeT Beit Midrash, reveal that without scaffolded instruction about supporting and challenging, many havruta partners not only engaged in little direct challenging, but they rarely engaged in explicit supporting in order to help their partners further develop the ideas on the table.[10] (Even with scaffolding, it takes times for partners to learn how to use these practices well.) Partners might say, "I agree" or "I like that idea." While those kinds of comments can be quite motivating generally, they do not help strengthen specific ideas. As teachers, we understood that if havrutot engaged in more explicit supporting moves, they could actually work with one another to focus on a given idea, strengthening and developing it as much as possible. In the end, they might find that the idea is very compelling or not actually so strong, but they would make this determination after having intentionally worked with it and not abandoned it prematurely.

The use of these practices for the sake of developing more compelling interpretations also helps highlight the ethical-relational dimension of this work that we discussed in Chapter Three. The work of havruta is not about defending one's own idea or about "winning." It is about being willing to enact a commitment to all three havruta partners: the text, one's human partner, and oneself. Taking time and care to revisit the text, listen deeply to it, and give it voice demonstrates a commitment to it. Supporting and/or challenging one's partners ideas, instead of merely focusing on one's own ideas, demonstrates a sense of responsibility to the other by constructively engaging with his ideas and making them stronger. In this way, havruta text study entails each partner taking responsibility for both partners' learning.

Laurent Daloz, a scholar in the field of adult learning and mentoring, lays out a framework for understanding the relationship between support and challenge. He explains that when both

---

[10]   See Orit Kent, *Interactive Text Study and the Co-Construction of Meaning*, and Orit Kent, "A Theory of Havruta Learning," for specific examples of how this plays out. Kent also illustrates through havruta cases the ways in which supporting and challenging are intertwined practices, and how the text challenges the human partners' thinking. For a broader discussion of havruta norms and modes of discussion, see Orit Kent, "Interactive Text Study: A Case of Hevruta Learning."

support and challenge are low, there is little growth. When support is increased and challenge stays the same, there is the risk that the learner will merely confirm her ideas and not really explore anything different. When challenge is increased and support remains low, the learner may retreat. Finally, when support and challenge are increased in an "appropriate mix," growth can occur.[11] Like Daloz, we posit that at its best, havruta will include a high level of both supporting and challenging. This can build and reinforce the havruta's commitment to a collaboration in which they respectfully work together to strengthen ideas. Through supporting each other's ideas, they can build them up as much as possible, and through challenging them, they can determine what does and does not work in a particular interpretation and consider alternatives that may be better. The end result of balancing high support with high challenge is interpretations that are more fully developed, as well as positive working relationships.[12]

The Lesson

Having recognized the value of supporting and challenging and the need to help our students learn how to engage in these practices in more productive ways, we developed a havruta lesson that explicitly focused on teaching supporting and challenging, with a protocol for engaging in both.

The three-hour lesson described below includes a mini-lesson on supporting and challenging, havruta text study to develop an interpretation of a text, an in-class exercise to practice supporting and challenging, a larger group debriefing, and written reflections on the experience. The overall lesson gives students a language and a process for working on their textual interpretations together, while also helping them cultivate these two specific practices for future use as havruta learners. The lesson assumes that students have already done some amount of work on learning how to interpret a text with a havruta partner.

---

[11]   Laurent Daloz, *Mentor, Guiding the Journey of Adult Learners*, 208.

[12]   There are possible scenarios where a *havruta* could develop a more compelling interpretation but sacrifice its working relationship in the process. This is not the goal since such a sacrifice will short change future interpretive endeavors for this pair and is therefore short-sighted.

> *Overview of Lesson*
>
> Part I: Mini-lesson introducing the practices of support-
> ing and challenging
>
> Part II: Text study in havruta to develop textual interpre-
> tations
>
> Part III: Text study in havruta to practice supporting and
> challenging and refining initial interpretations
>
> Part IV: In class debrief and/or written reflections on the
> experience of Part III.

Part I: Mini-lesson

The mini-lesson contains three big ideas, which explain and justify why supporting and challenging are important, and why they might be hard to do:

- Supporting and challenging are key to learning with our havruta partners, colleagues, and students.
- Challenging a fellow learner can be especially difficult and is coun-tercultural.
- Supporting and challenging are part of the ethical dimensions of havruta learning.

We begin by framing the overall importance of both supporting and challenging as crucial to our learning, and in our relationships with our havruta partner, professional colleagues, and students.[13] We explain that in the particular context of havruta learning, supporting and challenging can help refine ideas as they are being developed: How is this idea working, does it really stand up in the text, can we develop it further, or is there another direction that we want to go in? We connect being challenged to the experience of disequilibrium and

---

[13] This is our opportunity to "hook" our particular students—that is, class-room teachers—by arguing for the significance of these practices in their own professional lives. There is much we say that does not directly relate to the context of teacher education and is relevant to all those learning havruta text study.

comment on the role of disequilibrium in havruta and learning more generally.[14]

We also discuss why challenging is a countercultural activity, especially in many sub-cultures in the United States where people are taught to be polite (especially in classroom contexts) and see being polite as good and in contrast with being someone who challenges others. The mini-lesson tries to normalize student anxiety by naming the fact that challenging is not what they are used to doing, and in some cases it may even be the opposite.

The third idea that we highlight in the mini lesson is the ethical-relational dimension of supporting and challenging—namely, that in havruta learning, we can not simply think about ourselves and our own ideas. Rather, we have a responsibility to both closely study the text, and to help our partners with their own learning and with the development of their ideas. One way we help our partners' learning is by supporting and challenging their ideas in the spirit of trying to strengthen their interpretations.

We then distinguish "challenging and supporting" from "agreeing and disagreeing," further highlighting the ethical nature of this work and emphasizing that it is our responsibility to challenge and support one another regardless of whether we agree or disagree. The larger goal is to flesh out ideas and come to a more compelling interpretation.[15] Our goal is make students feel more comfortable challenging and supporting by helping them understand that these practices are meant to be disentangled from personal feelings and focus on the overall development of compelling interpretations.

Finally, we close the mini-lesson by defining each of the practices and providing specific language prompts that can be used to support and challenge.[16] First, we define supporting in the context of

---

[14]   Internal disequilibrium is something that can occur when we are faced with conflicting ideas, which may render our own views and cognitive structures unstable.

[15]   Peter Elbow's work on methodological doubting and the "believing game" and "doubting game" highlight the importance of taking on a role in the spirit of working together in order to engage in supporting, even when we disagree, and in challenging, even when we agree. Peter Elbow, *Embracing Contraries* (New York: Oxford University Press, 1986).

[16]   The is an example of what Pamela Grossman and her colleagues calls "decomposition." Pamela Grossman et al., "Teaching Practice: A Cross-

havruta as encouraging one's havruta partner in developing the ideas she has on the table, identifying particular words that indicate one is paying attention (e. g. a simple "yes" or "hmm," which signals to one's partner that her ideas may be worthy of further consideration) and doing proactive things, like asking specific clarifying questions to flesh out an idea or saying, "Please tell me more about your idea."[17] Another way to support is to offer supporting evidence, e. g. "I see you are saying this... and here's some evidence that supports your idea." We acknowledge that most people are less accustomed to thinking about supporting in a proactive, intentional way, and we also disconnect support from how one feels about one's partner or even her ideas.

Next, we discuss the practice of challenging, which we define as questioning ideas on the table. There are two primary ways to challenge. First, there is questioning the current ideas under discussion, asking what is missing from the interpretation and/or drawing attention to contradictions between the interpretation and the text: to simply ask "Is that idea supported by the text?" is often a provocative and generative question. There is another type of challenging, in which partners offer alternative ideas or interpretations—for example, "I have a different idea..." or "Here's another way of understanding these textual details." We remind students that while they may associate challenging with a more argumentative and debate-like stance, this is not the goal in our context, and in fact zero-sum debates often shut down opportunities for learning. We share with students anecdotes of havrutot that have engaged in this kind of argumentative challenging and how this negatively affected their ability to explore their ideas fully. The point of challenging is to help each other step back and think through ideas in order to consider weaknesses in the ideas as well as alternative interpretations, all in the service of developing the strongest possible interpretation.

Professional Perspective," *Teachers College Record* 111.9 (2009): 2055–100. In this lesson, the teacher decomposes the practices of supporting and challenging, breaking them down into their discrete elements so that students can become familiar with all that they entail.

[17] This is a phrase that I learned from Eleanor Duckworth as a way to help learners elaborate their thinking. For Duckworth, a key to the learning process is making room for learners to explain their thinking. "The idea is to listen, to have learners tell us their thoughts" (Eleanor Duckworth, ed., *"Tell Me More": Listening to Learners Explain* [New York: Teachers College Press, 2001], 181).

The mini-lesson as a whole introduces students to specific language to use in order to practice supporting and challenging—and specific language is very important for students who are first learning these practices. As novices, they have a host of things to pay attention to and get better at. By having language to experiment with, they can put the practices into use without first having to figure out how to say what they want to say. The mini-lesson leaves students with an overall sense of purpose and some concrete moves to try out. In future lessons, we continue to remind students of our definitions of supporting and challenging, and give students language prompts to use in their havruta work and to examine the effect of using these language prompts on their resulting interpretations.[18] For many, incorporating these moves into their regular havruta repertoire requires creating new habits of interaction.

Part II: Text Study in Havruta to Develop Textual Interpretations

Following the mini-lesson, we introduce the supporting and challenging exercise that students are supposed to use as they study the text of the day with their partner. The exercise has three steps. The first step is reading the story and figuring out what it is about. This is obviously not unique to engaging in the practices of supporting and challenging, but is a necessary precondition for students to be able to use the practice of supporting and challenging productively. They need time to become familiar with the text, develop their first interpretations of it, and know it well enough to be able to effectively support or challenge their partner's interpretations—and to have a chance to develop some ideas about the text before those ideas are closely examined by their partner.

Below are the written directions that we distribute, along with the Talmud text in both Aramaic and English.[19]

---

[18]   For a discussion of the moves made in havruta to bring the text and the human partner into the discussion, and the ways in which the interpretive/intellectual and interpersonal/social moves ultimately overlap, see Orit Kent, "Interactive Text Study: A Case of Hevruta Learning."

[19]   See also Appendix 9.

Part II. *Study guidelines*[20]

A. Closely read the text. A close reading entails considering the details of the story and how they contribute toward the larger meaning of the story. This means you may want to read the text a number of different times. A close reading also entails understanding what happens in the story and finding explanations for why the people in the story choose to do or say what is stated in the text.

B. Articulate what you understand the story to be about (this is not the same as paraphrasing a story). You and your havruta partner may share one interpretation or have different interpretations.

C. Write down your interpretation on a piece of flip chart paper.

    1. "According to our understanding, this story is about…"

    2. This interpretation enables us to explain the following details of the story:

Although we have previously explored in class what a close reading entails, we do not assume that all students will remember the exact details of the classroom discussion. Therefore, in Step A we provide them with specific instructions to explore both the plot of the story and its larger meaning, which requires rereading the text and noticing all of its details, and analyzing how those details contribute to the text's meaning. The distinction in Step B between what they understand the story to be about and mere paraphrasing has also been elaborated earlier.

Step C, in which students write down their interpretations so that they can continue working on them and share their ideas with other havruta pairs, is an essential prerequisite for working on supporting and challenging. Since havruta work is oral, all too often once the havruta time is over, the ideas seem to evaporate. By asking students to write down their ideas, we not only help them capture their havruta work on paper but challenge them to pull their thinking

---

[20]   See Chapters Four and Five for some similar text study questions.

together coherently. Students can write down their own individual interpretation or their joint interpretation, depending on what they generated in the previous step. In this step, the task reviews what ought to be included in a fleshed-out interpretation by asking students to do two things: (1) write out what they think the story is about and (2) point to details in the story that their interpretation of the story explains. In other words, the task asks for an interpretation about the larger meaning of the story, inviting students to connect this larger whole to the different parts of the text (and thereby reinforcing the idea that interpretations are grounded in evidence).

Part III: Text Study in Havruta to Practice Supporting and Challenging

Part III of the lesson is the main exercise to give students practice developing their facility with supporting and challenging one another. They once again sit in pairs, but this time they switch partners and meet with someone new. Each student in the pair has an opportunity to present his/her interpretation—either the joint interpretation or his/her individual interpretation developed in the previous havruta—to a new colleague. Each student also has the opportunity to serve as a "critical colleague," supporting and challenging the presenter's interpretation.[21] The work of articulating one's interpretation and developing it further is itself a challenging task, as is the responsibility to support and challenge an interpretation. This task separates the roles of presenter and critical colleague so that students, in this learning context, can practice each with full focus, though these roles will generally be combined in the course of a less structured, "natural" conversation during havruta text study.[22]

---

[21]   For a discussion of the idea of "critical colleagueship" and its importance, see Brian Lord, "Teachers' Professional Development: Critical Colleagueship and the Role of Professional Communities," in *The Future of Education Perspectives on National Standards in America* (New York: College Entrance Examination Board, 1994), 175–204.

[22]   One additional pedagogic strategy for their reinforcement is modeling performance of these practices prior to students' own engagement with them. This can be done by setting up a "fishbowl," with two instructors or two volunteers (who are coached by the instructors in real time in front of the group) using the task in front of the whole group.

Part III Study Guidelines:
a. Choose someone in the room you haven't studied with yet.
b. One of you will serve as a presenter of an interpretation and the other one will serve as a critical colleague/havruta.

Your role as a presenter is to:
1. Articulate your interpretation of what the story is about and to explain how you arrived at these ideas
2. Listen and reply to your colleague's questions
3. Probe/reinforce/revise your interpretation of the story.

Your role as a critical colleague/havruta is to:
1. Actively listen to your colleague's interpretation so that you are clear about what s/he is saying. You might ask the following questions: "Am I understanding you correctly that you are reading this part of the text to mean X?"
2. Probe your colleague's interpretation by asking clarifying questions such as: "You said X; how did you get to this idea?; You said X, could you tell me more about what you mean by that?" When you feel the need, don't hesitate to probe the answers to these questions as well.
3. Support and reinforce your colleague's interpretation by offering additional cues in the story and/or reasons which may support his/her interpretation. For example: "Would you say that when it says X, this reinforces your point...?"
4. Challenge the interpretation of your colleague by pointing to details in the story which the interpretation does not address or which may contradict the interpretation. For example, "In the text it says X, how do you make sense of this part according to your interpretation? How do you account for...?; Why do you say that? How does that fit with what was just said? I don't really get that; could you explain it another way or give me an example?"
5. Offer good reasons why your colleague's interpretation is not compelling enough in your view or is in fact very compelling.

The task above delineates steps for each person to go through in each of the roles, and provides language to use at each of the steps. The role of the critical colleague is particularly complex. The critical colleague is asked to go through five steps: active listening, probing, supporting, challenging, and evaluating. The first step is to actively listen to their new partner's ideas, since there can be no real discussion until both partners understand what is under discussion. Probing is essentially a part of active listening, since it helps clarify understanding, but we identify it separately to help insure that the critical colleague gives her partner some time to speak, listening quietly before asking a lot of questions. After both partners have a clear understanding of the interpretation on the table, we ask the critical colleague to look for ways to support the interpretation and thereby make it stronger (so they can make the idea on the table as strong as possible before they challenge it). We then have students challenge the interpretation on the table and find its weak points—not for the purpose of proving the other person "wrong" but to work together to develop the strongest interpretation possible. We have students wait to make a final evaluation of the interpretation until they have gone through all of the preceding steps, and thus have worked with the interpretation and understand its strengths and weaknesses.

While separating out these steps is artificial, it helps students notice each of the elements and allows them to try out each one. When students are first learning these practices, they often skip one or more elements in the task or get stuck in one place. For example, many students do not probe their partner's interpretation in order to clearly understand it and skip right to supporting or challenging questions, but in order to effectively either support it or challenge it they must first understand it. Sometimes students will remain in the step of active listening for their entire havruta. While it can be very helpful in giving someone time to develop an idea, exclusive use of active listening does not engage the knowledge and insight of the listening partner, which would allow him/her to draw attention to new details in the text, strengthen the interpretation, or help reformulate it. Some students do not engage in both supporting and challenging, choosing instead to do just one, in part because students sometimes find it difficult to switch from seeing all the strengths of an interpretation to moments later needing to identify and argue all its weaknesses. (While making this switch is ultimately an important capacity to be fostered, we sometimes break up the task into two sessions, giving students a chance to initially practice each part separately.)

Part IV: Students' Oral and Written Reflections on the Task

Part IV gives students an opportunity to reflect on their experience of being a presenter and a critical colleague through classroom discussion and written reflections. This is a crucial step in the lesson, and a place where a great deal of learning occurs. It is a tempting step to skip when there are time constraints, but in our experience the crux of the learning occurs in this step, which allows students to revisit what they did in step III, noticing their own behavior and how it contributed towards or got in the way of their partner's successful interpretive work. Below, we will use student reflections (in both classroom discussions and written reflections) in which various havrutot[23] discuss the benefits and difficulties of these practices, and what they learned about themselves and the work of partnered text study from trying to use them, highlighting some of the key ideas that often emerge for students in the lesson on supporting and challenging.

Moving Beyond Habit and Inclination

Susan and Stacy[24] are two students who participated in the same class discussion reflecting on what it was like to enact the roles of critical colleague and presenter. Susan begins her reflection by highlighting the difficulty she had with the critical aspect of her role: "I actually found it really challenging to be a critical havruta. I don't think I did a very good job, I had a very hard time coming up with questions to ask and ways to challenge her [Stacy's] thinking when I was just listening [to her interpretation] …" In her written reflection, she also notes that she has a tendency to agree without questioning and needs to practice asking better questions. A transcript of their havruta session confirms that, while Susan worked hard to come up with clarifying

---

23   All these examples are taken from the Beit Midrash Project of the DeLeT program.

24   The three havruta pairs whose reflections we present in this section happen to consist of six women. The experiences they articulate are common to both women and men with whom we work.

questions to draw out Stacy's ideas, and took copious notes and did an excellent job listening to Stacy, she did not make explicit supporting or challenging comments that could have helped strengthen Stacy's interpretation.

Stacy's reflections reveal the opposite tendency; she notices that she tends to move to challenge her partner before she has really listened and understood what the other person means:

> I found it challenging to force myself to go back and clarify what [you meant] because I assumed I understood what you were saying. Because the first step was to clarify and ask probing questions, I had to force myself to go back and make sure I knew what you were saying before I challenged, because I had challenging thoughts that popped into my head while you were talking but that wasn't my role at that point. So I found it hard to remove myself first and focus on what you were saying and only after I really knew what you were saying, to come back.

In her concluding written comment, Stacy also reports: "I have learned how important it is to understand fully what the other person means to say before challenging or even supporting. When I forced myself to understand her points better, I was able to ask better, more focused challenging questions because I had a basis for them."

Susan's participation in the task helped surface her tendency to not question—a challenge not only in her work with her havruta, but in her work as a teacher; in the class discussion, she commits herself to working on asking her own students more questions. For Stacy, this task helped her experience and reflect on the importance of listening in order to effectively work with a havruta, and the connection between listening to another and being able to ask good questions of that person and thereby productively challenge their ideas. Both recognized that working to move past their natural tendencies would improve their ability to help draw out and sharpen their partner's interpretations.

*The Challenges of Challenging and the Interpretive Benefits
of Challenging and Supporting*

Cindy and Mary demonstrate how this exercise helps students become aware of both areas that they need to work on (as we have seen above) and the ways in which their use of the practices of supporting and especially challenging help them develop more textually grounded interpretations with their havruta partners.

Mary writes as follows: "It was very hard for me to challenge Cindy about anything at first. I didn't want to sound mean. But since we had to, I challenged a few ideas she had and because of that, we ended up having a great conversation about the text." She goes on to notice that this positive impact on their interpretive conversation was a result of stretching herself to challenge: "Usually when I discuss things with people, I tend to agree with what they are saying, even if I don't whole-heartedly agree. Today, even though I did agree with a lot of what Cindy said, I tried to bring up other opinions or point out parts of the text that differ with what she said and I thought that helped a lot." In the cultural context in which she operates, in which challenging is not a norm and not seen as something we do for another's benefit, as well as in the context of her individual inclinations, Mary, too, is called upon to stretch herself in taking on the role of critical colleague. Challenging Cindy, even when she agrees with her, is in the end something Mary finds helpful to their learning. She writes: "Something important I've taken away [from being the critical colleague] is having the experience of not always agreeing with what everyone says. It's not enough to simply have my own [potentially challenging] ideas—I have to voice them and share them for me and others to learn more!"

Cindy observes how one of Mary's challenges in the end helped her find further supporting evidence in the text for her idea: "She had challenged an idea of mine by presenting a verse that didn't seem to coincide with it at first but by bouncing ideas off of one another, we were able to work out how that verse could fit in with my interpretation." In this case, what started out as challenging becomes supporting, demonstrating the idea that challenging and supporting are intertwined. Cindy also explains how Mary's clarifying questions helped her: "It was challenging as a presenter for me to sometimes articulate my interpretation. However, by asking clarifying questions, Mary helped me to organize my thoughts into words that made sense."

Many students comment on the fact that they are uncomfortable with challenging and/or have a hard time coming up with challenging questions, and that even if they try to challenge their partner, they can't do it when they agree with their partner because they have trouble separating the practice of challenging from disagreeing. Within the framework of this particular lesson and exercise, Mary is able to overcome her discomfort and embrace her role as critical colleague. Once in that role, she can challenge Cindy, even when they agree. This allows both Mary and Cindy to learn more as a havruta pair. The idea and experience of taking on a role in the service of another's learning will also be useful to them as prospective teachers, when they will need to take on the role of teacher on a daily basis.

Like many havruta learners, Cindy found it hard to take on this role, especially when it involved challenging Mary when agreeing with her. She writes, "...I found it difficult to refrain from simply offering support rather than challenging her to find more instances to reinforce her point. It was a lot easier when I disagreed." She more easily challenged Mary when they did not agree, and in her written reflections she underscores the importance of challenging one's partner to back up their interpretation based on the text: "Something I think I did well was to push Mary to go back to the text and defend her ideas. She would give an interpretation or an explanation and I would challenge her to explain why she had that idea and what from the text influenced her thoughts."

From her angle, Mary writes about the benefits of Cindy's challenges: "I found it very helpful when Cindy questioned some of my interpretations because it really made me think about why I interpreted something a specific way and that led to me changing my opinions about a few things in the text...[The practice of challenging] helps us clarify our positions and delve deeper into aspects of the texts that we hadn't visited before." Cindy, who initially had a harder time challenging, became aware of her learning curve, and both she and Mary note the benefits of challenging and of being challenged, profiting from pushing themselves to function as critical colleagues for each other.

*Developing An Awareness of the Importance of Listening
and How Havruta Partners Impact Each Other's Learning*

Nancy and Laurie's reflections highlight their new sense of the importance of listening to each other's ideas and having a clear sense of what the other is saying, and also reflect insight into the ways havruta partners impact each other's learning.

Laurie describes how, as a critical colleague, she followed the order laid out in the exercise, first listening and clarifying and gradually building up to challenging Nancy. She writes: "It is important when being the challenger to let the person finish explaining before challenging them." For Laurie, listening to Nancy seems to serve two purposes: it allows her to really understand what Nancy is saying so that she can work with her to make her interpretation stronger, by both offering constructive support and challenging, and it communicates respect to her partner, which is important to the overall working relationship of the havruta. Indeed, Laurie reports that she challenged in a "comfortable and respectful way while still trying to push my partner's thinking." Nancy, too, specifically highlights Laurie's respectfulness as having been very helpful to her when she presented her ideas.

For her part, Nancy reports that listening—"[letting] Laurie speak without interrupting her"—is something she found to be very challenging: The importance of simply listening, letting someone else initially spin out an idea without interruption, is something that many students become aware of through this exercise, and they often comment on how hard it can be to do.

Students also grapple with the impact on their learning partner—and their partner's learning—of their own actions. Nancy raises a point of tension for her: "When do you decide if the purpose of challenging is for the sake of Laurie's interpretation or for the sake of Laurie learning a new interpretation?" This is a very important question about text study in havruta and the impact that partners can have on each other's emerging interpretations. If you are committed to listening to your partner and trying to support your partner's idea, the havruta could go in one direction; if you move quickly to challenging and building a new idea, the initial idea can be quickly lost. There are no simple answers to Nancy's question. However, it is very important for havruta participants (and prospective teachers) to become aware of this tension, and of their impact on the development of their learning partners' ideas and on their final textual interpretations.[25]

Conclusion

What can we learn about teaching the practices of supporting and challenging from considering these students' reflections? Why are these practices often so hard to enact?

In their written reflections, many students comment that they find challenging to be "challenging." Some are used to being agreeable and do not want to risk offending others; some have a hard time formulating questions in the moment. Others find it difficult to challenge their partners when they agree with their ideas. Some have a hard time challenging because they believe that, ultimately, there is a multitude of good interpretations, making it difficult for them to distinguish good interpretations from less useful interpretations.[26]

Students' reflections about challenging point to both the difficulties they face enacting this practice and a strong case for its benefits—and thus for creating space to teach this as a central practice of havruta work. As we noted earlier, research on learning points to the importance of constructive conflict in developing ideas and intellectual skills; our experience as teachers of texts point to the usefulness of engaging in constructive challenging in order to refine ideas. As good collaborative learners and as prospective teachers, it is beneficial to gain experience taking on a role in which supporting others' learning involves raising questions and pushing others to refine their responses, not simply agreeing and being nice.

The separate practice of supporting is also difficult for students, although this comes through less clearly in their written reflections and more clearly in their actual havruta work. This may be because we have not always called out supporting as a distinct practice as spe-

---

[25]   This question is also tied to more general interpretive questions such as: How long should one stick with any given interpretation and how does one decide to discard an idea?

[26]   It is important to provide students with tools for evaluating interpretations so that they will be better equipped to determine what and how to challenge. On the evaluation of interpretations and a session designed to help students learn that practice, see Chapter Seven.

cifically and strongly as we have done with challenging (although we have consistently depicted challenging as something that "supports" the other's learning). But we believe that this is also a function of how comfortable students generally are with the *idea* of supporting—so much so that they do not realize how rarely in practice they proactively and skillfully support their partners' interpretation, not just affirming what they hear.

When teaching these practices, it is important to remember that "supporting" and "challenging" are loaded terms in our culture. The idea of offering support generally carries a positive valence (with the connotation of providing what a person seems to be asking for or obviously needs), while challenging usually carries a negative valence (or certainly an adversarial connotation). These associations complicate the use of these two practices, making students uncomfortable challenging their partners, and leading them to habitually offer acts of support that may help their partner feel good but do not strengthen the ideas on the table.[27]

In addition, a primary activity that complicates supporting and challenging is "interrelating viewpoints."[28] When one havruta partner hears another partner's ideas, if she is trying to listen and collaborate with her partner, she will try to relate her partner's ideas to her own. It is not as easy to relate viewpoints that are different, and the process can feel hard and uncomfortable, resulting in a sense of disequilibrium. To relate different viewpoints, partners need to engage with ideas different than their own, confront those differences, and possibly stretch and reconfigure their own ideas and ways of thinking. This relates to one aspect of what it means in philosophical terms

---

[27]   The idea that challenging is something negative was reported by students in the Beit Midrash for Teachers. In a related vein, Courtney Cazden writes that students report not liking arguments (*Classroom Discourse, The Language of Teaching and Learning*, 2nd edition [Portsmouth, NH: Heinemann, 2001], 132). Furthermore, there is a diverse body of literature on the issue of conflict avoidance. See, for example, Charles Goodwin, "Conversation Analysis," *Annual Review of Anthropology* 19 (1990): 283–307; and David Johnson, Roger Johnson, and Karl Smith, *Academic Controversy*. The latter specifically discuss the prevalence of "concurrence seeking" behaviors in which groups tend to avoid disagreements.

[28]   See Douglas Barnes and Frankie Todd, *Communication and Learning Revisited: Making Meaning through Talk*, 147–48.

to expand one's horizon,[29] or in psychological terms to accommodate one's schema, and thereby develop new frameworks or schemas for making sense of the world. This is how readers not only clarify their existing understandings but also develop new ones. In addition, being able to be aware of this process of interrelating viewpoints, and to see how your partner's ideas do and do not fit with your own prior thinking, is necessary to be able to genuinely hear their ideas and effectively both support and challenge them, mining how their thinking fits with yours and noting the clear gaps.

Finally, to engage in explicit supporting and challenging that is constructive seems to require a high level of metacognitive awareness of the work that the havruta is doing from moment to moment.[30] Each partner must be able to continually step back and say: There's this idea on the table. How might I strengthen it? And what might some compelling alternatives be? Each partner must also be able to monitor her own commitment to various ideas on the table in order to maintain "active uncertainty"[31]—actively pursuing ideas but not as ends in themselves, and thus being willing to consider and strengthen alternatives. Students' reflections on this exercise reveal their embryonic awareness of their use of supporting and challenging, an important step toward students being able to monitor their havruta interactions

---

29   See Chapter Eight.

30   When one has metacognitive awareness, one can step back, reflect on one's performance and revise it accordingly, both during the actual performance and after. Metacognition has been shown to be a critical part of learning and is important for use throughout havruta work, not just when supporting and challenging. However, both the delicate nature of these practices and that fact that it is so hard for people to call upon them and use them productively makes it particularly important to be able to develop metacognitive awareness of when and how one uses these practices. For more on metacognition, see David Perkins, *Smart Schools, Better Thinking and Learning for Every Child* (New York: Free Press, 1992) and John D. Bransford, Ann Brown, and Rodney Cocking, *How People Learn: Brain, Mind, Experience and School*.

31   Robert Kegan and Lisa Lahey, *Seven Languages for Transformation: How the Way We Talk Can Change the Way We Work* (San Francisco: Jossey-Bass, 2001), 135. Kegan and Lahey describe this stance as "not paralysis and indecision, but holding of one's own view tentatively (…) seeking clarity, via honest inquiry." For Kegan and Lahey, this stance is critical to being able to make conflict and disagreement a source of learning.

in real time. Their reflections also reveal that these are demanding practices and that students need many opportunities to practice them over time.

Dewey writes, "Experience does not go on simply inside a person... A primary responsibility of educators is (...) that they recognize... what surroundings (or methods) are conducive to experiences that lead to growth."[32] Students paired with one another will not naturally engage in supporting and challenging each other's ideas in substantive and constructive ways. It is the responsibility of educators to help students cultivate such practices through the design of the learning environment and the teaching we do in it. In this context, students can draw on the resources of all three havruta partners and engage in learning that is not "accessible to individuals working alone."[33] Finally, the use of these practices contributes to a classroom environment that emphasizes the ethical-relational aspect of learning, in which partners and classmates care enough about one another's growth that they take each other's ideas seriously and engage with them, in order to make each other's thinking and learning as compelling as possible.

---

[32]   John Dewey, *Experience and Education*.

[33]   Mara Krechevsky and Ben Mardell, "Four Features of Learning in Groups," in *Making Learning Visible: Children as Individual and Group Learners*, ed. Project Zero and Reggio Children (Cambridge, MA and Reggio Emilia, Italy: Project Zero and Reggio Children, 2001), 292. The quote comes from Krechevsky and Mardel's discussion of the value of group work. While group work and paired work are two different but related endeavors, both, when done, allow space for learning that would not occur if people were simply studying on their own.

The limits of interpretation coincide with the rights of the text.
Umberto Eco, The Limits of Interpretation

And then the interpretations—30,000 different interpretations!
Soren Kierkegaard

Chapter Seven:
Evaluating Interpretations

We now turn to a final but central interpretive practice: the evaluation
of the interpretations generated during that study.

In the three last chapters, we discussed the core practices
of havruta text study that are central to the development of sound
textual interpretations: the asking of open questions, fostering continuous open examination of the text; the subtle but significant aspects
of listening that, among other things, help the learner become aware
of and react to the receptive/projective process of interpretation, in
order to avoid its potentially misleading impact; and the supporting
and challenging of a havruta partner's textual interpretations, helping
each other revise and refine those interpretations. We will focus in this
chapter on how students come to be able to take in multiple textual
interpretations, and how they together deal with and evaluate different interpretations that are rarely all correct or of equal value and heft,
and which in fact may be in direct conflict.

In our teaching, we explicitly tell students that they do not have
to agree on one shared textual interpretation. In fact, we often insist
that they develop more than one interpretation of the same text. Yet
despite these injunctions, the collaborative task of havruta learning
fosters a naturally consensus-like synergy, at the end of which students
often agree upon one jointly constructed textual interpretation. This
is particularly true for students who are new to havruta learning.
Sometimes each havruta partner ends up supporting a separate interpretation, and occasionally, a particular student ends up maintaining
more than one interpretation herself. More commonly, it is after their
havruta learning time, in a larger classroom discussion, that students
have to contend with multiple interpretations.

The mere existence of different interpretations of a text can elicit interesting reactions. For example, we have seen students silence
themselves after listening to the interpretations of their peers, feeling
that their interpretation was not worthy enough to be shared with the
rest of the class. We also have seen instances in which students gladly
shared their different interpretations in the hope that it would be identical to the teacher's, who was expected to offer the final, authoritative
interpretation of that text. In other settings, we have heard teachers
say that guiding students to offer many and different interpretations
is actually the goal of the lesson. In their view, havruta text study is
a powerful instrument used to help each student develop his own
interpretation of traditional texts. Making these different interpretations visible not only supports the recognition of each student's voice,
but also helps the students see that "different people have different
ways of understanding things" and that "Judaism has more than one
voice," which, these teachers report, had not been the students' previous experience with Jewish learning.

From our own perspective, accounting for and knowing what to
do with alternative interpretations is a key element of what we mean
by teaching students to become self-conscious havruta learners. It is
essential that they achieve a conceptual understanding of the phenomena they encounter in havruta text study and cultivate practical
methods of engaging those phenomena in productive ways. In other
words, the very phenomenon of multiple interpretations demands
that we help students account for it. As will be explained presently,
unlike teachers who might identify the generation of multiple interpretations as an educational goal in itself, we want students to learn
to respond to the existence of multiple interpretations in a productive
way, by evaluating which of these interpretations may be stronger or
weaker (without necessarily coming to a the conclusion about which
are "right" or "wrong").

Below, we present our own views on multiple interpretations,
grounded in philosophical hermeneutics, for which this phenomenon
is an outcome of both, the indeterminacy of written language and the
readers' different horizons. We also include a sample lesson of a teaching strategy based on Wolfgang Iser's theory of gap-filling.[1] The lesson

---

[1]   Wolfgang Iser, *The Act of Reading*.

is designed to help students respond to the existence of multiple interpretations through the practice of evaluating them.

In the Presence of Multiple Interpretations

When considering the possibility of multiple interpretations of a text,
we must consider both how the students approach them and how we,
the faculty, approach them. In addressing the first question, while
we do not pretend to offer an exhaustive representation of students'
beliefs and attitudes on the issue, schematically speaking, we find that
responses are spread along a wide spectrum ranging from relativist
and reductionist to dogmatic attitudes.

The Relativist-Reductionist Approach

"All interpretations are equally valid" is a common view expressed
by havruta learners. Whether this is due to the belief that we do not
possess meaningful criteria by which we can discriminate between
interpretations (a relativist approach) or that a textual interpretation can be reduced to the values and beliefs that each reader brings
to the text (a reductionist approach), this statement reflects a seem-
ing comfort with the idea that multiple interpreters breed multiple
interpretations, without needing to do anything other than to note
this.

Students with a relativist approach hold that opinions and
beliefs are largely subjective matters, and that this is certainly the
case when it comes to the interpretation of texts (especially those that
come to us from a distance in time, making any attempt at a definitive
interpretation pointless). They believe that there are no shared and
common objective ground or criteria by which interpretations can be
evaluated; consequently, all interpretations are seen as equally valid,
foreclosing the possibility of any comparative or qualitative evaluation.

However, students who adopt such an approach sometimes
become very defensive of their own interpretations, leading them to
a more reductionist approach. While this might at first glance appear
to be in conflict with the idea that all interpretations are equal, it
reflects the reality that, among equals, a given learner will be especially

committed to her own interpretation, as it is, after all, an expression of her very self. This might be explained by the investigative, open, and active type of havruta text study that allows learners to generate their own interpretations, conferring a sense of ownership over the interpretive process and, over time, a growing sense of entitlement to interpret traditional texts.

While we generally view this as a positive outcome of havruta text study, it may also reinforce a defensive attitude, the subtext of which could be rendered as follows: Since interpretation reflects the reader's reading of herself into the text, to question the validity or the quality of an interpretation is perceived as questioning the learner's right to express her personal view. Alternatively, it implies questioning of her persona, her beliefs, and her value as a human being. These students thus tend to perceive any criticism or questioning as a lack of respect, or worse, a personal attack. Sometimes they may say, "Different people have different beliefs and therefore come up with different interpretations."[2] For these students, the very attempt to evaluate the quality and strength of an interpretation presents a problem.[3]

The Objective-Foundationalist View

At the other end of the spectrum, we find students who, even when studying narrative texts that are both laconic and evocative, assume an

---

[2]   This type of expression reflects views that are common in the sociopolitical realm, for example, "Everyone is entitled to their own opinion, and no opinion is inherently better than any other." This is a position where reality, in this case the text, is referenced in the light of one's situated finite and historical perspective. As an overall stance, Seyla Ban-Habib coined it as "situated universality": see Seyla Ben-Habib, *Situating the Self: Gender, Community and Postmodernism in Contemporary Ethics* (New York: Routledge, 1992), 3.

[3]   An additional aspect of this attitude lies in the use of the word "respect," when it is interpreted to refer only to the other's right to express herself. In dialogic theories, however, respect for another does not allow for non-engagement but requires careful observation: "To respect someone is to look for the springs that feed the pool of their experience" (William Isaacs, *Dialogue and the Art of Thinking Together* [New York: Doubleday, 1999], 110).

objectivist view of interpretation—that is, that a text holds (only) one true interpretation, which it is their task as readers to retrieve. Often, this approach is also foundationalist—that is, accompanied by a focus on authorial intention or the assumption that interpretation without any presuppositions is possible if one relies on "objective" methods of interpretation. Students who hold an objectivist and/or foundationalist view can become dismissive of alternative interpretations, feeling that only one can ultimately be correct. For these students, having multiple interpretations in a classroom creates a problem that needs to be solved.

Let us contrast these views with the view of interpretation that underlies our approach, as discussed in Chapter Two. Grounded in philosophical hermeneutics, we move away from a narrow and restricted search for authorial intention, aiming rather for the "world" of the text. In this view, the text is an autonomous source of meaning, open to new engagements, interpretations, and appropriations of meaning that are produced through a reciprocal interaction between learner and text. However, this notion of textual autonomy and the learner's projections into the text does not give the reader *carte blanche* to bend interpretation in any direction he wishes. Rather, the text imposes limits on the scope of legitimate interpretations.[4]

As in the relativist and reductionist approaches, we operate on the premise that the learner not only retrieves but also constructs the meaning of a text—but we hold that textual interpretations still allow for considered judgment based on evidence and reasoning. Indeed, while experience and the history of interpretation clearly show that many texts are irreducible to a sole meaning, this does not imply that

---

[4]   As mentioned in Chapter Two, by not reducing the meaning of a text to authorial intention or objectivist historical explanations, texts become the object of multiple interpretations. By grounding havruta text study in philosophical hermeneutics, we identify three major reasons for the phenomenon of multiple interpretations. First, it is a natural outcome of the polysemic nature of written language; see Paul Ricoeur, *Interpretation Theory: Discourse and the Surplus of Meaning* (Fort Worth: Texas Christian University Press, 1976). Second, every interpretation is also impacted by the historical, limited and changing horizons of the interpreter; see Hans-Georg Gadamer, *Truth and Method*. Finally, reading and interpreting is a performative activity in which the reader fill gaps in the text; see Wolfgang Iser, *The Act of Reading*.

there are no incorrect interpretations. A relative evaluation of interpretations is key. In Ricoeur's words, "an interpretation must not only
be probable, but more probable than another. And there are criteria
of relative superiority which may easily be derived from the logic of
subjective probability."[5] While it is true that there is more than one
way to interpret a text, it is not true that all interpretations are equal or
even acceptable. According to Ricoeur:

> If it is true that there is always more than one way of constru-
> ing a text, it is not true that all interpretations are equal... The
> text is a limited field of possible constructions. ...It is always
> possible to argue against an interpretation, to confront interpre-
> tations, to arbitrate between them and to seek for an agreement,
> even if this agreement remains beyond our reach.[6]

Finding the right balance, in which multiple interpretations are
accepted so long as they stand up to the evaluative scrutiny of the
reader, is one of our aims in teaching students to deal with the multitude of interpretations they will encounter in their studies.[7]

In our view, the criteria for evaluating a text lie in terms of the
genre of the text, its context, and its time and place. Likewise, interpretations should be well grounded in textual evidence. Finally, the
evaluation of different interpretations should also include heightened

---

[5]   Paul Ricoeur, *Hermeneutics and the Human Sciences*, 213. For Ricoeur,
        "validation is an argumentative discipline comparable to the juridical pro-
        cedures of legal interpretation" (*From Text to Action*, 175). He concedes that
        the validation of which he speaks with respect to texts is "closer to a logic of
        probability than to a logic of empirical verification" (ibid., 212). Thus, our
        use of the term "evaluation" to render the relative aspect of this activity and
        distance ourselves from what might be understood as "verification."

[6]   Paul Ricoeur, *From Text to Action*, 160.

[7]   One of the foundational principles of philosophical hermeneutics provides
        an alternative to nihilism, by claiming that it is possible for people to get
        beyond their current perspectives and to engage with something other
        than those perspectives. This is possible not despite but because people are
        grounded in language, which transcends their individual finitude. See for
        example Nicholas Davey, *Unquiet Understanding: Gadamer's Philosophical
        Hermeneutics* (Albany: State University of New York Press, 2006).

awareness of and examination by the interpreter of the meaning with which he has filled the gaps in the text.

Broadly speaking, this approach does justice to the actuality of competing interpretations without succumbing to relativism. It values, when possible, discrimination between stronger and weaker interpretations, while not taking a foundationalist or objectivist approach because, in the final analysis, it considers these interpretations to carry a certain amount of indetermination. Indeed, there can be reasonable interpretations about which people legitimately disagree, without the ability or even desirability of coming to any straightforward resolution.

Thus, in our approach to havruta text study, we aim to help students become aware that the reality and even desirability of multiple interpretations does not imply avoidance of examination and evaluation and, whenever appropriate, invites a judgment that is relative rather than absolute. We expect them to become self-evaluative and take advantage of alternative interpretations to help revise and improve their own. Practically speaking, this means providing students with the skills to examine different interpretations and distinguish between more or less compelling ones. To this end, we have designed learning experiences of which the following is but one example. This particular lesson and the instructional strategy is intended to emphasize the reciprocal influence of reader and text, through Wolfgang's Iser's concept of gap-filling (a concept we discussed in Chapter Two) and the use of textual evidence in making qualitative distinctions among varying interpretations.[8]

---

8   While grounded in philosophical hermeneutics, the approach to text study that underlies our approach to havruta text study is also close to literary theories like that of Abrams: see Meyer Howard Abrams, "A Note on Wittgenstein and Literary Criticism," in *Doing Things with Texts: Essays in Criticism and Critical Theory*, ed. Meyer H. Abrams (New York: W. W. Norton & Co, 1989), 73–87. Similar to Sophie Haroutunian-Gordon, we differ from theoreticians like Harold Bloom and Stanley Fish in that we assume that that the reader's preconceptions turn the text into a radically *undetermined* object, and that textual interpretations are the outcome of the interaction of the constraints imposed by the content of the text, the reader's preconceptions, and the practices and dynamics that characterize the textual interpretation process. See Sophie Haroutunian-Gordon, *Turning the Soul: Teaching through Conversation in the High School*, 196, note 2; Harold Bloom, *The Anxiety of Influence: A Theory of Poetry* (New York: University Press,

Learning to Evaluate Interpretations

We begin with a mini-lesson in which students are introduced to the concept of gap-filling, a central concept in understanding the sources of multiple interpretations and the need for evaluation. Next, students engage in a four-step text study activity built on havruta learning in order to experiment with gap-filling in connection with the evaluation of interpretations. Finally, students provide a written reflection in which they process what they have learned about the phenomenon of multiple interpretations and the evaluation of textual interpretations.

The Mini-Lesson

We begin the lesson by writing a question on the board as well as what may be one of the shortest stories ever:

What does the act of reading involve?

"When he woke up, the dinosaur was still there." [9]

We ask students to explain the story. Not surprisingly, we get a range of very different possible explanations. We note out that when people study the same text, they often end up offering different interpretations. We then ask the students how they account for this. Students typically note the lack of information in this story to account for the different interpretations offered and the need to make a number of inferences to help make sense of what is written.

We then introduce them to Iser's concept of gap-filling as a tool to help conceptualize the reciprocal and dynamic relationship between text and learner and to evaluate different interpretations. For Iser, reading is a performative act in which both the reader and the text play an active role. It is an activity in which the reader actively engages

---

1973); Stanley Fish, *Is there a Text in this Class? The Authority of Interpretive Communities* (Cambridge, MA: Harvard University Press, 1980).

[9]   By Augusto Monterroso.

in a reciprocal relationship with the text, whose perceived gaps and indeterminacies function as the key nexus point for the reader-text relationship. The gaps function as a pivot on which the whole reader-text relationship hinges. A weak interpretation would be one in which the learner fills in the gaps while ignoring what the words or sentences of the texts tell him; a strong one, in which she does so with attention to what appears in the rest of the text. Sometimes, as learners, we have to readjust our fillings-in based on what we encounter in the text or what we know about its historical or cultural context. At the same time, since it is the learner who fills in the gaps from within a range of possible meanings, more than one interpretation is to be expected by different learners. This allows us to consider which particular interpretation might be more compelling in terms of which gaps it fills and how it relates to other specific elements of the text.

We also explain how Iser's concept accounts for the phenomenon of multiple interpretations without taking a relativist or reductionist view of textual interpretation. Indeed, gaps create a significant element of indeterminacy in texts. Thus, the likelihood is that not only the more evocative a text is but the more significant its gaps, the more interpretations it will engender. In filling them, readers draw on their own background knowledge and life experience, yielding different interpretations. At the same time, the text uses its structure, the information it does provide, and the choice of words it uses to convey autonomous information to impose its own limits so that readers are not entirely free to fill in its gaps any way they want. It follows that the looser the textual anchor of the fillings, the weaker the quality of the interpretation.

We have found it helpful to locate this approach to reading in juxtaposition with two other familiar examples of reading: reading a dictionary and reading a Rorschach test.[10] (Although it is rare that an individual's interpretive efforts operate on the sole basis of either of the two extreme views represented, they operate as useful points of contrast.) We situate reading as grounded in "gap-filling" in the dia-

---

[10]   Cook and Kent discuss the way these approaches play out in classroom teaching and how teachers can reframe their work to focus on "interpretive experience" and "interpretive exercises." See Allison Cook and Orit Kent, "Doing the Work: Interpretive Experience as the Fulcrum of Tanakh Education."

gram below to serve three purposes: first, to provide students with
a map and a language with which to talk about the topics of reading,
meaning, and interpretation; second, to illustrate the connection
between assumptions about the practice of reading and views about
multiple interpretations; and finally, to illustrate how reading as gap-
filling invites evaluation of interpretations.

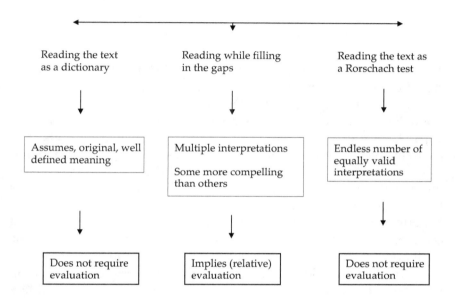

In this representation, we identify one extreme approach, "reading the text as a dictionary," which in the context of havruta text study
both compares reading to translating the Hebrew text into English.
This approach reflects a narrow view of interpretation, reducing it
to the level of paraphrasing. At the other extreme, we identify the
approach of "reading the text as a Rorschach test" (an extreme example
of the relativist and reductionist approaches), in which interpretations
are solely the product of what a reader projects onto the text, yielding
an infinite number of possible interpretations, all equally compelling
and valid by the mere fact that they were generated. We ask students
to describe what they think textual study would look like if it was
performed merely as reading the dictionary or as a Rorschach test.
To make these two extreme types of reading more tangible, we often
have students enact them in the following way: we provide a short text
and ask them to offer a reading of that text while limiting themselves

to strict paraphrasing—that is, by replacing most words using a the-saurus. Then, we ask them to choose three to four nouns in that same text and to offer a number of free associations that make connections between these nouns, without any consideration for the meaning of the rest of the text.

The Practice: Evaluating Textual Interpretation

This part of the lesson, consisting of several steps, uses havruta text study to help students begin the process of gap-filling to produce a range of interpretations that they can then evaluate and improve upon. First, students generate textual interpretations, pinpointing the gaps. A short exercise then makes their processes of gap-filling visible to themselves and to others. In the third step, students are exposed to each other's interpretations, which they then take turns evaluating. Finally, students engage in a comparative and evaluative process to refine the quality of their own interpretations. This entire process is performed in havruta pairs, which, through oral explanations and collaborative examination, makes the process of gap-filling and the evaluation of interpretations much more tangible and explicit.

In the example below, we use the same rabbinic text as in Chapter Four because it is particularly helpful in making gap-filling visible:[11]

---

[11]   See Appendix 2 for our discussion about information and guidelines pro-vided for the study of text in havruta pairs. For this particular text students are provided with the following information: "Rav (*stands for Rabbi*) Papa: (died 375) was a Talmud scholar and teacher who lived in Babylonia. He was a student of both Rava and Abaye. He led the yeshiva (the academy where people study) in the city of Nehardea and over time he trained many students. Rav Papa was a wealthy man and it is said that whenever he com-pleted studying a tractate from the Talmud he held a large party at which he invited his ten sons and many other people. *R. Shimi bar Ashi* (fourth cen-tury) was a close disciple of Abaye. After the passing away of his teacher he attended Rav Papa's yeshiva. The term *fell on his face* is a ritual and usually private practice during which people expressed their personal prayers."

1. Rabbi Shimi bar Ashi used to attend (the classes) of R. Papa

2. and used to ask him many questions (*Alternative translation:* many difficult questions).

3. One day he observed that Rabbi Papa fell on his face [in prayer] and he heard him saying, "May God preserve me from the embarrassment caused by Shimi" (*Alternative translation:* from the insolence of Shimi.)

4. The latter thereupon vowed silence and questioned him no more.

(*Tractate Ta'anit, 9a*)

The text is presented after having been separated into lines, leaving a fair amount of space above and beneath each line. Students are invited to engage in the textual practices they have already learned (e. g., multiple readings, paraphrasing the text). They are then provided with the following task in order to help them focus on the gaps in the text:[12]

Discuss any information that seems to be missing, i.e., which makes the story somewhat ambiguous and/or might have helped you to better understand what is going on.

Purposefully looking for and articulating what seems to be missing information in a text is not something learners do spontaneously. The reader's natural tendency is to unconsciously fill in the gaps. The assignment above helps slow down that process and make it visible. It is designed to help students reside in some kind of twilight between a possible comprehensive understanding of what the story is about and an awareness of what the missing pieces of information are in order to concretize their understanding of the existence of inevitable gaps in the text.

---

[12]   See Appendix 10 for a copy of the full document.

As in previous classes, students are then asked to offer at least one interpretation that they estimate to be compelling and to complete the following sentence:

> "I/We believe that this story is about... It says that..."

Students already know that the "I/We" signifies that either each havruta learner can offer her own interpretation or both havruta partners can co-construct one shared interpretation.

The following are two examples of interpretations we have collected from students who worked with this particular text.

Rina's interpretation of the story is as follows:

I believe the story is about the role of the teacher in the classroom. The text takes for granted that the role of students is twofold: first to be proactive by asking questions so that they understand what the teacher says ("and asked many questions"). Second, to ask questions that build on what the teacher taught so that the idea are further explored and developed, even if this is challenging for the teacher ("and asked him difficult questions").

It is my understanding that through this story, the text wants to tell us that teachers who do not fulfill their role, for withdrawal and lack of engagement, which consequently harms the student's learning. This text is addressed to teachers: It is a critique of certain teachers' stances when they disregard students' questions.

Steve, who was not Rina's havruta partner, interpreted the text as follows:

I believe the story is about the student's self-awareness of his interactions with his teacher (and classmates) in the classroom.

It is my understanding that through this story, the text wants to tell us that students should be aware of their teacher's expectations and aims in the classroom, and should not assume that their own learning is the only thing that matters. Until he heard the prayer, Rabbi Shimi wasn't aware that he had embarrassed his teacher. The embarrassment may have been caused by Rabbi Shimi interrupting Rabbi Papa's flow of thought, or by preventing him from fully developing the ideas he wanted to present during class. This text is addressed to students: It attempts to make them aware of their teacher's role, expectations, assumptions, and objectives in the classroom, and the fact that they may not overlap with those of the student.

The second assignment is designed to make the actual activity of filling in the gaps visible, both to the learner as well as to others. Students are asked to insert two sentences (not more) into the text that would help convey their understanding of the story. We limit the task to two added sentences to help students pinpoint what they believe to be the most important gaps to be filled in. The handwriting between the printed lines on the page creates a strongly visible quality to those fillings. In addition, students are asked to describe as specifically as possible what in the text or elsewhere in their knowledge prompted them to add these two sentences. It may have been something written in the text, something implied in the text, any previous knowledge they may have, something that happened during their havruta learning, or some previous experience and/or view of similar life situations. This reflective analysis is designed to help students experience in a tangible way Iser's description of the ways in which both elements of the text and elements brought by readers to the text interact and infuse what they add to it—the fillings—during the interpretive process. The list of examples is designed to help students realize the variety of resources a reader draws on to fill in these gaps.

Rina represented her interpretation with the following sentences added into the text:

> Rabbi Shimi bar Ashi used to attend (the classes) of Rabbi Papa and used to ask him many questions. One day he observed that Rabbi Papa fell on his face [in prayer] and he heard him saying, "May God preserve me from the embarrassment caused by Shimi." The latter thereupon vowed silence and questioned him no more. **Rabbi Papa realized how his hasty behavior had put an end to Rabbi Shimi's active learning. He went to him and encouraged him to ask questions during class.**

Steve visualized his interpretation with the following fillings:

Rabbi Shimi bar Ashi used to attend (the classes) of Rabbi Papa **because of his respect for his teacher. Unfortunately, he** used to ask him many questions. One day he observed that Rabbi Papa fall on his face [in prayer] and he heard him saying, "May God preserve me from the embarrassment caused by Shimi." The latter thereupon vowed silence and questioned him no more. **This, in turn, led to Rabbi Shimi's ability to begin listening to the profound words of his teacher Rabbi Papa and ultimately to deepening his understanding.**

These examples illustrate how Rina and Steve can offer two opposing interpretations of the text while the fillings they offer are more than reasonable and in sync with the text.

In the third stage of the lesson, we want students to be exposed to and examine alternative interpretations generated by their fellow students, and then to evaluate these interpretations as well as their own. This exercise is meant to help students realize how the gaps can be filled in different ways, but also to examine to what extent the ensuing interpretations are based on solid textual evidence, integrating as many details of the story as possible.

Each pair meets with another to evaluate each other's respective interpretations. They exchange the sheets with their interpretation (s) and insertions. First, each pair discusses separately the feedback they will be providing to the other havruta pair. They prepare their feedback with the help of the three following points:

* Provide feedback as to what elements of the interpretation you find compelling. Indicate the elements of the story that make sense in the context of this interpretation.

* Indicate which elements of the story are not addressed or are only partially addressed by this interpretation.

* Share further comments or suggestions which expose strengths or weaknesses in the quality of the interpretation.

By inviting students to look for both compelling as well as missing elements, we hope to cultivate an approach to textual interpretation that is relative (stronger or weaker) rather than absolute (right or wrong). The first two tasks have more of a directive character, as they have students focus on textual evidence, or at least on good anchors in the text, to help sustain the interpretation. The third task is broader and invites students to explore what additional elements might reinforce or weaken the suggested interpretations.

We believe that for feedback to be productive it is not enough for the provider to know how and about what she should be giving feedback; the quality of the feedback encounter can be increased when the *addressees* are also aware of what it entails to *listen* to feedback. Therefore, each havruta pair is also asked to prepare for their role as listeners. To that end, we provide them with the following description:

> The goal of listening to the evaluation of your interpretation is to help you improve and/or revise it. For this process of evaluation to work, please do not argue or respond to the comments when you receive your evaluation. Rather, listen carefully to what is said. You will have time to process these comments with your havruta partner and decide how you want to address them. You may want to ask the other havruta pair for clarification questions.

Again, the language that is used in these guidelines is designed to set the tone and cultivate the stance that is at the basis of havruta text study in general and textual evaluations in particular. It sets the goal of the evaluative feedback as striving for a relative improvement (that is, helping to improve or revise) rather then to find out who is right and who is wrong. It positions listening to feedback in contrast to arguing or having to respond. As opposed to a potentially defensive attitude on behalf of the listener, it aims to cultivate an investigative stance by inviting students to ask for clarification. It also makes clear the staged separation between the need to be receptive to the evaluative feedback and a later opportunity to think about how to address the points made by the evaluators. Finally, by having each havruta pair take upon themselves the role of evaluator as well as listener, it reinforce the sense that both of these activities are inherent in what we believe good havruta learning looks like.

At the conclusion of each of these times for mutual feedback, the havruta pairs regroup separately. They are then given time first to evaluate the various interpretations they have been exposed to in this exercise. They then take advantage of the evaluations and comments they have received, as well as their own heightened awareness of what elements make for stronger or weaker interpretations, to re-examine, refine, or revise their own interpretations. For this purpose, we provide them with the following tasks:

> * *Evaluation*: discuss with your havruta which of the interpretations you have been exposed to so far (yours included), you find more or less compelling and why.
>
> * If you decide to change your interpretation, please write your new interpretation: "I/We believe this story to be about… and that it tries to say that…"
>
> * Explain what has caused you to change your interpretation and why you find this one to be more compelling.
>
> * If you decide not to change your interpretation, explain how you address the comments and questions presented to you.

The various steps of this lesson embody its central idea. It is important to be able to account for the phenomenon of multiple interpretations from a theoretical point of view, but even more important is the practical consequences of acknowledging the phenomenon. Being brought into the presence of alternative interpretations is not an end in itself. Rather, it provides each learner with a unique opportunity to deepen and enrich the development of compelling interpretations in a self-evaluative way. Close attention to one's own gap-filling is the first step. Next, the evaluation of alternative interpretations, while pointing out concrete features that make them more or less compelling, provides insight as to what would make for better interpretation. Finally, since the point of the exercise is the identification and development of what each havruta learner considers to be the most compelling interpretations, rather than holding onto his or her own interpretation, they are invited to revise, strengthen, or change the interpretation (s)

they are ready to consider as the most compelling based on the evaluative process.[13]

Student Reflections

The lesson ends with an opportunity for students to reflect on the
new insights they may have gained from this exercise. We ask them
to articulate what they have learned about the phenomenon of multiple interpretations and what they now think makes for compelling
textual interpretations. In reading student reflections following this
lesson, we are interested in what kinds of connections students make
and what kinds of questions arise for them. This gives us a window
into what students take away from the lesson and also helps us build
on those insights in future lessons.

For instance, the following examples reflect a heightened awareness of the multiplicity of valid textual interpretations, but without
grounding this observation in a relativist/reductionist approach. Mike
writes:

> I've learned that a text can look so different when approached
> and re-approached. This is the value of looking over the text
> multiple times.

Josh expresses a similar awareness:

> I noticed myself rereading and questioning the text. I found this
> to be a passage that could be interpreted in a number of ways,
> and as such it is important that one pays close attention to the
> wording and the connotation of these words... This text also
> piqued my curiosity and left me wondering about the various
> interpretations and explanations there might be for it, and how
> they relate to my own thoughts and findings.

Varda reflects a heightened awareness not only of the need to
avoid offering hasty interpretations, but also of the complexity of the
interpretive process, which involves both reader and text:

---

[13]   See Appendix 11 for an alternative model in which textual interpretations
are collectively evaluated by the entire class.

It is not enough to assume, after a cursory reading, that
Rabbi Papa was short-tempered and a "bad teacher," nor is it
appropriate to assume that Rabbi Shimi bar Ashi's lines of questioning were innocuous. The extremity of Rabbi Papa's reactions
demands that a student imagine all the possible scenarios that
might have caused such a reaction. I find that I try to examine
a text from as many possible angles as my personal biases will
allow, while at the same time drawing from my current knowledge about the characters, historical period, and society to make
the best assessment of the text.

Another student, Rebecca, identified this lesson with "slow
reading" and writes about the interpretive benefits of such a reading
in helping make visible the author's assumptions as well as hers:

I learned how to read slowly. I learned about the assumptions
of authors, as well as my own assumptions when reading a text
and how to make my assumptions explicit.

We also see in student reflections how their conception of what
constitutes a good interpretation and a good interpreter has been
informed by the lesson. For Shira, for example, the practice of evaluating one's own as well as another's interpretations seems to have
become central to what it means to interpret a text:

Someone who is a critical reader and who can listen to other
perspectives and know why they do or why they do not hold
them. A good interpretation is one that is supported by the text.

For Daniel, this lesson elicits a fresh formulation of the themes
addressed in previous classes. In this case, he reflects on his understanding of the text as partner:

Text as a partner means that we make sense of the text by using
all that it has to offer us. Text as partner happened when we
were asking questions [about the text] and had to add sentences
to it. This exercise forced us to become partnered with the text.

Finally, some degree of confusion is not only an inevitable part
of learning but also a frequent outcome of this particular lesson, in

which there is an attempt to raise students' awareness of some of the more subtle aspects of the evaluation of textual interpretations. This is aptly described by Rose:

> The process [of text interpretation] has limits but those limits are vague. The line is blurry. I am still confused about where the line is and if it shifts, depending on the person.

We have found this lesson to be particularly rich in that it addresses several important aspects of havruta text study. It has students examine their beliefs about textual interpretation while touching upon broader cultural issues like aspects of dogmatism, relativism, and the right to have one's own or many opinions, along with the understanding that this does not have to prevent critical and rational examination and evaluation.[14] It also mirrors the development of textual interpretation as an activity that is neither a strict application of one method nor a free process of associations. Rather, it situates the development of interpretation closer to an art form, in which there is room for personal creativity and diversity together with an expectation of accountability based on a shared rationality. This framework, in which personal creativity and diversity are paired with accountability, is grounded in the concept of the reader's foreknowledge of the interpretive process, as explained in philosophical hermeneutics, as well as on Iser's concept of "filling in" of the text's blanks. While both theories offer an explanation as to how the same text can generate several interpretations, they also help us realize how the richness of students' pre-knowledge can initiate a wide variety of interpretations, making it more challenging to discern among less or more compelling ones.

Although we keep reminding students that to generate a sound interpretation of a text does not imply that they identify with the ideas conveyed in the interpretation, students may naturally want to hold on to the interpretation they have developed to a point where they become a little dogmatic in their attitude. Thus, another important idea of havruta text study enacted in this lesson is that the center of the

---

[14]   For an example of the connection between people's thinking about text interpretation and this kind of cultural issues, see Dan Stiver, *Theology after Ricoeur: New Directions in Hermeneutical Theology* (Louisville, KY: Westminster John Knox Press, 2001).

learner's concern is expected to be the generation of compelling interpretations, rather than to be concerned that the interpretation would
solely be "theirs." Not only is the feedback of others important, but
being exposed to alternative interpretations may also impact, enrich,
and alter one's own interpretation.

Likewise, both the topics and the lesson described in this chapter embody the kind of learning that we strive for in havruta text
study. As already mentioned, we expect havruta learners not only to
be attentive but also to account for diverse elements and recurring
phenomena they encounter in havruta text study. Our task as teachers
is to design learning strategies that provide students with an opportunity to experience key theoretical concepts, in this case Iser's concept
of gap-filling. By making students the enactors of the concept of gap-
filling and by putting them in the role of evaluators, we hope to bring
to center stage those aspects of textual interpretation, and also hope
that over time students may adopt them as an inherent practice of
havruta text study.

When havruta learners reach a point where they each separately
or jointly hold any number of textual interpretations they have found
to be compelling enough in the sense discussed in this chapter, they
can be said to have achieved the first phase of havruta text study.

Far from saying that a subject, who already masters his own being-in-the-world, projects his own understanding into the text, I shall say that to conduct a good conversation with a text is the process by which the revelation of new ways of being gives the subject new capacities for knowing himself.

The interpretation of a text culminates in the self-interpretation of a reader who thenceforth understands himself better, understands himself differently, or simply begins to understand himself.

Paul Ricoeur, Hermeneutics and the Human Sciences

Chapter Eight:
Dialoguing with Texts and Partners

We began our exploration of havruta text study by proposing a two-phase approach. The first step was characterized by the joint attempt of havruta partners to "make the text speak"—that is, to co-construct compelling textual interpretations (through textual, interpersonal, and intrapersonal interpretive practices designed to serve that goal). This chapter now addresses the second phase of havruta text study, characterized by a dialogical engagement of the learners with the ideas submitted and questions raised by their encounter with the text. The type of havruta text study we aim to cultivate is not confined to "mastery" of the text or "the students' understanding of the text's meaning" (to paraphrase common pedagogic language), in which the text might well remain an object that students can describe but with which they have not truly engaged. In contrast, in our approach to havruta text study, the text is a true dialogical partner, and thus it is necessary to identify the relevant features of that dialogue.

Earlier in this volume, we used the metaphor of text as a partner to emphasize that a text has something to say, the discovery of which is the learner's primary task. In addition, we presented the text as an *active* partner, indicating the reciprocal interaction between text and learner that characterizes the interpretive process. However, it is in the second phase of havruta text study that the notion of "text as partner" reaches its fullest critical meaning. Here, the text adopts, as it were, features of a human conversational partner: It sets a topic for the conversation, offers a view or takes a stance on the topic, and poses a question to its interlocutors, inviting them to respond to what is said. Havruta text study requires the learner's intentional and active responses to these invitations.

The word "dialogue" is intended to capture the intricacies of this particular engagement. We therefore confine this term to the second phase of havruta text study, despite our acknowledgment that vivid verbal exchanges of information and ideas take place between havruta partners when they co-construct textual interpretations during the first phase. Too often, terms like "dialogue" are used in classrooms to refer merely to random or turn-taking exchanges of opinions. A clarification of what a dialogue with a text and havruta partner entails here and is meant to achieve is therefore necessary. We begin by identifying and discussing key features of such a dialogue, then discuss examples of learning tasks designed to help students enact them.

Enactment of Dialogue in Havruta Text Study

In havruta text study, we aim to cultivate learners of texts who are not removed spectators but rather engaged participants in dialogue with the text and with their havruta partner, who genuinely desire to hear what texts and co-conversants have to say to them and articulate what they have to say to the text and to their partner. As Gadamer would have us understand, such a dialogue focuses on the subject matter under discussion at a time and in such a way that the study partners are vulnerable, both in their expression of self as well as in their openness to encountering new ideas.[1]

From that perspective, an essential element of learning that can be achieved through dialogue with the text and havruta partner is the learner's critical awareness of her habitual understanding of the studied topic. As part of this process, the learner experiences something of a "defamiliarization," or even a temporary rupture, in her usual

---

[1]   Jean Grondin provides an analysis of four types of understanding in Gadamer's work: understanding as an intellectual grasp, as a practical know-how, as agreement, as application and as translation. See Jean Grondin, "Gadamer's Basic Understanding of Understanding," in *The Cambridge Companion to Gadamer*, ed. Robert J. Dostal (Cambridge: Cambridge University Press, 2002), 36–51.

ways of thinking, which brings her to interrogate, examine, revise, and ground or transform her thinking and open herself to the possibility of new worlds. In that process, by the text and/or havruta partner, she might come to question what she once took for granted, or on the contrary, reinforce her views in the light of the dialogue with text and havruta partner. This is all to say that the aim of havruta text study in this sense is to lead each learner toward a more reflective and critical viewpoint and a deeper self-consciousness.

This conceptualization of dialogue is captured in Ricoeur's concept of self-understanding. For him, textual study "culminates in the self-interpretation of a subject who thenceforth understands himself better, understands himself differently, or simply begins to understand himself."[2] In other words, if the first phase of havruta text study is designed to lead to the development of sound interpretations, its second phase should be designed to lead the learner to deeper self-understanding. To that end, havruta text study should encourage each learner to engage in a self-reflective process designed to help him achieve this personal synthesis on the basis of the dialogues experienced. Thus, we identify self-understanding as a dialogical and intrapersonal goal, as represented by the circular arrow in the diagram.

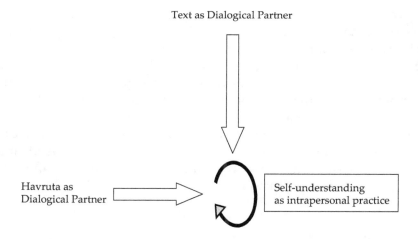

Text as Dialogical Partner

Havruta as
Dialogical Partner

Self-understanding
as intrapersonal practice

---

2   Paul Ricoeur, *Hermeneutics and the Human Sciences*, 158–59.

However, any attempt to trace systematic steps that would auto-matically lead to self-understanding is doomed to fail. The first phase of havruta text study is defined by a relatively tangible goal—co-con-structing textual interpretations—which allows for an analytical and relatively systematic discussion of interpretive practices that may be conducive to achieving this goal. Yet a parallel approach to the dialog-ical phase of havruta text study would be problematic. The dynamic of dialogue is much more open-ended and illusory, and does not end in any tangible "product." The nature of dialogue is associative, as one idea often elicits new directions of thought and unexpected argu-mentations or insights. As teachers of havruta text study, we do not have students "structure" their dialogue, as it would suffocate what makes that dialogue alive, dynamic and unpredictable. Instead, we ask ourselves what features of dialogue with text and havruta partner are necessary to make it conducive to self-understanding as defined earlier, and which practices can facilitate the cultivation of this stance or state of mind

Textual Dialogical Practices

As we saw earlier, the textual interpretations that havruta learners have come to articulate represent the "world" of the text. We saw that this "world" should not be identified with the intention of the author or with the historical situation common to the writer and his original readers. Instead, it is understood as the view or perspective that the text presents, "as the direction of thought opened up by the text"[3]— or, for Gadamer, the text's presentation of a world that also provides a response to a question, which we only understand "when we under-stand the question to which it is an answer."[4] This helps us identify a first dialogical textual practice: namely, reconstructing the question to which the text is an answer.[5]

---

[3]   Paul Ricoeur, *Interpretation Theory: Discourse and the Surplus of Meaning*, 92.

[4]   Hans-Georg Gadamer, *Truth and Method*, 370.

[5]   Ibid., 370. The text projects a question without having to have a special syntac-tical questioning distinction. See Gadamer's "Semantik und Hermeneutik," quoted in Thomas Schwarz Wentzer, "Toward a Phenomenology of

Following Gadamer, dialogue is not about reaching an agreement with the text so much as allowing for the emergence of a new understanding of the subject matter by the learner. Consequentely, an important element of dialogue is for each partner to recognize the value of ideas that are alien or opposed to their own; "while holding on to his own arguments," each learner should be "able to weigh the counterarguments."[6] Thus, a second textual practice consists of trying to understand the reasoning behind the text's perspective and allowing for the merits of such reasoning, even up to the point that one's own presuppositions might be transformed.[7]

A third practice consists in the learner's articulation of his personal answer to the question that is posed by the text. This, following Gadamer, is the power and the value of the study of texts, especially traditional texts:

Questioning: Gadamer on Questions and Questioning," in *Gadamer's Hermeneutics and the Art of Conversation: International Studies in Hermeneutics and Phenomenology Vol. 2*, ed. Andrzej Wiercinski (Berlin: Lit Verlag, 2011), 246. See also: "Reconstructing the question, to which the meaning of a text is understood as an answer, merges with our own questioning. For the text must be understood as an answer to a real question" (Hans-Georg Gadamer, *Truth and Method*, 374).

[6]   Ibid., 388–9. Also, "If we put ourselves in someone else's shoes then we will understand him" (ibid., 305). And further: "Each opens himself to the other person, truly accepts his point of view as worthy of consideration and gets inside the other to such an extent that he understands not a particular individual but what he says (...) Such an opening does not entail agreement but rather the to and fro play of dialogue" (ibid., 347). It should be noticed that Jacques Derrida criticizes this type of apparent good will to being open to the opinion of an other, as a manipulation expressing a will of power. See Diane P. Michelfelder and Richard E. Palmers, eds., *Dialogue and Deconstruction: The Gadamer-Derrida Encounter* (Albany: State University of New York Press, 1989), 162–75.

[7]   For Gadamer, any interpretation of a text consists of a dialogue between past and present. When confronted with a text, we listen to its unfamiliar voice, allowing it to question our present concerns. At the same time, what the text "says" to us will depend on the kind of questions we are able to address to it as well as on our ability to reconstruct the "question" to which the text itself is an "answer," for the text itself is also a dialogue with its own history. This type of dialogue with text enacts the view that the present is only understandable through the past, with which it forms a living continuity. At the same time, the past cannot be grasped but from our own partial historical viewpoint within the present.

The most important thing is the question that the text puts to us... The voice that speaks to us from the past—whether text, work, trace—itself poses a question and places our meaning in openness. In order to answer the question put to us, we, the interrogated, must ourselves begin to ask the questions.[8]

It is in this sense that learning bridges past and present, as the learner in the present is expected to contribute his own view in an open and evolving dialogue with the past. In doing this, the learner will have to compare the similarities and/or differences between his own and the text's view. Likewise, as part of the dialogue with the text, he may raise questions or challenge the text's view as well as revise or expand his own in the light of the text's view. In doing this, a clear distinction between what is perceived to be the text's and the learner's ideas is established. At the same time, it is from that awareness that the learner opens himself to unfamiliar ideas and may allow himself to be changed.

Interpersonal and Intrapersonal Dialogical Practices

All of the dialogical textual practices are in some sense applicable as interpersonal practices as well. For instance, differences in the respective views of both havruta learners should be articulated. One learner can then deepen the understanding of his havruta partner's view by having her reconstruct the question to which her perspective offers an answer. Each learner should allow their havruta partner to challenge with an alternative view or argument, and should have an opportunity to weigh the havruta partner's arguments without necessarily having to agree with them. Finally, each learner should also be able to offer his own ways of thinking and challenge his havruta partner's view.

These textual and interpersonal practices are not exhaustive, but in our view they are essential in promoting self-understanding, which also makes them in some sense intrapersonal practices as well. They emphasize dialogue as involving a fair amount of readiness to allow one's own views and values to be questioned, not simply each

---

8   Hans-Georg Gadamer, *Truth and Method,* 374.

participant having their say and being heard. In Gadamer's words, it implies the learner's readiness to put himself "at risk."[9] This emphasis contrasts with both the all-too-frequent competitive feel of havruta learning in traditional settings, and with the hands-off stance of those havruta learners who identify solely with their personal beliefs, closing themselves up to any "risk" by claiming at the outset that "different people have different views."

The dialogical view of havruta learning, in contrast, invites learners to expose themselves to the potential limitations of their own views, eventually providing them with new insights and helping them acknowledge some of their preconceptions. In many ways, this is the dialogical foundation of havruta text study: the presence of both a human and a textual partner in the learning exchange can contribute something to learning that may help the learner open up beyond the confines of his own limited views. This idea is well captured by Gadamer:

> The mere presence of the other before whom we stand helps us to break up our own bias and narrowness, even before he opens his mouth to make a reply. That which becomes a dialogical experience for us here is not limited to the sphere of arguments and counter-arguments the exchange and unification of which may be the end meaning of every confrontation. Rather... there is something else in this experience, namely, a potentiality for being other that lies beyond every coming to agreement about what is common.[10]

At this point, we offer a non-exhaustive list of some of the dialogical practices of havruta text study as follow:

---

[9]   Ibid., 388.

[10]   Diane P. Michelfelder and Richard E. Palmers, eds., *Dialogue and Deconstruction: The Gadamer-Derrida Encounter*, 26.

Dialogical Practices of Havruta Text Study

Textual practices * Reconstruct the text's question * Understand the reasoning of the text * Answer the question from a personal point of view * Compare personal and text's ways of addressing the question * Challenge the text's view and/or revise one's own view
Interpersonal practices * Give reasons for havruta partner's views * Offer one's own views to havruta partner * Compare havruta partner's and own views * Challenge havruta partner's view and/or revise one's own view[11]
Intrapersonal practices * Re-examine of learner's ideas and own preconceptions in light of dialogue with text and havruta partner * Remain open to and work actively towards self-understanding that is the result of the above practices

Cultivating Dialogical Practices

Special havruta lessons can also be designed to help students learn and experiment with dialogical practices (despite the dynamic and unpredictable aspects of dialogue and, as we have said previously, a less tangible outcome than is expected with interpretive practices yielding textual interpretations). In the rest of this chapter, we choose to discuss an example of a different pedagogic strategy, in the form of written assignments that are integrated into regular classes when students are already more experienced with the first phase of havruta text study. The written assignments are designed to slow down various parts of the dialogical phase with the goal of both facilitating and making its central components visible through enactment of dialogical practices. We illustrate their enactment with samples collected

---

11   In Chapter Six, challenging is discussed as an interpretive practice. Focusing on the meaning of the text, it helps foster textual interpretations. As a dialogical practice, challenging focuses on the havruta partner's personal views on the matter that is discussed. Thus in this phase, the student will not be expected to use textual evidence in challenging his havruta partner.

from learners, in a class in which they studied the text involving Rabbi Shimi and Rabbi Papa (see Chapter Four).

Overall, our aim in helping students experiment with these dialogical practices is to help them get used to articulating distinctions between what they understand the text to say and what they have to say, and between what their partner has to say and what they themselves have to say. In addition, in their dialogue with text and partner, we want them to develop constructive arguments, rather than to merely vanquish the (textual or havruta partner) opponent and/or limit themselves to a simplistic "I agree/disagree" response. Finally, we expect them to proactively uncover, examine and perhaps even revisit any view or pre-conception they may hold on the topic that is discussed.

The following are examples of tasks that are designed to have students experiment with textual and intrapersonal dialogical practices.[12] The first task involves reconstructing the text's question.[13] An example of this task follows:

Please go back to the textual interpretations you have generated, filling in the prompts

I/We believe this text to be about....

And the text says that.....

Together with your havruta partner, please try to articulate what might have been the question to which these two lines are an answer.

While this is not an easy task, we have seen many instances in which it has helped students revise their interpretations, pushing them to refine their ideas with more precise wording and understanding.

---

[12] In this chapter, we have chosen to discuss the design of learning tasks for the dialogical encounter between learners and text. Almost identical tasks are designed for the use of dialogical practices between havruta learners, especially when they express different views on the matter discussed. For example, the question "What alternative viewpoint is presented by the text?" can be reframed as "What alternative viewpoint is presented by your havruta partner?"

[13] See also the template in Appendix 2 for annotated discussion of dialogical practices.

The second task is identifying the text's reasoning and replying to it. Students are provided with the following instructions:

> Using your havruta partner as a sounding board, discuss each of your interpretations as a point of view worthy of consideration, even though you may not agree with it. Discuss possible reasons one might support this point of view. The following question may guide your work in giving the text reason:
>
> • What alternative viewpoint is presented by the text?
>
> Then, articulate your own view of the matter and compare:
>
> • How would *you* address the text's question?
>
> • In what ways might the text's perspective be better than yours?
>
> What might the strengths and weaknesses of this view be?
>
> Can you think of any reason why your ideas are similar/different, more compelling and/or worthy than those offered by the text?

This task has the students enact a number of the textual practices described above. Implied in these questions is a clear separation between the student's and text's points of view. It encourages the students to open themselves up to new perspectives without agreeing to accept them. The first question ("What alternative way of looking is presented by the text?") encourages students to cultivate a receptive approach toward a view they may not agree with, while the next three questions invite the articulation of their own views and a comparative analysis of the different views.

Following is the example of Karin, who already had four years of teaching experience in a public school before enrolling in the teacher education program in which this class took place.[14] We bring Karin's

---

[14]   Collected in the context of the Melamdim program, in 2011. Translated from Hebrew.

relatively long answer to illustrate her use of the different tasks and guiding questions in conducting her dialogue with the text (words derived from the guiding questions are italicized):

> *I understand the text to* address teachers, of which Rabbi Papa happens to be only an example. *The text expresses* a strong empathy with the student, Rabbi Shimi, who is eager to learn and asks many questions. *The text criticizes* the teacher as being so self-absorbed with his uncomfortable feelings, that he overreacts (by invoking God's help) and causes the student to stop asking questions and thus to learn as he used to.

> *The question I believe to be at the basis of this text* is, "What should teachers consider when the public image they desire to cultivate of themselves is threatened by their professional shortcomings?"

> *The text criticizes* teachers who because of their personal/narcissistic concerns, and perhaps their inadequacy, harm students' learning instead of looking for constructive initiatives that might help solve the problem.

> *As a teacher, I do not* necessarily empathize with this view *because* I know too well from my own experience how often students can cause annoying situations and elicits teachers' bad feelings. The reality in the classroom is such that there isn't always time to handle the issues, or to adopt solutions that seem to be available "right there," on the spot. This may create a great sense of distress by teachers, an emotional place from which it is not always so easy to depart.

> *And yet, I can see the perspective* offered by the text. After all, isn't the major task of a teacher to care about students' learning? *Perhaps the text challenges us* to ask ourselves, if we, teachers, are making enough distinctions in our emotional reactions? For example, is there something to be said for the distinction between students whose behaviors hinder their own and their classmates' learning, and those students who may cause us, and perhaps classmates, bad feelings, but only because they are

eager to learn? *I could see* how the text offers *a different perspective* than mine, a perspective that might counterbalance my own.

On second thought, I believe *my view is different* than the text's in that I am placing myself in the concrete, day-to-day role of the teacher. *The text, on the other hand,* adopts a value or philosophical perspective by emphasizing the higher purposes to which a teacher is committed.

The text's answer is something like: Make sure that the outcome of your intervention won't cause the student to be less engaged. I, on the other hand, would address the question by saying: As a teacher it is good to be reminded of my mission, and of the fact that I should not take personally everything that happens to me. And yet, I would like to refine the text's answer, which does not take enough into consideration situations in which teachers are emotionally overwhelmed and thus reach out for radical solutions.

It goes without saying that, given its open-ended dynamic, an oral dialogue could not have yielded this kind of well-structured reflection. Karin's written response presents a rich example, much above the average of what we have generally seen students produce. Her writing clearly demonstrates a distinction between her own ideas and what she understands the text's ideas to be. She weighs the text's perspective, but it brings her to articulate her own. She adopts central dialogical phrases that indicate her perception of the text as a dialogical partner ("The text criticizes"; "the text challenges us") and juxtaposes it with her own perspective ("I"; "my view"). She allows herself to adopt the text's perspective and explain its reason ("I can see the perspective offered by the text"; "a different perspective than mine"). Still, she goes back to her own perspective ("On second thought") offering a new distinction between both views.

Like the interpretive practices, the dialogical practices of havruta text study can only be acquired over time. The assigned tasks may feel artificial, in the sense that they unnaturally slow down what dialogue would seem to be about: a dynamic, unstructured exchange of ideas. And yet, the same rule that applies to the other parts of our project applies here as well: It is by a recurrent and slow learning process that students learn to identify the practices, experiment with them, and reflect on their experiences, over time integrating them more naturally into how they conduct dialogues, both with texts and with their havruta partner.

Finally, a last task focuses on the intrapersonal practice of self-understanding. It is designed to provide students with the opportunity to examine what they have learned through dialogue. Learning, in this context, encompasses any expanded understanding of oneself vis-à-vis the topic discussed. The student may end up realizing that he disagrees with the text's claim. His learning will then refer to his refined understanding of the reasons for this disagreement. Alternatively, the student may come to revisit and change her view as a consequence of the dialogue. Pinpointing what in the dialogue caused her to change her opinion would be the essence of her learning. In either case, being engaged in dialogue helps the student realize some of the implicit preconceptions (e. g., beliefs, values, understandings) by which she operates and which shape her thinking. She may then want to revise her preconceived ideas, reinforce her identification with them, or some combination of the two.

Here is an assignment given to promote self-understanding (which we have found to be successful towards that end):

> Please write about the following and be ready to share with your havruta partner:
>
> • One important thing you've learned about the topic through the dialogue you have had with the text.
>
> • Has anything in your own view on this topic been altered, reinforced, or enriched as a consequence of this exchange?
>
> • What new questions do you have about this topic as a result of this exchange?

Following are three students' written reflections, selected because they reflect the conceptual distinctions we made through the dialogical practices are expressed. Sarah, a 23-year-old student teacher, writes:

> This text invites me to see things from a different perspective, namely the teacher's. It helps me become aware of what might

be expectations, feelings, and considerations of a teacher in the classroom. For instance, Rabbi Papa may have come to his class with the intention of teaching a certain number of ideas. Certain types of questions (e. g. questions that require a significant amount of time to be addressed) might simply be considered by the teacher as not serving his goal and distractive. I do not necessarily agree with the way Rabbi Papa handled the situation, but the text invites me to empathize with teachers' predicament.

Sarah was able to adopt the basic features of dialoguing with text. She has learned to "see things from a different perspective," in this case by putting herself in the teacher's place. We also hear an echo of her attempt to "give the text reason,"[15] by looking at the story not only from a general textual perspective, but from the perspective of the text's main character, Rav Papa. Sarah reflects a clear awareness of the distinction between the perspective offered by the teacher, Rav Papa, which she says she can "empathize" with, and his behavior, with which she disagrees.

Overall (and similar to Karin), Sarah's reflection expresses the key elements that define this type of a dialogical relationship with the text.

- A clear distinction between the text's perspective and her own
- Empathy with the perspective of another point of view (mediated here through a literary character, Rav Papa) despite disagreeing with it
- The ability to "inhabit" different perspectives (e. g., student, teacher).

Similar insights are reflected in Josh's reflection, which indicates a heightened awareness as a result of the text study:

> Thanks to this dialogue with the text, I have come to better appreciate the fact that a teacher also comes to class with his own agenda and priorities. I believe after this text study, I am a little more sensitive to teachers' subjective feelings, emotions, and aims.

---

15   A term inspired by Gadamer which we've used in Chapter Two.

Josh also refers to a heightened awareness of his own beliefs, as another result of his conversation with the text:

> At the same time, this exchange has reinforced my strong belief in the need to create a learning culture in which students feel free to ask questions, either because they don't know something or because they see their role in moving the class forward through (difficult) questions.

Like Sarah, Josh also learned to differentiate between empathy and condoning a specific behavior:

> With all my empathy for Rabbi Papa's position, there are better ways for teachers of conveying emotions and concerns to students than the one he used.

Finally, through his conversation with the text, Josh became aware of a new aspect of teaching, which he articulates in practical terms:

> One new question I have relates to the strategies a teacher can use to communicate his choices during the lesson (e. g. not to address questions) while identifying additional settings where such questions can be addressed. This would prevent students from becoming disengaged as a result of refraining from posing questions.

Suzanne, a third member of the class, uses the exercise to share her appreciation of students different from herself.

> As a learner, I do not identify with Shimi, because I think I am unlikely to be the one asking many questions during class. However, I generally appreciate having someone like Shimi in the class, who has no qualms interrupting the teacher to ask questions, because I find a discussion-oriented class more rewarding than a lecture.

For Suzanne, the character of Shimi helped her locate herself in relation to other students in the classroom. While she sees Shimi as a very different kind of student than the one she believes herself to be, she is able to articulate his contributions to her and others' learning. It is exactly this ability to articulate what she gained from dialogue with the text that these exercises aim to develop.

The confrontation between participants' strongly-held opinions is a common attribute of traditional havruta text study, and in our own model we do not expect students to neutralize their personalities or opinions, vis à vis either their human partner or text partner. And yet, to the extent that their interactions with either partner remains a clash of personalities or an exchange of opinions only, dialogue will not be achieved. What we have hoped to emphasize through the examples discussed in this chapter is that one of the points of dialogue is to allow one's opinion to be matured by opening oneself to partners whose views differ from one's own. In that regard, the student who has grown into a havruta learner through dialogue has cultivated what Gadamer calls a "consciousness of effective history."[16] Not only is he aware of preconceptions he holds, but the word "effective" indicates the understanding of the continuing impact of these preconceptions on him, and an awareness of the contingency of his beliefs such that he has learned to hold them loosely, with openness to change, when he encounters alternative views.

One could argue that the kind of reflection we invite seems to reinforce the students' subjective distanciation from the text (e. g. "One important thing you've learned *about* the topic through the dialogue you have had with the text"). In fact, the structuring of dialogue through written tasks, as discussed in this chapter, reflects the inherent tension between the didactic and the dialogical dimensions of our approach to the teaching of havruta text study. Specific tasks are designed to teach students how to proceed so that dialogue might occur. Of course, a dialogically-oriented person might well find what to say and what to ask in the midst of the encounter itself.

Is our work best described as "teaching havruta text study," or rather as "helping students become mature havruta learners"? We frame most of our design of "havruta lessons," in which students learn specific havruta practices, in the spirit of the former, believing they will lead to the latter. Not surprisingly, it is in our attempt to help students learn the subtle aspects of dialogue with havruta partner and text that we feel an increased tension between the design of particu-

---

[16]   Hans-Georg Gadamer, *Truth and Method*, 27–8.

lar tasks and the cultivation of a fundamental dialogical attitude by the students. We believe that this tension is inherent to what we are trying to achieve and thus requires its own ongoing pedagogical attention over time, the use of written assignments representing only one strategy among others in the cultivation of this essential attitude and stance in havruta text study.[17]

---

[17]   For a discussion of ways that study guidelines can both support and constrain havruta learning, see Orit Kent, *Interactive Text Study and the Co-Construction of Meaning.*

Where a conversation is successful, something remains for us and something remains in us that has transformed us. (…) Only in conversation can friends find each other and develop that kind of community in which everyone remains the same for the other because they find the other in themselves and find themselves in the other.

Hans-Georg Gadamer, "The Incapacity for Conversation"

The creation of meaning out of an experience is at the very heart of what it is to be human. It is what enables us to make sense of and attribute value to the events of our lives.

Carol Rodgers, "Defining Reflection"

CHAPTER NINE:
THE EDUCATIONAL VALUE OF HAVRUTA TEXT STUDY

In the first chapter of this volume, we acknowledged that students and educators hold many different ideas as to the purposes and benefits of havruta text study. They may feel that havruta study contributes to a better understanding of the text, or that it is desirable to maintain the historical continuity of this traditional Jewish learning format. They may see it as a venue for nurturing a learning environment that celebrates multiple and personal interpretations. Having presented and discussed at length a particular model of havruta text study, the time has come for us to address this subject as well.

The two following questions will help us explore this issue: To what educational end shall we cultivate havruta text study in contemporary educational settings? And what is the value of cultivating the dispositions and skills associated with this mode of learning? We believe these questions to be particularly important for practitioners in the field for whom havruta text study is not a given, as it is in traditional yeshiva settings (albeit without many of the assumptions, practices, and goals reflected in our own approach). Given that it must compete for time and resources, any learning format should be examined in the context of broader educational aims.[1] Through a nearly

---

[1]   We have seen a number of people and institutions begin to engage in havruta text study only to stop once the novelty of a romanticized view of this tradition has passed. For a discussion of various pedagogical ratio-

decade-long cyclical process of teaching, researching, and designing havruta text study, we have come to articulate, refine, and reframe our own views on these questions (even as answering them remains a work in progress).

To begin with, it is necessary to state that the benefits of havruta text study may not be obvious to the contemporary teacher. While on one hand, havruta text study seems to line up with a modern orientation toward collaborative and constructivist theories of learning, the intensive work required by this type of text study goes against the grain of widespread cultural patterns of learning. For instance, as educators, we must consider that we operate in an age of visual learning, in which the eye becomes trained to "consume" what it sees rather than to contemplate it.[2] In this regard, it is worth noting Nietzsche's sharp contrast between what he identified as (then) modern cultural attitudes toward reading and his own understanding of what it means to read:

> I admit that you need one thing above all in order to practice the requisite art of reading, a thing which today people have been so good at forgetting... you almost need to be a cow for this one thing and certainly not a "modern man": it is rumination.[3]

Contemporary learning settings continue to value compact, well-presented information, unlike the inherently open-ended investigative

---

nales that sustain havruta text study in professional schools see Elie Holzer, "What Connects 'Good' Teaching, Text Study and Havruta Learning? A Conceptual Argument."

[2] See for example Michel Henry, *Barbarism* (New York: Continuum, 2012). This is increased by the new communication technologies which at times emphasize the access to information rather than what to do with it. Also, the inflation of words used in contemporary culture seriously questions the possibility of conducting this type of text and havruta based dialogue. See Marc J. LaFountain, "Play and Ethics in Culturus Interruptus: Gadamer's Hermeneutics in Postmodernity," in *The Specter of Relativism: Truth, Dialogue and Phronesis in Philosophical Hermeneutics*, ed. Lawrence K. Schmidt (Evanston, IL: Northwestern University Press, 1995), 206–23.

[3] Friedrich Nietzsche, *A Genealogy of Morality* (Cambridge: Cambridge University Press, 2006), 9.

approach required by havruta text study.[4] Process-oriented views like our approach to havruta text study stand in sharp contrast to the strong orientation of measurable outcomes and what Jean-Francois Lyotard calls "performativity," which is very important to a vast majority of educational policy makers.[5]

Havruta text study is also time-consuming for both teacher and students and thus competes for one of the most precious educational resources: time. Moreover, it requires sophisticated intellectual and interpersonal skills and forms of knowledge, the acquisition of which can only be developed over an extended course of study. This places it at odds with many of the rather pragmatic goals of contemporary education, which is typically geared to prepare students to succeed in a competitive society oriented toward individual and collective financial success.

In contrast, our model of havruta text study, rooted as it is in the dialogical principles of philosophical hermeneutics, recognizes the educational value of uncertainty, processes, and fallible judgments. It is characterized by the love and pursuit of wisdom (in the Greek and the Jewish senses) and not only by the possession of knowledge. Above all, its educational success is marked by the cultivation of beneficial habits and dispositions of mind and heart. The idea of havruta

---

4   Similar reflections on the value of certain forms of literature and of history studies of texts have been expressed by various intellectuals. See, for example, Iser (1997), on literature: "The question arises as to why we may need this particular medium, especially in view of the fact that literature as a medium is put on a par with other media, and the ever-increasing role that these play in our civilization shows the degree to which literature has lost its significance as the epitome of culture. The more comprehensively a medium fulfills its sociocultural function, the more it is taken for granted, as literature once used to be. It did indeed fulfill several such functions, ranging from entertainment through information and documentation to pastime, but these have now been distributed among many independent institutions that not only compete fiercely with literature but also deprive it of its formerly all-encompassing function. Does literature still have anything to offer that the competing media are unable to provide?" See also David Tracy, who discusses the challenge of historical consciousness for text-based traditions in *Plurality and Ambiguity: Hermeneutics, Religion, Hope* (Chicago: University of Chicago Press, 1987).

5   For the philosophical underpinnings of the pragmatists and technical view of knowledge see Jean-François Lyotard, *The Postmodern Condition* (Minneapolis: University of Minnesota Press, 1979).

text study constitutes, then, an educational, epistemological, and even economic challenge to prevailing cultural norms and approaches, creating further need to reflect on its potential educational purposes, benefits, and value.

In this concluding chapter, we refer back to the hermeneutical foundations of this work to discuss the potential of havruta text study to transform learning, providing a most important rationale for its cultivation in contemporary education. We then discuss the potential formative effects of the practices that derive from havruta learning—that is, helping havruta learners cultivate fundamental human qualities such as intellectual openness, ethical sensitivity, critical thinking, self-awareness, and responsibility for one another's learning. We then return to the laboratory where this work began, in a program of professional development for teachers, in order to discuss how these formative effects may specifically contribute to teachers' professional dispositions and skills.

Havruta Text Study and Transformation

Modes of Engagement

We see in havruta text study a significant potential for transformative learning, and it is particularly because of this that we promote it as teachers and researchers. To explain what we mean by transformation, we must first acknowledge a major contrast between the way text study has been conceptualized in traditional forms and settings, and the way we conceptualize it on the basis of the theoretical orientation that permeates this volume.

From a historical perspective, text study served not only as a method of acquiring knowledge about the Jewish tradition, but also as a devotional activity believed to have a transformative impact on its practitioners' values and beliefs. People studied traditional texts not only in order "to know," but also to be guided and inspired. Beliefs in the metaphysical or inspired origins of these texts also likely played a role in individuals' receptiveness to undergoing some type of transformation through their studies.[6]

---

[6]   The transformative effects of text study pertain to actions, beliefs, character development etc. For examples in the Jewish tradition, see for example

Today, however, as members of secular societies, people typically do not imbue traditional texts with metaphysical origins. Nevertheless, the concept of transformation continues to be associated with text study, not due primarily to the inspired origins of the text but because of the transformative potential of readers' engagement with texts. This shift is, in part, a result of the "hermeneutic turn" — the growing awareness of the impact of processes of interpretation in literature and philosophy, emphasizing and inviting a refined attention to the *ways* people engage in meaning making in general and with texts in particular.[7] Thus, for Gadamer, the fundamental purpose of philosophical hermeneutics is learning *how* to relate to things.[8] Nicholas Davey's characterization of this shift aligns with our own educational focus regarding havruta text study:

> As encounters with texts (and others) are lived, learning from experience derives not just from that which is encountered but from the character of the encounter itself.[9]

The Zohar, Part II, 99 a and b; Moshe Idel, *Language, Torah and Hermeneutics in Abraham Abulafia* (Albany: State University of New York Press, 1989); Benjamin Gross, *L'âme de la vie: Hayyim de Volozhyn* (Paris: Verdier, 1986). See also different meanings attributed to Torah Lishma study: Norman Lamm, *Torah lishmah: In the Works of Rabbi Hayyim of Volozhin and His Contemporaries* (New York: Yeshiva University Press, 1989). Compare also to the concept of Lectio Divina in Christian traditions.

[7] This is of course only one important change that has occurred. Broadly speaking, different literary and hermeneutical theories emphasize different foci, such as the text, the author's intention, the reader, or the reading process. See Anthony C. Thiselton, *New Horizons in Hermeneutics: The Theory and Practice of Transforming Biblical Reading*; Mario J. Valdes, *Phenomenological Hermeneutics and the Study of Literature* (Toronto: University of Toronto Press, 1987). See also Wolfgang Iser, *The Act of Reading*; Hans Robert Jauss, *Aesthetic Experience and Literary Hermeneutics* (Minneapolis: University of Minnesota, 1982); Hans Robert Jauss, *Toward an Aesthetic of Reception* (Minneapolis: University of Minnesota, 1982).

[8] Duska Dobrosavljev, "Gadamer's Hermeneutics as Practical Philosophy," *Facta Universitatis: Series Philosophy, Sociology and Psychology* 2.9 (2002): 606.

[9] Nicholas Davey, *Unquiet Understanding: Gadamer's Philosophical Hermeneutics* (Albany, NY: State University of New York Press, 2006), 6.

The attention to modes of engagement in literary theory and philosophical hermeneutics is especially appealing for those practitioners for whom, following John Dewey, the radical dichotomy of educational means and ends becomes blurred.[10] Modes of engagement are evaluated in their own right on the basis of their educational impact and as a locus of learning. The three parts of the havruta learning triangle emphasize the modes and quality of the encounters between learner, text and havruta partner, and are embedded in the practical pedagogical elements of havruta text study. It is here that we find several important areas of potential transformation.[11]

Transformative Perceptions

The potential for transformation is built into the havruta encounter by virtue of the fact that both the havruta partner and the textual partner may present the learner with different views, values, or beliefs. From an educational point of view, this transformation constitutes an "epistemic shift," in the sense that we are concerned not only with a student's mastery of a given text but with how the student understands herself in light of her engagement with the text and her havruta partner's ideas. In the words of Sandra Schneiders—who has published several works on spirituality and theology—the effect of such an engagement can be

> analogous to the effect on the audience of participation in a play. Watching the play participatively is an act of interpretation that terminates in the transformation of the viewer through the aesthetic experience itself. The transformation can be made explicit afterward and can even result in some decisions and actions to be carried out later, but it is itself not something added on to

---

10   For a philosophical discussion of this distinction and the type of knowledge it assumes, see Joseph Dunne, *Back to the Rough Ground: Practical Judgment and the Lure of Technique* (Notre Dame: University of Notre Dame Press, 2001).

11   This idea is inspired by the work of Nicholas Davey, *Unquiet Understanding: Gadamer's Philosophical Hermeneutics*. His analysis of philosophical hermeneutics has helped us refine and articulate some of the more fundamental aspects of havruta text study.

the interpretation but the terminating moment of the interpretation itself.[12]

It is this dialogical aspect that carries significant potential for perceptual transformation, as we have discussed in relation to the second phase of havruta text study.[13] Indeed, we believe that the most important learning that takes place during havruta text study occurs in the differential space that emerges when a person engages with a text and/or a havruta partner. It is in this space that the learner is exposed to alternative perspectives, which must be considered without necessarily becoming his own. It is in this space that the difference(s) between perspectives are disclosed and sharpened, and that the learner's perspective is enriched and/or altered, thus undergoing transformation.[14]

In other words, implicit in the dynamics of havruta text study is an opportunity for learners to emerge thinking differently. As we discussed in Chapter Eight, the concept of self-understanding captures this idea. It is marked by the learner's recognition of the difference between what he thought or believed before the havruta text study encounter and what he thinks or believes afterwards.

This view of learning contrasts with perceptions of havruta text study in which both partners are considered to have accomplished their task merely by acknowledging the differences between their own, their partner's, and/or the text's views. This is often reflected in expressions like "I like/do not like the idea of this text"; "I notice that the text/you and I have different views on the matter and that's ok"; "different people have different interpretations"; or "well, let's agree that we have different takes on this." Without any further engagement, these expressions are not more than acknowledgment of facts, which

---

[12]   Sandra Schneiders, *The Revelatory Text: Interpreting the New Testament as Sacred Scripture* (San Francisco: Harper Collins, 1991), 196.

[13]   See Chapter Eight. In another powerful expression, Ricoeur says that interpretation implies "a moment of dispossession of the egoistic and narcissistic ego." Paul Ricoeur, *Interpretation Theory: Discourse and the Surplus of Meaning*, 94.

[14]   For a related learning and literary theory which sheds light on the transformative aspects of havruta discussion, see Orit Kent, *Interactive Text Study and the Co-Construction of Meaning.*

allow the participants to hide, avoiding having to open themselves to other perspectives. They foreclose further thinking and discussion, especially in cases of disagreements. They prevent a learning opportunity that may lead to self-understanding.

In contrast, to ground havruta learning in philosophical hermeneutics actualizes the view that understanding is not an individual achievement. Rather, learning occurs through recognition of disagreement, or at least of challenges in one's understanding. It is only in this kind of learning dynamic that what Nicholas Davey calls "disruptive experiences" can occur, offering each partner the opportunity to change and be changed.[15]

The accomplished havruta learner comes to appreciate that the value of a perspective becomes apparent only when it is challenged and brought into community with others. He has learned to avoid the self-comforting satisfaction that results from a reluctance to have his beliefs, interpretations and ideas challenged. Instead, he learns the power of questioning and being questioned by others for learning.

We might say that havruta text study aims to broaden the subjective perception of the learner, leading him to acknowledge his dependence on others, be it a text or a partner, and perhaps, following Gadamer, something about his human limitations. We are talking here about an existential recognition highlighting that understanding is usually and ideally a mutual or collective achievement.[16]

This approach reflects a central aspect of our view of Jewish learning that is built on fundamental conversations: a diachronic conversation through a dialogical engagement with traditional texts (canonical texts and their subsequent interpretations), and a synchronic conversation through a dialogical engagement with contemporary fellow men and women. Through these conversations, havruta text study promotes learning that engages two aspects of our cultural condition:

---

15   Nicholas Davey, *Unquiet Understanding: Gadamer's Philosophical Hermeneutics*, 7. This term echoes John Dewey's "felt difficulty," without which no learning can occur.

16   In the words of James Risser: "Understanding comes not from the subject who thinks, but from the other who addresses me (…) It is this voice that awakens one to vigilance, to being questioned in the conversation we are" (*Hermeneutics and the Voice of the Other: Re-reading Gadamer's Philosophical Hermeneutics* [New York: State University of New York Press, 1997], 208).

It places historical distance from previous generations at the center of learning, growing, and self-understanding, while simultaneously recognizing one's own understanding (always mediated by one's historical present) as an existential characteristic of learning.

In that regard, the discourse that prevails at times in circles of Jewish education, emphasizing the dichotomy between the learner's autonomy and the text's authority, advances what we consider to be a false dichotomy that can prevent the kind of hermeneutical engagement that ideally lies at the heart of deep learning. It is, in our view, a mistaken approach that does not encourage the student to learn through an open and potentially transforming engagement with texts and others.

Against this dichotomy between personal autonomy and textual authority, postmodern identity theory tends to resist any impulse that would erase difference or otherness. The self is thought of not as an autonomous entity, but as radically interpersonal, continuously confronted with the presence of the Other.[17] As in any encounter, denial or dismissal of the Other is always an option, as is a kind of "polite acknowledgment" in which havruta and text partners are recognized but not engaged with—a kind of relativism of indifference. In that regard, relativist approaches in which all views are equal and none are held with passion or preference end up in non-engagement. In contrast, the dialogical concept that lies at the center of our work entails fruitful and meaningful engagement with these two "Others"—that is, the havruta partner and the textual partner—resisting either an oversimplified reduction of their alterity to oneself or a comfortable surrender to that alterity.[18]

---

[17]   Michael Theunissen, *The Other: Studies in the Social Ontology of Husserl, Heidegger, Sartre and Buber* (Cambridge, MA: MIT Press, 1984), 1. "Other" is capitalized to signal the radical alterity that resides in the encountered person or text.

[18]   It should be noticed that by emphasizing the role of pre-knowledge and the impact of historical and cultural perspectives in people's encounters with texts, we suggest an alternative to two traditions of learning texts in Jewish education: one that is at times characterized by a naïve overconfidence in method, as for example certain historical approaches, which confine meaning to historical explanation, and one that is characterized by a non-reflective, ahistorical reading of biblical and talmudic texts and their later interpretations. We believe that both approaches fail to recog-

Rather than a false dichotomy that forces us to choose to be either a blind follower of the text or its critic, havruta text study calls for an enlarged concept of learning, one that includes taking responsibility to first make the text speak, and responsibility for one's own learning as well as for that of one's havruta partner. In that regard, havruta text study offers a model for the education of the self that is the outcome of relationships with others. For teachers, this means going beyond the educational mission of "helping students find meaning in the text."

This view of learning and self encourages the cultivation of a person who feels indebted to the engagement with others (texts as well as people), rather than perceiving himself as a purely autonomous individual seeking to consume whatever is offered that he might find "relevant" or interesting. It undermines the pretensions of the self-founding and self-knowing *cogito*, positing a model of human identity not as autonomous subject, but one that can discover meaning and begin to understand himself only through engagement with the linguistic mediations of others (cultural symbols, texts and persons).

Havruta Text Study and Formative Practices

Practices have so far been amply discussed as instruments for establishing textual interpretations and conducting dialogues with text and havruta partner. Yet, in a more subtle way, the practices are also what fuel the actual relationships between havruta learners and text, as suggested by the arrows of the havruta learning triangle. Here, we underline another aspect of the practices, namely their *formative*

---

nize the social and historical factors that shape our understanding. For a thorough discussion of various interpretive orientations in the study of Bible, see Barry W. Holtz, *Textual Knowledge* (New York: JTS Press, 2003). For a similar systematic discussion of orientations to Talmud study, see Jon A. Levisohn, "A Menu of Orientations Towards the Teaching of Rabbinic Literature," *Journal of Jewish Education* 76.1 (2010): 4–51. Also relevant in that regard is Ricoeur's notion that there has been a false dichotomy opposing tradition as prior understanding vs. criticism as an "eschatology of freedom": see Paul Ricoeur, "Hermeneutics and the Critique of Ideology," in *The Hermeneutic Tradition from Ast to Ricoeur*, ed. Gayle L. Ormiston and Alan D. Schrift (New York: State University of New York Press, 1990), 332.

aspects—that is, their potential to help cultivate different perceptions, sensibilities, and ethical dispositions in the learner. While the
transformative aspects of havruta text study are merely nurtured by
the dynamics created by the engagement with different views presented by both havruta and text partners, the actual ongoing and
self-conscious performance of the practices can more directly cultivate
qualities like sensitivity, listening, wholeheartedness, open-mindedness, vulnerability, responsibility, and ethical commitment, and in this
way provide us with an additional educational end worthy of being
promoted by havruta text study.[19]

Drawing on Zagzebski, we view disposition as the expression of
both the heart and the mind.[20] Disposition characterizes one's behavior in encounters with both textual and human others. Disposition
(defined as the marriage between skills and attitudes) can be nurtured and become a stable trait of character through habituation in
ongoing practices of moral behavior.[21] In the context of our work on
havruta text study, we characterize an ethical disposition as consisting
of habits that can be cultivated in and through both interpretive and
dialogical practices.

[19]   Building on the work of Martin Buber, Ronald Arnett also indicates the
         connection between dialogic learning and character building through con-
         versation. That is, the characteristics of the conversation as well as who
         the partners become are essential to what is learned. See Ronald C. Arnett,
         Communication and Community: Implications of Martin Buber's Dialogue
         (Carbondale, IL: Southern Illinois University Press, 1986).

[20]   Linda T. Zagzebski, *Virtues of the Mind: An Inquiry into the Nature of Virtue
         and the Ethical Foundations of Knowledge* (Cambridge: Cambridge University
         Press, 1996).

[21]   "Virtue for Aristotle is not a state of mind but a disposition—which means
         being permanently geared for acting in a certain way even when you are
         not acting at all. (…) It is that our actions create the appropriate states of
         mind" (Terry Eagleton, *After Theory* [New York: Basic Books, 2003], 135).
         Emilio Betti believes that philosophical hermeneutics fosters open-minded-
         ness and receptiveness. It nurtures tolerance, mutual respect, and reciprocal
         listening. See Emilio Betti, quoted in Anthony C. Thiselton, *Hermeneutics*
         (Grand Rapids, MI: William B. Eerdmans Publishing Company, 2009), 6–7.

Sensitivity to the Other

The encounter with a text and havruta partner requires that the learner fully immerses herself in it. As a first step in the interpretive process, the learner must acknowledge that the text presents something in its own voice, demanding sensitivity to its otherness. Gadamer character-izes this immersion through an evocative series of terms, all of which reflect personality traits. These terms underline the fundamental rela-tional aspects of havruta text study and how these cannot be entirely separated from the full personality of the learner:

> A person trying to understand something will not resign himself from the start to relying on his own accidental fore-meanings, *ignoring* as consistently and *stubbornly* as possible the actual meaning of the text until the latter becomes so persistently audi-ble that it breaks through what the interpreter imagines it to be. Rather, a person trying to understand a text is rather *prepared for it to tell him* something. That is why a hermeneutically trained consciousness must be *sensitive to the other* of the text from the beginning."[22]

This sensitivity is explicitly emphasized in the first phase of havruta text study, when we use language like "the text as a partner," "making the text speak," or "lending your voice to the voiceless text." It is further encouraged by having havruta learners engage in prac-tices like questioning the text or learning to listen to the text and their havruta partner. Sensitivity to otherness is, of course, also central to the dialogical phase of havruta text study, during which learners learn to examine and give reasons for views provided by either the text or the havruta partner—views which may be radically different from their own.

---

[22]   Hans-Georg Gadamer, *Truth and Method*, 269.

Listening

The type of conscious close reading of the text and the engagement in multiple readings with a havruta partner that we promote makes the processes of listening increasingly visible, and can thus help havruta learners reduce their tendencies to subconsciously project meanings onto the text. Moreover, over time havruta learners develop a sense of the weakness of certain interpretations, of the hastiness that sometimes goes into the process of making meaning of a text. This is another way in which students refine their listening skills, learning to appreciate the nuances of quality among different interpretations.

Over the years, we have heard from students that through havruta text study, they have learned the importance of listening to a text on its own terms, before rushing in with premature assumptions or forcing it to conform to their own expectations. They become more aware of the facility with which a reader can opt for convenient or self- affirming interpretations, and of how this is often true in human conversations as well. Thus, they find themselves adopting practices like paraphrasing and asking open questions in casual and professional conversations. They note that they have come to appreciate that listening to understand is more than just hearing.[23]

Wholeheartedness

Havruta learners who are wholehearted fully dedicate themselves to make their textual partner speak before delving into criticizing her ideas. They are cognizant of the text's vulnerability as it can easily be misinterpreted, or worse, manipulated by the reader's interest. A wholehearted learner makes a deliberate effort to orient her energy toward what is specifically expressed by her havruta partner, and she takes it seriously before attempting to diagnose or criticize it. The practices that we have discussed call for this kind of dedication to the text and to one's partner—for example, our recurring focus on

---

[23]   See Miriam Raider-Roth and Elie Holzer, "Learning to be Present: How Hevruta Learning Can Activate Teachers' Relationships to Self, Other and Text"; Orit Kent, *Interactive Text Study and the Co-Construction of Meaning*.

interpretive practices for revisiting, revising, and improving textual interpretations, and on making sure that, through dialogical practices, the havruta partner's personal view is fully understood before it is challenged.

Open-mindedness

Open-mindedness refers to a genuine desire to give one's full attention to a variety of views and alternative possibilities. Openness and good will, requirements of a genuine conversation, are demonstrated when "one seeks instead to strengthen the other's viewpoint so that what the other has to say becomes illuminating."[24] This willingness to grant authority to another view is a precondition for dialogue. It expresses the shared concern for understanding, and a recognition that others can teach us about a subject matter so that it is only through our dialogical engagement with them that we can reach our own self-understanding. It also expresses a fundamental moral attitude: As Jane Roland Martin puts it: "The ability to take the point of view of another is a basic element of morality itself."[25]

In cultivating open-mindedness, the havruta learner recognizes the possibility of error or limited perspective even in beliefs that are important to him. The engagement with the text and the havruta partner might generate a variety of new and possibly alternative views about the topic at hand, as participants become aware of each other's (and the text's) horizon. Because it requires an attempt to view a given subject from the other's perspective, havruta text study rests on a mutual commitment to engage with the other's claims, regardless of whether one ultimately rejects or accepts them.[26]

---

[24]   Diane P. Michelfelder and Richard E. Palmers, eds., Dialogue and Deconstruction: The Gadamer-Derrida Encounter, 55.

[25]   Quoted in Sarah Lawrence-Lightfoot, *Respect: An Exploration* (Reading, MA: Perseus Books, 1999), 236.

[26]   According to Gadamer, to encounter a text is ideally to encounter an other who breaks into one's ego-centeredness and gives him something to understand. See Hans-Georg Gadamer, *Reflections on My Philosophical Journey: The Philosophy of Hans-Georg Gadamer* (Chicago: Open Court, 1997), 46.

Open-mindedness is involved in both phases of havruta text study. In the first phase, havruta learners engage in supporting their havruta partner's interpretations, for example, by providing additional textual evidence, even when they are not convinced by that interpretation. In the second phase, this disposition is addressed when havruta learners give the text and/or the havruta partner reasons for their view.[27]

Vulnerability

While acknowledging the preconceptions that one invariably brings to the text, Gadamer submits that for the true learner, such preconceptions are vulnerable to the learning encounter—"an opinion and a possibility that one brings into play and puts at risk."[28] Texts,

---

27   Openness in conversation means recognizing "in advance the possible correctness, even the superiority of one's conversation partner": quoted in Robert Bernasconi, "'You Don't Know What I'm Talking About': Alterity and the Hermeneutic Ideal," in *The Specter of Relativism: Truth, Dialogue, and Phronesis in Philosophical Hermeneutics*, ed. Lawrence K. Schmidt (Evanston, IL: Northwestern University Press, 1995), 187. Further: "That is the essence, the soul of my hermeneutics; to understand someone else is to see the justice, the truth, of their position. And this is what transforms us. And if we then have to become part of a new world civilization, if this is our task, then we shall need a philosophy which is similar to my hermeneutics, a philosophy which teaches us to see the justification for the other's point of view and which thus makes us doubt our own" (Dieter Misgeld and Graeme Nicholson, eds., *Hans-Georg Gadamer on Education, Poetry and History* [Albany: State University of New York Press, 1992], 192).

28   Hans-Georg Gadamer, *Truth and Method*, 388. Thus, conversation in which one does not put oneself at risk is not a genuine conversation (ibid., 303). On the power of text interpretation to provoke self-understanding, Wolfgang Iser has written: "If a literary text does something to its readers, it also simultaneously reveals something about them. Thus literature turns into a divining rod, locating our dispositions, desires, inclinations, and eventually our overall makeup. The question arises as to why we need this particular medium. Questions of this kind point to a literary anthropology that is both an underpinning and an offshoot of reader-response criticism" (*Introduction to Prospecting: From Reader Response to Literary Anthropology* [Baltimore: John Hopkins University Press, 1989], VII). For a hermeneuti-

especially those with evocative characteristics, as well as a dialogue partner, have the potential to challenge the learner's preconceptions and to invite him to expand himself: "It is impossible to make ourselves aware of a prejudice while it is constantly operating unnoticed, but only when it is, so to speak, provoked. The encounter with a traditional text can provide this provocation."[29]

In the havruta text study encounter, the learner willingly allows herself to be challenged or provoked by the subject matter as well as by her havruta partner. This experience brings her previous understanding to the foreground and provides her with an opportunity to uncover some of the unarticulated mental habits by which she had initially come to understand the issue at hand. The student learns that she can become more aware of her projections and thus engage in revising them.

This disposition is actively focused on in the last phase of havruta text study, particularly when students actively and purposefully engage in reflection and address the question, "Has anything in your own view on this topic been altered, reinforced, or enriched as a consequence of this dialogue?"

Responsibility and Ethical Commitment

Successful havruta text study is characterized by the ability to take a high level of responsibility for oneself (one's beliefs and ideas; one's learning) as well as for the other (his beliefs and ideas; her learning). Good havruta text study does not preclude heated exchanges, especially when there is a sense of mutual caring and commitment in place; the learner must both stand up for himself and care about the other. The latter is especially emphasized by the central place we give to the ethical-relational dimension of havruta learning. It is attended to in the special learning activities we design as well as in our framing

---

cal and educational conceptualization of the concept of "putting at risk" in the context of the study of Jewish texts, see Elie Holzer, "Choosing to Put Ourselves 'at Risk' in the Face of Ancient Texts: Ethical Education through the Hermeneutical Encounter."

[29]   Hans-Georg Gadamer, *Truth and Method*, 299.

of practices like supporting and challenging as interpretive practices, when the learner helps the havruta partner refine his interpretations, and as dialogical practices as she helps the partner ground or refine his personal views on the topic of discussion.

By emphasizing the formative effects of practices, we locate moral education in the practice of havruta learning itself, beyond the confines of the topics and themes that are being studied, thus offering an alternative to dichotomous educational views, which differentiate between means and ends. Following neo-Aristotelian traditions of ethics and learning, it is the learner as a person and the relationship between how he learns and the type of human being he strives to be, that lies at the center of the educational value we attribute to havruta text study.[30] Indeed, to grow into a havruta text study learner is to cultivate a complex set of abilities, awareness and refined consciousness.[31] It is from this perspective that we characterize havruta text study as having the potential to be a fundamentally human and humanizing activity.[32]

This approach to havruta text study represents a marriage between our view of Jewish learning and a certain type of liberal humanist education.[33] Both are grounded in the belief that a learner should be flexible and open-minded, prepared to have his beliefs questioned, and ready to be transformed through dialogues with oth-

---

[30]   Joseph Dunne, *Back to the Rough Ground: Practical Judgment and the Lure of Technique.*

[31]   See David Carr, "Rival Conceptions of Practice in Education and Teaching," *Journal of Philosophy of Education* 37.2 (2003): 253–66. This view of education is grounded in Jewish and neo-Aristotelian views of ethics and of learning, in which it is assumed that one's interiority and actions are intertwined and impact one another. Particularly interesting in that regard is Aristotle's concept of the virtuous person as someone who consciously and knowingly chooses the virtuous action, and has the disposition to accomplish that action. This concept echoes the accomplished self-aware, responsible, and skillful havruta learner we are aiming to help cultivate.

[32]   For an example of how havruta text study gets to be conceptualized as a humanizing activity, see Elie Holzer, "'Either a Havruta Partner of Death': A Critical View on the Interpersonal Dimensions of Havruta Learning." For a similar view of learning as a humanizing activity, see George Steiner, *Real Presences* (Chicago: University of Chicago Press, 1991).

[33]   We identify Gadamer and Ricoeur's work as a type of liberal humanism.

ers and texts. Both assume that openness to an encounter with the unfamiliar and the unexpected is crucial for learning and existential self-knowledge. Both assume a complex relationship of the learner with his beliefs, as he strongly identifies himself with them and yet is ready to put them at risk in dialogue.[34] Both operate on the view that existential meaning-making occurs through dialogical encounters with texts and people, past and present. Finally, both challenge radical separations between means and ends, between pedagogy and goals, between learning as an intellectual and an existential activity, and between the instrumental and the ethical-formative dimensions of learning.

To summarize, our model of havruta text study requires a deep emotional, intellectual, and self-conscious involvement on the part of the learner. Beyond pragmatic goals like mastery of the text, the acquisition of learning skills or building community, we believe that the major educational values of havruta text study lie in its potential for transformative learning, and in the possibility that the dispositions which its practices help cultivate will impact the learner's ways of perceiving and interacting in life, not only within the confines of the classroom.

Havruta Text Study in Teachers' Professional Development

We now return to the original purpose and context of our research. The major impetus for the development of our work has been our teaching in programs designed for teachers' professional development, chief among them the DeLeT program at Brandeis University. At the outset, we introduced havruta text study into the professional development of teachers in Jewish education for the following reasons:

    a. It embodies a traditional value of Jewish learning, represented by the term *torah lishma*, studying for the sake of learning itself.

---

34   In fact, it is only when strongly held beliefs are put into this type of "risky" dialogue that true transformative learning can occur. Indeed, lightly held convictions being challenged by the text and/or havruta partner would not be really significant for the learner.

b. It offers a learning format that helps democratize the study and interpretation of Jewish texts, and has the potential to provide students with an increased sense of agency and self-confidence. We find these qualities particularly important for teachers, whose vocation consists, among other things, in conveying a historical, cultural, and/or religious tradition to the next generation.

c. As teacher educators, we believe that teachers should have first-hand experience with the complexity of meaningful text study and havruta learning if they want to be able to help students or other teachers engage in similar activities.

d. Havruta text study reflects the type of dialogical, investigative, self-reflective, and responsible learning that we are interested in promoting in these professional programs.

Over the course of our research at the Mandel Center for Studies in Jewish Education, we have come to realize the formative aspects of this particular model of havruta text study, and more specifically how certain features of havruta text study are especially relevant to the teaching stance cultivated by these teacher education programs. Thus, havruta text study became a "site" for cultivating dispositions for teaching, in both emerging teachers studying in DeLeT and veteran teachers participating in programs like the Mandel Teacher Educators Institute. Our experience has reinforced our belief that the type of study and engagement cultivated in havruta text study can provide teachers with an experiential microcosm, in which they can learn something about how people interact through learning. Such an understanding is central to the work of teaching.[35]

Let us compare some characteristics of havruta text study with their counterparts in dispositions for good teaching:

- Listening to what the text/ havruta partner/ students have to say.

---

[35] For examples of how teachers draw on what they learn through havruta text study experience in their teaching stance and practice, see Miriam Raider-Roth and Elie Holzer, "Learning to be Present: How Hevruta Learning Can Activate Teachers' Relationships to Self, Other and Text"; Orit Kent and Allison Cook, "Havruta Inspired Pedagogy: Fostering an Ecology of Learning for Closely Studying Texts with Others."

- Awareness of preconceptions toward text/havruta partner/students and readiness to revise them.
- Openmindedness towards another perspective provided by text/havruta partner/students.
- Being aware of—and ready to revisit—one's preconceptions as a havruta learner/as a teacher.
- Tolerance and patience for ambiguity in havruta learning/in the teaching-learning relationship.
- Accountability toward text/havruta partner/students.

Listening

Genuine listening to students' ideas and to their "world" is an essential characteristic of the kind of teaching promoted in the DeLeT program.[36] Listening to students means, first and foremost, listening to what they say in relation to the subject matter at hand. Together with an awareness of one's preconceptions, a teacher ought to strive to develop the capacity to reduce her tendency to subconsciously project meanings onto what the student is saying, for example, by using techniques like paraphrasing with the goal of checking her understanding with the student.

Wholeheartedness

Wholeheartedness entails receiving what is expressed by someone else and taking responsibility for attending to it—taking it seriously—before attempting to diagnose or criticize it.[37] Teachers who are wholehearted give their full attention to the matter at hand and the

---

[36]   Sharon Feiman-Nemser, "Beit Midrash for Teachers: An Experiment in Teacher Preparation."

[37]   Neil Noddings, "Caring and Competence," in *The Education of Teachers*, ed. Edward Griffen (Chicago: National Society of Education, 1999), 205–20; Neil Noddings, *Caring: A Feminine Approach to Ethics and Moral Education* (Berkeley: University of California Press, 2003).

ways by which students encounter and make sense of what is studied. Giving full attention and taking what students say seriously is as central to good teaching as it is to havruta text study, where one is taking responsibility for her partner's learning.

Open-mindedness

A genuine desire to listen and give full attention to a variety of views and new possibilities is a central element of teaching when it is conceptualized as including students' construction of meaning, which often generates a variety of new or alternative views. Open-mindedness assumes that these views ought to first be considered on their own merits, before being deemed "right" or "wrong." Open-mindedness also includes the possibility that one may come to recognize the error of his beliefs, even those he holds most dear. For example, teachers who are open-minded take pains to examine the rationales behind subjects often taken for granted.[38]

Awareness of Ones' Own Preconceptions

We understand teaching as a practice that entails elements of uncertainty from which one is called to learn. Teachers therefore need to learn to be open to articulate and revise some of their unexamined preconceptions about the subject matter at hand, about students, and about teaching in general.[39] Becoming aware of one's preconceptions, being willing to go from a stance of knowing and certainty to not-knowing and uncertainty, and the readiness to revise one's preconceptions, are all key qualities of good teaching.

---

[38]   See, for example, Kenneth M. Zeichner and Daniel P. Liston, *Reflective Teaching: An Introduction.*

[39]   Deborah L. Ball and David K. Cohen, "Developing Practice, Developing Practitioners, Toward a Practice-Based Theory of Professional Education."

Tolerance and Patience for Ambiguity

Teaching that takes seriously the construction of ideas by students is often characterized by moments of ambiguity. Because of the somewhat more open orientation of this type of teaching, ideas are not constructed and presented in a linear way. Often, ideas evolve in a back and forth or circular movement between teacher, learners, and subject matter. Full articulation of ideas is often an outcome of such a process and takes time to be achieved. Thus, this view of teaching requires that both teachers and learners learn to tolerate and cope with moments of ambiguity. This requires a fair amount of patience, as understanding is not immediately achieved but an outcome of a constructive process. Clearly, tolerance for ambiguity and the need to postpone immediate "understanding" characterize the type of hermeneutical conversation we have discussed for havruta text study as well.

Accountability

In the framework of havruta learning, meaning is not simply provided by a text but requires the work of interpretation. During this process, the learner is required to attend to various types of textual evidence in order to build and sustain his or her interpretation. Our view of teaching requires a similar disposition on the part of the teacher to seek concrete evidence of learning by students.

Broadly speaking, meaning making is not only central to text interpretation but to teaching as well. In other words, teachers are not only engaged in their own conversation with text and partner, they are also engaged in interpreting what students say and do. Teachers make decisions based on these interpretations. For example, they are trying to help students make meaning when they engage with the subject matter from the perspective of their own horizons. Studying, engaging with, and assessing the various interpretations that are created in their own havruta learning experiences can provide teachers with an intensive and open-ended process in which they learn something about how people (as exemplified by themselves and their havruta partners) interpret, make meaning, and find relevance over time.

Havruta Text Study as an Educational Philosophy

On the basis of the educational values discussed in this chapter, havruta text study has the potential to develop a discipline of ethical attunement and educative self-cultivation[40] as well as being a helpful pedagogical tool for the professional development of teachers. Looking back at our journey with havruta text study, we see it transformed from a traditional learning activity centered on an authoritative corpus of received texts into a self-reflective and potentially humanizing activity.

The ideal outcomes of havruta text study discussed in this chapter reflect a broader philosophy of learning, echoed in the writings of Michael Oakshott, a philosopher of traditional liberal education. According to Oakshott, to be truly human, people must claim, appropriate, and then dwell in the rich heritage of their culture—a world of meanings, not of things. Entering this world "is the only way of becoming a human being, and to inhabit it is to be a human being."[41] In this work of becoming human, students learn to engage in conversation with their inheritance and its many voices—what Oakshott calls its various modes of thought or distinct idioms of human self-understanding. These voices reflect humanity's achievements in science, literature, the arts, politics, economics, and philosophy. Oakshott captures the role of working with texts as follow:

> Learning to read or to listen is a slow and exacting engagement, having little or nothing to do with acquiring information. It is learning to follow, to understand and to rethink deliberate expressions of rational consciousness; it is learning to recognize fine shades of meaning without overbalancing into the lunacy of "decoding"; it is allowing another's thoughts to reenact themselves in one's own mind; it is learning in acts of constantly surprised attention to submit to, to understand and to respond to what (in this response) becomes a part of our understanding of ourselves.[42]

---

40   See Michael Fishbane, *Sacred Attunement: A Jewish Theology* (Chicago: University of Chicago Press, 2008), a book which has influenced our work.

41   Michael Oakshott, *The Voice of Liberal Learning: Michael Oakeshott on Education* (New Haven: Yale University Press, 1989), 45.

42   Ibid., 69.

Similarly, Oakshott understands the primary aim of liberal education as helping the student become a full participant in the human "conversation." The term "conversation," as used by Oakshott, refers to engagement with texts and people, without which no deeper understanding and growth is possible. It means to partake in "the art of this conversation in which we learn to recognize the voices, to distinguish their different models of utterance, to acquire the intellectual and moral habits appropriate to this conversational relationship and thus to make our *début dans la vie humaine.*"[43]

We have seen how havruta text study embodies these characteristics, and in that regard, havruta text study reflects a microcosm of one potential philosophy of Jewish education. It is characterized by a holistic view: it fosters habits of the mind, the hand and the heart; it cultivates dispositions needed for a full life; it has a special salience for educators in their personal and professional development; and it assumes that learning through dialogue is a worthy way to live. Havruta text study aims to cultivate a learner who grows through dialogical encounters with the past—represented in traditional texts—and the present—represented by fellow learners and the learning community. No doubt, these views, beliefs and assumptions reflect a certain philosophy of life, culture, and education. It will be the task of future research to undertake the further exploration and articulation of the Jewish, religious, and humanist traditions and values that provide additional wellsprings feeding such a view and of how they might be elaborated to enrich our educational endeavors in general, and havruta text study in particular.

---

[43]   Ibid., 39. On additional uses of the concept of conversation as transformational, see Sophie Haroutunian-Gordon, *Turning the Soul*. For the use of conversation in theological discourse, see David Tracy, *The Analogical Imagination: Christian Theology and the Culture of Pluralism* (New York: Crossroad, 1981).

Appendix 1

(For Chapter Three)

Selected Texts for Havruta Lessons:

Pedagogical and Scholarly Considerations

For the specially designed havruta lessons in which students experiment with various havruta text study practices, we typically select
short narrative texts from the literary genre of talmudic legends
known as *midrash aggadah*. There are several pedagogical reasons for
this choice based on the formal literary aspects of these texts.

To begin with, many of these texts are relatively accessible in the
sense that they do not require prior knowledge of complex legal concepts from talmudic literature. Additionally, they are usually short,
allowing for a comprehensive study of the text in a relative short
period of time. They also often have a strongly evocative nature; while
they often seem to offer a straightforward meaning, students soon discover after repeated readings that the text is more complex than they
had thought and lends itself to more than one interpretation. The literary qualities of the genre and the need to further investigate the text
are particularly conducive for students experimenting with the interpretive practices of havruta text study. Finally, as we have illustrated
throughout the book, narrative texts lend themselves particularly to
the treatment of the text as a partner which "suggests" a particular
view or an idea about a topic. As a result, they offer rich opportunities
to practice the dialogical aspects of havruta text study.

In addition to the formal literary qualities of these texts, in
selecting them for the special havruta lessons we also consider their
thematic aspects. Often, we select texts having themes with a direct
connection to learning, to learning in pairs, or even more specifically
to havruta learning practices. For example, the asking of questions
seems to be a key element in the text we selected for practicing open
questions (see Chapter Four). When this is the case, the thematic ideas

in the text infuse the students' discussions and reflections as they experiment with the practice.[1]

There is also a scholarly basis upon which we build our selection and use of talmudic legends. From within the vast literature of *midrash aggadah*, we often select what have been characterized as "miniature stories"[2]: uniquely short stories, just a few lines long, which are characterized by many of the features mentioned above. Our selections draw on interesting developments that have occurred during the last three decades in the scholarship of talmudic literature. Under the influence of hermeneutic and literary theories, talmudic legends have come to be conceptualized as "literary-artistic creations."[3] In this approach, the legends are viewed as purely fictional and didactical. This last point is important as it invites the reader to explore the potential ideas that were intended to be conveyed by the legends' authors, which provides us with a scholarly ground for having students frame the meaning of the text as both "being about..." but also as "saying that..." (see Chapter Four).

This scholarly approach suggests that the interpretation of talmudic legends benefits from the tools and concepts of literary analysis. A literary approach considers structure, the relation between the parts and whole, the use of metaphors and repetitions, the choice of nuanced vocabulary in the dialogues, imposed silences of the literary characters, and the omission or the deferral of information. Indeed, since

---

[1]   It is, of course, not feasible to link every aspect of havruta text study with a traditional text addressing that same topic. When available, we prefer to select short legends or metaphoric text. Their evocative nature offer more possibilities for students' imagination, consideration, and thus interpretive engagement with the ideas. For an elaborated discussion on this approach to the use of texts for educational purposes, see Elie Holzer, "Conceptions of the Study of Jewish Texts in Teachers' Professional Development."

[2]   Jonah Fraenkel, *Iyounim beolamo haruchani shel sippur haaggadah* (Tel Aviv: Hakibbutz Hameuchad Publishing House, 1981); Jonah Fraenkel, *Darkhei haaggada vehamidrash* (Masada: Yad LeTalmud, 1991); Jonah Fraenkel, *Sippur haaggadah: Ahdout shel tohen vetzura* (Tel Aviv: Hakibutz Hameuchad, 2001); Yair Barkay, *Hasipur haminyaturi* (Jerusalem: Ministry of Education, 1986).

[3]   Jeffrey L. Rubenstein, *Talmudic Stories: Narrative Art, Composition and Culture* (Baltimore: Johns Hopkins University Press, 2003).

the pioneering work of Fraenkel and Meir,[4] scholars have engaged in careful readings of rabbinic stories using a variety of tools of literary analysis.[5]

Rabbinic stories from the *midrash aggadah* often share common features. They use minimal descriptions of the world beyond the immediate context of the narrative, and they pay little explicit attention to the characters' emotions.[6] These literary characteristics intensify interpretive effects like Iser's gap-filling and Gadamer's projection of preconceptions, which are precisely those aspects of the interpretive process of which we want students to become aware.[7] We weave similar literary approaches into the textual interpretation assignments we give students. We invite them, for example, to articulate what information is missing, and to consider if and how literary devices like the characters' inner dialogues, the need to imagine the character's emotions, or the entire structure of the story might provide us with clues and keys as to its meaning.

Fraenkel also stresses the "internal self-containedness" of the talmudic legend, by which he means that the literary piece stands on it own, providing all the information needed for the ideas it is designed to convey.[8] Although other scholars, like Rubinstein,[9] disagree with him, for the pedagogical purposes of these havruta lessons we are comfortable with Fraenkel's view (that is, we believe these narratives are sufficiently self-contained for the kind of textual understanding we are seeking) and invite students to delve into the isolated texts we selected.

---

[4]   Jonah Fraenkel, *Darkhei haaggada vehamidrash*; Jonah Fraenkel, *Sippur haaggadah: Ahdout shel tohen vetzura*; Ofra Meir, *The Acting Characters in the Stories of the Talmud and the Midrash* (Unpublished doctoral dissertation, Hebrew University, Jerusalem, 1977); Ofra Meir, "The Story as a Hermeneutic Device," *American Journal of Scientific Research* 7–8 (1982–83): 231–62.

[5]   Daniel Boyarin, *Carnal Israel: Reading Sex in Talmudic Culture* (Berkeley and Los Angeles: University of California Press, 1995); Adamiel Kosman, *Massekhet gvarim: Rav vehakatzav veod sippurim* (Jerusalem: Keter, 2002); Jeffrey L. Rubenstein, *Talmudic Stories: Narrative Art, Composition and Culture*.

[6]   Jonah Fraenkel, Darkhei haaggada vehamidrash.

[7]   Wolfgang Iser, *The Act of Reading*; Hans-Georg Gadamer, *Truth and Method*.

[8]   Jonah Fraenkel, *Darkhei haaggada vehamidrash*.

[9]   Jeffrey L. Rubenstein, *Talmudic Stories: Narrative Art, Composition and Culture*.

Readers acquainted with talmudic literature may, however, object to our decision to disconnect the legend from its original talmudic context, which they argue eliminates important cues that the learner may use in developing an interpretation. Indeed, scholars who work on talmudic narratives and legends show how the literary and legal contexts of these texts are critical to interpretations of their meaning.[10] Our approach, however, is based on the near-universal scholarly view that most of these stories and legends had a "life of their own" before their inclusion in the flow of the Talmud's discussions, making it reasonable for our purposes to use these texts in our havruta lessons out of their (later) talmudic context.

10   Yehuda Brandes, *Aggadah lemaaseh: Iyounim beagadot hazal besugiyot hevra, mishpacha veavodat hashem* (Jerusalem: Elinor Library and Beit Morasha Publications, 2005).

Written Guidelines for Havruta Text Study

Throughout this book, we have often noted that havruta text study practices are best learned over time and as the outcome of ongoing opportunities to experiment with them. Consequently, in addition to our specially designed "havruta lessons," in which students are given the opportunity to focus on specific practices, we also make a point of looking for practical ways of alerting students to and surfacing their awareness of those practices during regular classes in which they spend time learning in havruta pairs.

A major pedagogic tool serving that goal is a list of written guidelines. It is designed to help students manage and monitor the various parts of havruta text study and help them engage in its practices. The specific items are not meant to serve as a questionnaire to be answered, but rather as signposts or reminders of practices to be performed. These templates should not be regarded as rigid structures, which have the potential to undermine the creative and sometimes unexpected directions of havruta learning. They allow for the fact that the exchange between a learners and a text is never strictly methodical, linear or replicable. Even when following a step-by-step procedure that is reflected in the guidelines, students are often—and should not hesitate to be—swept away by the details of their conversations and the images of the text as they comment and respond to them.

These guidelines are provided to new or relatively new learners of havruta text study, as well as to more experienced learners who have not been exposed to our more conceptualized, formative approach to havruta text study. For new learners, the guidelines may serve mostly as a practical aid by which they initiate themselves into the various features of havruta text study; guidelines support their experimentation with its flow and practices. For more advanced learners, the guidelines can slow down or undermine the "natural" and often unreflective way in which they have engaged in havruta learning until this point. Instead of following guidelines step-by-step, they may use them as a checklist that they consult at different points.

Below, we provide an annotated template of a set of written guidelines. It should be understood that different parts might be used, shortened or expanded in different contexts. The reader will note that the guidelines reflect the full scope of havruta text study and the two phases discussed in this volume, beginning with reading the text aloud and ending with self-understanding, the final integrative personal reflection. The written guidelines that cover the second phase of havruta text study reflect only those dialogical practices we consider to be central.

Finally, in our annotations, we also comment on our use of written guidelines to accustom the students to alternating between tasks they might perform collaboratively and tasks they may perform on their own. For instance, we want to help students acknowledge and appreciate the value of including private, silent time in the midst of havruta learning. As much as the co-construction of interpretations and the dialogue with ideas are important, it should not prevent students from taking time to think individually as well. Thus, inviting students to first articulate an idea by themselves helps them clarify their own individual ideas, which at times can be overshadowed by the collaborative learning dynamic. Likewise, alternating between individual and collaborative tasks is a device we use to help students experience how havruta learning can be fruitful in various ways. For example, they can fruitfully build on each other's different views and understandings not only in co-constructing them, but also by first bringing to the table each view separately after having had the time and the space to articulate it for themselves.

Written Guidelines for Havruta Text Study—A Template
(This example uses text discussed in Chapters Four, Seven, and Eight)

1. Background information	
Rav (*stands for Rabbi*) **Papa**: (died 375) was a Talmud scholar and teacher who lived in Babylonia. He was a student of both Rava and Abaye. He led the yeshiva (the academy where people study) in the city of Nehardea and over time he trained many students. Rav Papa was a wealthy man and it is said that whenever he completed studying a tractate from the Talmud he held a large party to which he invited his ten sons and many other people. **R. Shimi bar Ashi**: 4th century. Was a close disciple of Abaye. After the passing away of his teacher, he attended Rav Papa's yeshiva. *Fell on his face*: a ritual and usually private practice during which people expressed their personal prayers.	*Basic historical/conceptual background information about the text. E.g. biographical information about the literary characters and a definition of terms, concepts, or expressions with which students may not be familiar.*
2. Reading and Questioning the Text	
• Please take turns reading the text aloud. • Help each other paraphrase the text. • Discuss the possible parts of the story. • Read the text again. You may notice new details.	*This section encompasses the practices of reading discussed in Chapter Four. In this example, we use a number of expressions meant to activate the collaborative work: "take turns," "help each other," "discuss," "share."*

- Question the text: Share any questions you may have as you try to figure out "what's going on." For example: Why does the character say what he says? What exactly does a particular word or expression mean? How does this relate to what the text says elsewhere?
- Help each other ask *open* questions.

Our experience shows us that this emphasis in vocabulary is particularly important for new students of havruta learning, for whom it is natural to read silently on their own.

3. Making the Text Speak

a. *On your own*: Explore interpretations as to what you believe the story to be about. Be ready to provide strong textual evidence for your interpretations.

b. *Share* your interpretation (s) with your havruta partner. Consider using some of the following introductory phrases to present your interpretations: "I believe this story to be about..." and "it is saying that..."

This example illustrates how we help create private time to allow the student to first articulate her own interpretation. We use the words "[o]n your own" and "share" to indicate and emphasize these two distinct steps.
As discussed in Chapter Four, we provide specific language to help articulate the interpretations.

c. Paraphrase what you understand your havruta partner's interpretation to be and ask for confirmation or rectification.

Paraphrasing each other's interpretation is a practical listening technique designed to reduce the listener's projections.

d. Compare the different interpretations that are on the table and articulate to each other what their similarities and/or differences are.

We use phrases like "different interpretations" to reflect the working assumption that, given the nature of texts and interpretation, looking for more than one interpretation is a desirable goal.

	Comparing interpretations is intended to help students go beyond the acknowledgment of differences and help them look for the foundations of each interpretation.
e. Try to improve the quality of those interpretations by challenging and/ or supporting each other's interpretations and by responding to the challenges and support.	*Challenging and supporting are discussed in Chapter Six. We make sure to frame the goal of both as "improving the quality of the interpretations."*
f. Discuss with each other which of the interpretations might be the most compelling and explain your choices.	*The need to evaluate interpretations and provide reasonable explanations is discussed in Chapter Seven. Here, we use the phrase "which of the interpretations," emphasizing the interpretations as a common object of evaluation, rather than emphasizing the personal "belonging" of each interpretation to the particular student.*

4. Retrieving the Text's Question

Please go back to the textual interpretations you have generated. Together with your havruta partner, please try to articulate what might have been the question to which these two lines are an answer.

The conceptual basis for this question is discussed in Chapter Eight. The practice of "retrieving the text's question" is designed to move students to a perspective from which they might be able to better understand and appreciate the text, by viewing it as providing a possible answer to a question.

5. Giving the Text's Reason and Replying

Using your havruta partner as a sounding board, discuss each of your interpretations as a point of view worthy of consideration, even though you may not agree with it. Discuss possible reasons one might support this point of view. The following question may guide your work in giving the text reason:

• What alternative way of looking is presented by the text?

Then, articulate your own view on the matter and compare:

• How would *you* address the text's question?
• In what ways might the text's perspective be better than yours? What might the strengths and weaknesses of this view be?
• Can you think of any reason why your ideas are similar/different; more compelling and/or worthy then those offered by the text?

These questions are designed to help students identify and clearly articulate the differences between the text's view and their own. By replacing "the text" with "your havruta partner," these questions can also be used to evaluate the dialogue between the human havruta partners about their differing views. In any of these scenarios, the last two questions are designed to have students move from mere acknowledgment to critical judgment of these views.

6. Self-understanding

Please write about the following and be ready to share with your havruta partner:

• One important thing you've learned about the topic through the dialogue you have had with the text.
• Has anything in your own view on this topic been altered, reinforced, or enriched as a consequence of this exchange?
• What new questions do you have about this topic as a result of this exchange?

These questions are designed to help students reflect as concretely as possible in this final and most important part of havruta text study. Thus, the first task orients the student to only one specific (and in his view, important) insight he is taking away from the dialogue that has been conducted.

Yet the last question is designed to allow something about the topic to remain open for additional and future learning. This is in the spirit of Gadamer's definition of the experienced person who is characterized by a readiness for new experience.[1]

---

[1]   Hans-Georg Gadamer, *Truth and Method*, 362.

Appendix 3

(For Chapter Three)

This document is designed to help the student write reflectively about himself as a (future) learner of havruta text. The assignment provides information to teachers for use when they pair students up, as well as to both havruta partners in helping them learn about each other as learners.

Myself as a Havruta Learner

ASSIGNMENT

1. Introduction

Havruta study is a particular learning practice for studying Jewish texts in which you will learn to function as both a teacher and a learner. This type of text study will require you to read the text meticulously — not only to decipher what the text may be saying, but also to converse with the text and with your study partner.

Havruta study appears deceptively simple. In actuality, it is a practice that requires people to listen closely to and engage with their own ideas, their partners' ideas, and the ideas in the text, and to be open to revising their initial interpretations. This is hard work! Havruta study also requires participants to take responsibility for their own learning as well as their partner's learning by helping each other engage with and learn from the text. This means that when one person states an idea, the havruta partner cannot simply ignore that idea, but has a responsibility to respond to it in order to further the learning. Appropriate responses may range from asking questions to help clarify your partner's idea to offering an alternative interpretation with textual evidence. Being able to challenge less convincing interpretations (either your own or your partner's) in a respectful and informed way is *fundamental* to havruta learning.

Hereunder, you will find a list of features of good havruta study for you to familiarize yourself with.

Features of Good Havruta Text Study

Textual Practices

- Taking turns reading the text out loud
- Understanding the Hebrew or Aramaic version of the text
- Figuring out the structure of the text
- Articulating your interpretation of the text
- Revisiting the text many times in order to deepen your understanding and "test" your ideas

Interpersonal Practices

- Asking for help and/or looking up what you don't know and/or understand
- Helping your havruta partner put into words or express clearly what she is trying to say
- Listening closely to your havruta partner and asking questions to clarify what she is saying
- Probing your havruta partner's interpretations and statements
- Articulating and weighing the pros and cons of the various interpretations you and your havruta partner develop
- Being willing to defend an interpretation that you find compelling
- *Taking risks:*
     a. Challenging your havruta partner about her interpretation and statements
     b. Offering an interpretation that you are not 100% sure about
     c. Offering an interpretation which might lead the text to say something which you totally disagree with
- *Managing the work:*
     a. Paying attention to what helps your havruta learn
     b. Letting your havruta know what helps you learn
     c. Developing some shared norms for how you will work together and some strategies to improve your joint work. These might include strategies for providing feedback and for negotiating disagreements.

Your Assignment

Please write your answers to the following questions.

a. Think of yourself as a *learner*: describe two elements that makes learning satisfying for you.

b. Think of yourself as a *learner*: describe two elements that makes learning challenging for you.

c. What 2–3 things in the list of "Good Features of Havruta Study" do you perceive as being most challenging for you to perform? Explain why.

d. Think of yourself as *teacher*: Based on the list "Good Features of Havruta Study," describe 2–3 things that you believe you will be able to bring to havruta study that will be helpful for your partner's learning.

e. Think of yourself as a *learner* and a *teacher*: What do you do when circumstances cause you to "shut down?" When something in a text or with a learning partner offends or distances you, how do you usually react? How do you reconnect after such moments?

f. Please share two questions and/or concerns you have about havruta text study.

Please make sure to e-mail us a copy of your assignment and bring one extra hard copy to class as you will share it with your havruta partner.

APPENDIX 4

(For Chapter Three)

This document accompanies the session in which students are introduced to havruta text study as a learning format to be explored and reflected upon in and through their ongoing experience of it.

A. Please write first on your own and then share with your havruta partner:

According to your understanding, in what sense can havruta learning contribute to "better" learning?

What do you believe to be one important practice (that is, something you or both of you could do) that could promote this/these contribution (s)? Explain your choice.

B. Explore and discuss with your havruta partner:

An additional way to expand our thinking about those questions is by exploring what Jewish sources suggest. Today, we focus on one short talmudic statement. Please refer to the copy of the original text that you have on the accompanying handout. Please note that this talmudic text offers an interpretation of a biblical verse of metaphorical nature: "Iron sharpens iron, and a man sharpens the face of his friend" (Proverbs 27:17).

Also, FYI:

* Rabbi Hama son of Rabbi Hanina: 3rd century, Israel. Rabbi Hama directed a school.
* The term "questions of halakhah" means matters of Jewish law.
* The term "Torah scholars" refers to the students and scholars of the Jewish tradition.
1. Read *aloud* to each other Rabbi Hama's interpretation of the biblical verse and discuss:

Following this interpretation, what might be important effects of studying together that are conveyed by the metaphor of "iron sharpens iron"? (E.g. *This metaphor seems to suggest that learning together is important because* …).

2. Choose one of the effects the metaphor suggests to you. What would be an example of a *practice* (that is, something you or both of you could do) that those who study together should cultivate in order for this effect to take place?

C. Compare what you have learned from this text to what you wrote earlier (part A).
Are some of these ideas similar/different? Does anything stand out to you?

Appendix 5

(For Chapter Three)

The following document helps havruta partners monitor the encounter in which they share their written reflections on themselves as learners and as havruta learners.

As a reminder, the questions of your assignment were:

1. Think of yourself as a learner. Describe two strengths you possess as a learner—that is, qualities that make learning a satisfying and accessible experience for you.

2. Think of yourself as a learner. Describe what makes learning challenging for you. Explain why.

3. Think of yourself as a teacher. Describe two qualities you think you will be able to bring to havruta study that will be helpful for your partner's learning.

4. Think of yourself as a learner and a teacher: What do you do when circumstances cause you to "shut down?" When something in a text or with a learning partner offends or distances you, how do you usually react? How do you reconnect after such moments?

5. Please share two questions and/or concerns you have about havruta text study.

***

Meet your havruta partner
    a. Please meet with your havruta partner, exchange what you have written and read it silently to yourself.
    b. If needed, ask for clarification about what your partner wrote.

c. Based on what you wrote (but not limited to it), discuss with your havruta partner what you believe will be most helpful for your *own* learning during the havruta sessions.

Finally, write on your own about the following:
  a. What are two important things you have learned about your havruta partner as a learner?
  b. Reflecting about what you have learned about yourself and about your havruta partner as learners, what are two things you hope to work on over the next 3–4 havruta text study sessions? Please be as specific as possible about what you might do to contribute to your havruta partner's learning as well as your own. (For example, some people might want to work on their listening skills, specifically learning to listen to their partner's entire comments before responding; some people might want to work on being clear in articulating their own ideas; etc.)

Appendix 6

(For Chapter Four)

This document describes a model for engaging students in the practice of questioning, which we have found particularly helpful with participants who might need more guided assistance in this kind of exercise.[1]

It is designed around the use of specific questioning words, which provides an extra tool for students to practice questioning. First, we make the following quote from Rudyard Kipling accessible to students on a big poster:

> I keep six honest serving men
> (They taught me all I knew);
> Their names are What and Why and When
> And How and Where and Who.
>
> *Rudyard Kipling*

Then students are provided with the following guidelines:
- Using Kipling's six question words, ask questions about this text.
- Please be ready to share with the larger group two compelling questions, indicating first which of Kipling's question words you have used.

When we come back together as one group, we ask havruta pairs to share their questions with other havruta pairs or with the entire group. Sometimes we ask them to share these questions aloud, at other times we invite them to write down their questions on a flip-chart, which we make available to everyone in the room.

---

[1] This model was designed in a professional development seminar on havruta text study held in Rome, Italy in 2011 and has been used subsequently in additional settings.

The six simple question words provided in this model hold the potential to "open up" interpretation significantly. When we reconvene for students to report on their sessions, we ask each of them first to indicate which of Kipling's question words they used and only then to share their question. This practice slows down the reporting process and creates a heightened presence of both dimensions involved in the exercise: the actual questioning of text, and a metacognitive awareness of the ways in which certain key words can open fruitful lines of questioning.

APPENDIX 7

(For Chapter Five)

This text serves as background to the text in Appendix 8 (which is explored using the line-by-line method).

Rabbi Hananyah son of Hakhinai was about to leave for the house of study at the end of Rabbi Shimon ben Yochai's wedding. He said to him, "Wait for me until I come with you." He did not wait for him. He went and sat (studied) for 12 years in the house of study.

Rabbi Shimon used to send letters to his home and knew what was happening. R. Hananyah son of Hakhinai did not send letters home and did not know what was happening.

His wife sent him a letter saying: "Your daughter has reached the age to marry, come home and help her to get married." He did not return. Rabbi Akiba was inspired by heaven and said: "Whoever has a daughter to marry should return home."

By the time he came back, the streets of the town had changed and he did not know how to go to his house. He went and sat on the bank of the river. He heard young women calling to a certain girl: "Daughter of Hakhinai, daughter of Hakhinai, fill your jug and go." He said (to himself): "Infer from this that this girl is ours."

He followed her. His wife was sifting the flour. She lifted up her eyes and looked at him.

Her heart recognized him, she fainted and died.

He said: "Master of the universe, this poor woman, is this her reward?"

He besought mercy for her and she revived./ **And some say she revived.**

(Talmud, Tractate *Ketubot* 62a and sources from additional manuscripts in bold)

APPENDIX 8

(For Chapter Five)

1. R. Hama son of Bisa went away and spent 12 years at the house of study.	1. רבי חמא בר ביסא אזל יתיב תרי סרי שני בבי מדרשא.
2. When he came back he said: "I will not do what the son of Hakhinai did".	2. כי אתא אמר: "לא איעביד כדעביד בן חכינאי"
3. He therefore entered the (local) house of study and sent a message to his house.	3. עייל יתיב במדרשא שלח לביתיה
4. (Meanwhile) his son, R. Oshaya, entered, and sat before him	4. אתא רבי אושעיא בריה יתיב קמיה
5. He (Rabbi Oshaya) asked him questions about subjects of study	5. הוה קא משאיל ליה שמעתא
6. He (Rabbi Hama) seeing how well versed he (Rabbi Oshaya) was in his studies	6. חזא דמחדדי שמעתיה
7. became distressed (*weak; depressed*)	7. חלש דעתיה
8. "Had I been here," he said, "I would have had a son like this."	8. אמר: אי הואי הכא הוה לי זרע כי האי.
9. He entered his house	9. על לביתיה
10. His son came in	10. על בריה
11. whereupon he rose before him believing that he wished to ask him some (more) study questions	11. קם קמיה, הוא סבר למשאליה שמעתתא קא בעי
12. His wife said to him: "Is there a father who stands up before his son?"	12. אמרה ליה דביתהו: מי איכא אבא דקאים מקמי ברא?

Talmud, Tractate Ketubot 62b

Appendix 9

(For Chapter Six)

This document is used in the session in which students are first introduced to the practices of supporting and challenging.

Study Guidelines

Part I

    A. Closely read the text. A close reading entails consideration of the details of the story and how they contribute toward its larger meaning. This means you may want to read the text a number of times. A close reading also entails understanding what happens in the story and finding explanations for why the people in the story choose to do or say what is stated in the text.

    B. Articulate what you understand the story to be about (this is not the same as paraphrasing a story). You and your havruta partner may share one interpretation or have different interpretations.

    C. Write down your interpretation on a piece of flip chart paper.
        1. "According to our understanding, this story is about…"
        2. This interpretation enables us to explain the following details of the story:

Part II

    a. Choose someone in the room you haven't studied with yet.
    b. One of you will serve as a *presenter* of an interpretation and the other one will serve as a *critical colleague/havruta*.

Your role as a presenter is to:

1. Articulate your interpretation of what the story is about and to explain how you arrived at these ideas;
2. Listen and reply to your colleague's questions;
3. Probe/reinforce/revise your interpretation of the story.

Your role as a critical colleague/havruta is to:

1. **Actively listen** to your colleague's interpretation so that you are clear about what s/he is saying. You might ask the following questions: "Am I understanding you correctly that you are reading this part of the text to mean X?"

2. **Probe** your colleague's interpretation by asking **clarifying** questions such as: *"You said X; how did you get to this idea"?; "You said X, could you tell me more about what you mean by that?"* When you feel the need, don't hesitate to probe the answers to these questions as well.

3. **Support** and reinforce your colleague's interpretation by offering additional cues in the story and/or reasons which may support his/her interpretation. For example: *"Would you say that when it says X, this reinforces your point...?"*

4. **Challenge** the interpretation of your colleague by pointing to details in the story that the interpretation does not address or that may contradict the interpretation. For example, *"In the text it says X, how do you make sense of this part according to your interpretation? How do you account for...?; Why do you say that? How does that fit with what was just said? I don't really get that; could you explain it another way or give me an example?"*

5. **Offer** good reasons why your colleague's interpretation is **not** compelling enough in your view or **is** in fact very compelling.

Appendix 10

(For Chapter Seven)

This document is designed to have students make visible their interpretive insertions in the text as well as articulate their interpretation of the text.

Gap-filling

1. Rabbi Shimi bar Ashi used to attend (the classes) of R. Papa	‫1. רב שימי בר אשי הוה שכיח קמיה דרב פפא‬
2. and used to ask him many questions (*alternative translation:* many difficult questions).	‫2. הוה מקשי ליה טובא‬
3. One day he observed that Rabbi Papa fell on his face [in prayer] and he heard him saying, "May God preserve me from the embarrassment caused by Shimi." (*alternative translation:* from the insolence of Shimi.).	‫3. יומא חד חזייה דנפל על אפיה. שמעיה דאמר: רחמנא ליצלן מכיסופא דשימי.‬
4. The latter thereupon vowed silence and questioned him no more.[1]	‫4. קביל עליה שתיקותא ותו לא אקשי ליה.‬

Discuss any information that seems to be missing, i. e., which makes the story somewhat ambiguous and/or might have helped you to better understand what is going on.

***

I/we believe this story is about...

It says that ....

---

[1]   Talmud, Tractate Ta'anit 9b.

APPENDIX 11

(For Chapter Seven)

As an alternative to having havruta pairs provide feedback to each other, we have also designed a model that is appropriate for classes of less than 16 students. In this model, each havruta pair selects one interpretation among those they have generated. The original text is projected onto the screen and each havruta pair reads aloud the sentences they inserted within the text, which are then typed into the text. They also read aloud their interpretation of what the story is about. The other students then consult in havruta pairs, and prepare a brief evaluation of the interpretation, aided by the following guidelines:

    a. Indicate which elements of the story are not addressed or are only partially addressed by this interpretation.
    b. Share further comments or suggestions that expose strengths or weaknesses in the quality of the interpretation.

The havruta pair whose interpretation is being discussed is invited to listen and take notes but is asked to hold their responses until the end, with the exception of asking clarifying questions. The reason for this is to keep the focus on the evaluation, rather then moving into justification or argumentation. Later on, time is provided for the havruta pair to process these comments.

One advantage of this model is that it offers the teacher an opportunity to monitor and model the use of evaluative language as well as the social dynamics of evaluation. The teacher can then better contribute to fostering the creation of a supportive environment and a sense of collective effort within the learning environment.

Bibliography

Abel, Olivier. "Du Sujet Lecteur au Sujet Ethique." *Revue Internationale de Philosophie* 255 (2003): 369–85. (French)

Abrams, Meyer Howard. "A Note on Wittgenstein and Literary Criticism." In *Doing Things with Texts: Essays in Criticism and Critical Theory*, edited by Meyer H. Abrams, 73–87. New York: W. W. Norton & Co, 1989.

Althusser, Louis, and Etienne Balibar. *Reading Capital.* London: NLB, 1968.

Apel, Karl-Otto. "The Problem of Philosophical Foundations in Light of Transcendental Pragmatics of Language." In *After Philosophy: End or Transformation?* edited by Kenneth Baynes and James Bohman, 250–99. Cambridge, MA: MIT Press, 1987.

Aristotle. *Nicomachean Ethics.* Indianapolis: Hackett Publishing Company, Inc, 1999.

Arnett, Ronald C. *Communication and Community: Implications of Martin Buber's Dialogue.* Carbondale, IL: Southern Illinois University Press, 1986.

Assaf, Simha. *Mekorot letoldot hahinukh be Yisra'el: mitehilat yemehabenayim ad tekufat hahaskalah.* Tel Aviv: Devir, 1925. (Hebrew)

Auerbach, Ephraim E. *Hazal: Pirke emunot vedeot.* Jerusalem: Magnes, 1969. (Hebrew)

Ball, Deborah L., and David K. Cohen. "Developing Practice, Developing Practitioners, Toward a Practice-Based Theory of Professional Education." In *Teaching as the Learning Profession: Handbook of Policy and Practice*, edited by Linda Darling-Hammond and Gary Sykes, 3–32. San Francisco: Jossey-Bass, 1999.

Barel, Esti. *Vetalmud torah keneged kulam: Mabat migdari al limud hatorah bemidrashot beisrael.* Unpublished doctoral dissertation. Bar-Ilan University, Ramat Gan, 2009. (Hebrew)

Bandura, Albert. *Principles of Behavior Modification.* New York: Holt, Rinehart and Winston, 1969.

———. *Social Learning Theory.* New Jersey: Prentice Hall, 1977.

Barkay, Yair. *Hasipur haminyaturi.* Jerusalem: Ministry of Education, 1986. (Hebrew)

Barnes, Douglas, and Frankie Todd. *Communication and Learning Revisited: Making Meaning through Talk*. Portsmouth, NH: Heinemann, 1995.

Bauman, Zygmunt. *Life in Fragments: Essays in Postmodern Morality*. Oxford: Blackwell Publishers, 1995.

Beck, Isabel L., Margaret G. McKeown, Rebecca L. Hamilton, and Linda Kugan. *Questioning the Author: An Approach for Enhancing Student Engagement with Text*. Delaware: International Reading Association, 1997.

Ben-Habib, Seyla. *Situating the Self: Gender, Community and Postmodernism in Contemporary Ethics*. New York: Routledge, 1992.

Bernasconi, Robert. "'You Don't Know What I'm Talking About': Alterity and the Hermeneutic Ideal." In *The Specter of Relativism: Truth, Dialogue, and Phronesis in Philosophical Hermeneutics*, edited by Lawrence K. Schmidt, 178–94. Evanston, IL: Northwestern University Press, 1995.

Bernstein, Richard J. *Beyond Objectivism and Relativism: Science, Hermeneutics and Praxis*. Oxford: Basil Blackwell, 1983.

Bingham, Charles, and Alexander M. Sidorkin. *No Education Without Relation*. New York: Peter Lang, 2004.

Blanchot, Maurice. "The Infinite Conversation." *Theory and History of Literature, Vol. 82*. Minneapolis: University of Minnesota Press, 1993.

Bloom, Harold. *The Anxiety of Influence: A Theory of Poetry*. New York: University Press, 1973.

Blum-Kulka, Shoshana, Menahem Blondeim, and Gonen Hacohen. "Traditions of Disagreements: From Argumentative Conversations about Talmud Texts to Political Discourse in the Media." In *Coverage as Story: Perspectives on Discourse in Israeli Media. In honor of Itzhak Roeh*, edited by Moti Neiger, Menahem Blondeim, and Tamar Libes, 245–74. Jerusalem: Magnes Press, 2008.

Booth, Wayne C. *The Company We Keep: An Ethics of Fiction*. Berkeley: University of California Press, 1989.

Boyarin, Daniel. *Carnal Israel: Reading Sex in Talmudic Culture*. Berkeley and Los Angeles: University of California Press, 1995.

Brandes, Yehuda. *Aggadah lemaaseh: Iyounim beagadot hazal besugiyot hevra, mishpacha veavodat hashem*. Jerusalem: Elinor Library and Beit Morasha Publications, 2005. (Hebrew)

Bransford, John D., Ann Brown, and Rodney Cocking. *How People Learn: Brain, Mind, Experience and School*. Washington, D.C.: National Academy Press, 2000.

Brawer, Dina. *Havruta and Talmud Study: Peer Interaction in Critical Thinking*. London: University of London, 2002.

Breuer, Mordechai. *Ohale torah: Hayeshiva tavnita vetoldoteha*. Jerusalem: Merkaz Zalman Shazar Publication, 2004. (Hebrew)

Brown, Ann. "Communities of Learning and Thinking, or a Context by Any Other Name." In *Developmental Perspectives on Teaching and Learning Thinking Skills*, edited by Deanna Kuhn, 108–26. New York: Karger, 1990.

Brown, Steven M., and Mitchel Malkus. "Havruta as a Form of Cooperative Learning." *Journal of Jewish Education* 73.3 (2007): 209–26.

Buber, Martin. "Elements of the Interhuman." In *Martin Buber: The Knowledge of Man; Selected Essays*, edited by Maurice Friedman, 68–87. Baltimore: Humanity Books, 1988.

Burbules, Nicholas C., and C. Bruce Bertram. "Theory and Research on Teaching as Dialogue." In *Handbook of Research on Teaching*, edited by Virginia Richardson, 4th edition, 1102–21. Washington, DC: American Educational Research Association, 2001.

Carr, David. "Rival Conceptions of Practice in Education and Teaching." *Journal of Philosophy of Education* 37.2 (2003): 253–66.

Carr, Wilfred, and Stephen Kemmis. *Becoming Critical: Education, Knowledge and Action Research*. Lewes: Falmer, 1986.

Cavallo, Guglielmo, and Roger Chartier. *Histoire de la Lecture dans le Monde Occidental*. Paris: Seuil, 1997. (French)

Cazden, Courtney. *Classroom Discourse: The Language of Teaching and Learning*. Portsmouth, NH: Heinemann, 2001.

Clark, Thomas. "Sharing the Importance of Attentive Listening Skills." *Journal of Management Education* 23 (1999): 216–23.

Coates, Jennifer. *Women Talk: Conversation Between Women Friends*. Oxford: Blackwell Publishers, 1996.

Cochran-Smith, Marilyn, and Susan L. Lytle. *Inquiry as Stance: Practitioner Research for the Next Generation*. New York: Teachers College Press, 2009.

Cohen, David K., Stephen W. Raudenbush, and Deborah L. Ball. "Resources, Instruction, and Research." *Educational Evaluation and Policy Analysis* 25.2 (2002): 1–24.

Cook, Allison, and Orit Kent. "Doing the Work: Interpretive Experience as the Fulcrum of Tanakh Education." *Hayidion* (Summer 2012): 58–60.

Daloz, Laurent. *Mentor: Guiding the Journey of Adult Learners*. San Francisco: Jossey-Bass, 1999.

Davey, Nicholas. *Unquiet Understanding: Gadamer's Philosophical Hermeneutics*. Albany: State University of New York Press, 2006.

Derber, Charles. *The Pursuit of Attention: Power and Individualism in Everyday Life*. Oxford: Oxford University Press, 1979.

Dewey, John. *Democracy and Education: An Introduction to the Philosophy of Education*. New York: Free Press, 1966.

———. *Experience and Education*. New York: Collier Books, 1963.

Dobrosavljev, Duska. "Gadamer's Hermeneutics as Practical Philosophy." *Facta Universitatis: Series Philosophy, Sociology and Psychology* 2.9 (2002): 605–18.

Donoghue, Denis. *The Practice of Reading*. New Haven: Yale University Press, 1998.

Dori-Hacohen, Gonen. "Integrating and Divisive Discourses: The Discourse in Interactions with Non-Jewish Callers on Israeli Radio Phone-in-Programs." *Israel Studies in Language and Society* 3.2 (2011): 146–65. (Hebrew)

Dorph, Gail Z., and Barry W. Holtz. "Professional Development for Teachers: Why Doesn't the Model Change?" *Journal of Jewish Education* 66.2 (2000): 67–76.

Dorph, Gail Z., Susan S. Stodolsky, and Renee Wohl. "Growing as Teacher Educators: Learning New Professional Development Practices." *Journal of Jewish Education* 68 (2002): 58–72.

Duckworth, Eleanor. *The Having of Wonderful Ideas*. New York: Teachers College Press, 1996.

Dunne, Joseph. *Back to the Rough Ground: Practical Judgment and the Lure of Technique*. Notre Dame: University of Notre Dame Press, 2001.

Eagleton, Terry. *After Theory*. New York: Basic Books, 2003.

Elbow, Peter. *Embracing Contraries*. New York: Oxford University Press, 1986.

Feiman-Nemser, Sharon. "Beit Midrash for Teachers: An Experiment in Teacher Preparation." *Journal of Jewish Education* 72.3 (2006): 161–81.

Feuchtwanger, Ruti. *Becoming a Knower: Acquisition of Knowledge and Status by Religious Women Studying Talmud in Order to Teach*.

Unpublished doctoral dissertation. Bar-Ilan University, Ramat
Gan, Israel, 2011. (Hebrew)

Fish, Stanley. *Is There a Text in this Class? The Authority of Interpretive
Communities.* Cambridge, MA: Harvard University Press, 1980.

Fishbane, Michael. *Sacred Attunement: A Jewish Theology.* Chicago:
University of Chicago Press, 2008.

Fraenkel, Jonah. *Darkhei haaggada vehamidrash.* Masada: Yad LeTalmud,
1991. (Hebrew)

———. *Iyounim beolamo haruchani shel sippur haaggadah.* Tel Aviv:
Hakibbutz Hameuchad Publishing House, 1981. (Hebrew)

———. *Sippur haaggadah: Ahdout shel tohen vetzura.* Tel Aviv: Hakibutz
Hameuchad, 2001. (Hebrew)

Freeman, Donald. *Doing Teacher Research: From Inquiry to Understanding.*
Portsmouth, NH: Heinle & Heinle, 1998.

Freire, Paulo. *Pedagogy of the Oppressed.* New York: The Seabury Press,
1972.

Gad, Yair, Talia Sagiv, Sari Shimbursky, Sivan Akrai, and Maya
Lichtman. *Study of Learning Communities and Batei Midrash.* 2006.
http://avichai.org/wp-content/uploads/2011/01/learning-summ-
eng_0.pdf (accessed July 30, 2013).

Gadamer, Hans-Georg. *Reflections on My Philosophical Journey: The
Philosophy of Hans-Georg Gadamer.* Chicago: Open Court, 1997.

———. "Subjectivity and Intersubjectivity: Subject and Person."
Continental Philosophy Review 33.3 (2000): 275–87.

———. "The Incapacity for Conversation." *Continental Philosophy
Review* 39.4 (2006): 351–59.

———. *Truth and Method.* New York: Continuum, 1996.

Gadotti, Moacir. *Pedagogy of Praxis: A Dialectical Philosophy of Education.*
New York: SUNY Press, 1996.

Galef, David. *Second Thoughts: A Focus on Rereading.* Detroit: Wayne
State University Press, 1998.

Gallagher, Shaun. *Hermeneutics and Education.* Albany: State University
of New York Press, 1992.

Gillespie, Alex. "The Social Basis of Self-Reflection." In *The Cambridge
Handbook of Sociocultural Psychology,* edited by Jaan Valsiner and
Alberto Rosa, 678–91. Cambridge: Cambridge University Press,
2007.

Gilligan Carol. *In a Different Voice: Psychological Theory and Women's
Development.* Cambridge, MA: Harvard University Press, 1982.

Goodwin, Charles. "Conversation Analysis." *Annual Review of Anthropology* 19 (1990): 283–307.

Grondin, Jean. "Gadamer's Basic Understanding of Understanding." In *The Cambridge Companion to Gadamer*, edited by Robert J. Dostal, 36–51. Cambridge: Cambridge University Press, 2002.

Gross, Benjamin. *L'ame de la vie: Hayyim de Volozhyn.* Paris: Verdier, 1986. (French)

Grossman, Pamela, Christa Compton, Danielle Igra, Matthew Ronfeldt, Emily Shahan, and Peter Williamson. "Teaching Practice: A Cross-Professional Perspective." *Teachers College Record* 111.9 (2009): 2055–100.

Grossman, Pamela, Sam Wineburg, and Stephen Woolworth. "Toward a Theory of Teacher Community." *Teachers College Record* 103.6 (2001): 942–1012.

Habermas, Jurgen. *The Theory of Communicative Action.* Boston: Beacon Press, 1984.

Haroutunian-Gordon, Sophie. *Learning to Teach Through Discussion: The Art of Turning the Soul.* New Haven: Yale University Press, 2009.

———-. *Turning the Soul: Teaching through Conversation in the High School.* Chicago: University of Chicago Press, 1991.

Hawkins, David. "I, Thou, and It." In *The Informed Vision: Essays on Learning and Human Nature*, edited by David Hawkins, 48–62. New York: Agathon Press, 2002.

Heidegger, Martin. *Being and Time.* New York: Harper Perennial, 1962.

Heilman, Samuel C. *The People of the Book, Drama, Fellowship, and Religion.* Chicago: University of Chicago Press, 1987.

Heller, Marvin J. *Printing the Talmud: A History of the Earliest Printed Editions of the Talmud.* Brooklyn: Am Hasefer, 1992.

Helmreich, William. *The World of the Yeshiva: An Intimate Portrait of Orthodox Jewry.* New Haven: Yale University Press, 1982.

Henry, Michel. *Barbarism.* New York: Continuum 2012.

Hirsh, Eric D. *The Aims of Interpretation.* Chicago: The University of Chicago Press, 1976.

———. *Validity in Interpretation.* New Haven: Yale University Press, 1967.

Holtz, B. W., G. Z. Dorph, and E. B. Goldring. "Educational Leaders as Teacher Educators: The Teacher Educator Institute; A Case from Jewish Education." *Peabody Journal of Education* 72.2 (1997): 147–66.

Holtz, Barry W. *Textual Knowledge*. New York: JTS Press, 2003.

Holzer, Elie. "Allowing the Text to Do Its Pedagogical Work: Connecting Moral Education and Interpretive Activity." *Journal of Moral Education* 36.4 (2007): 497–514.

— — —. "Conceptions of the Study of Jewish Texts in Teachers' Professional Development." *Religious Education* 97.4 (2002): 377–403.

— — —."Choosing to Put Ourselves 'at Risk' in the Face of Ancient Texts: Ethical Education through the Hermeneutical Encounter." In *International Studies in Hermeneutics and Phenomenology*, edited by Andre Wiercinski. Berlin: LIT Verlag, 2013 (forthcoming).

— — —. "Educational Aspects of Hermeneutical Activity in Text Study." In *Modes of Educational Translation: Studies in Jewish Education,* edited by Jonathan Cohen and Elie Holzer, 205–40. Jerusalem: Magnes Press, 2009.

— — —." 'Either a Havruta Partner of Death': A Critical View on the Interpersonal Dimensions of Havruta Learning." *The Journal of Jewish Education* 75 (2009): 130–49.

— — —. "Ethical Dispositions in Text Study." *Journal of Moral Education* 36.1 (2007): 37–49.

— — —. "Teachers' Learning and the Investigation of Practice." *Mekhkarei Morashtenu* 2.3 (2004): 291–302. (Hebrew)

— — —. "What Connects 'Good' Teaching, Text Study and Havruta Learning? A Conceptual Argument." *Journal of Jewish Education* 72 (2006): 183–204.

Holzer, Elie, and Orit Kent. "Havruta Learning "What Do We Know and What Can We Hope to Learn?" In *International Handbook on Jewish Education*, edited by Helena Miller, Lisa Grant, Alex Pomson, 407–418. New York: Springer, 2011.

Hubbard, Ruth, Power Shagoury, and Brenda Miller. *Living the Questions: A Guide for Teacher-Researchers.* Portland, ME: Stenhouse Publishers, 1999.

Idel, Moshe. *Language, Torah and Hermeneutics in Abraham Abulafia.* Albany: State University of New York Press, 1989.

Isaacs, William. *Dialogue and the Art of Thinking Together.* New York: Doubleday, 1999.

Iser, Wolfgang. *Act of Reading: A Theory of Aesthetic Response.* Baltimore: Johns Hopkins University Press, 1978.

— — —. *Introduction to Prospecting: From Reader Response to Literary Anthropology.* Baltimore: John Hopkins University Press, 1989.

— — —. "The Reading Process: A Phenomenological Approach." *New Literary History* 3.2 (1972): 279–99.

Jauss, Hans Robert. *Aesthetic Experience and Literary Hermeneutics.* Minneapolis: University of Minnesota Press, 1982.

— — —. *Toward an Aesthetic of Reception.* Minneapolis: University of Minnesota Press, 1982.

Johnson, David, and Roger Johnson. *Cooperation and Competition, Theory and Research.* Edina, MN: Edina Interaction Book Company, 1989.

— — —. "Energizing Learning: The Instructional Power of Conflict." *Educational Researcher* 38.1 (2009): 37–51.

— — —. *Learning Together and Alone: Cooperation, Competition and Individualization.* Englewood Cliffs, NJ: Prentice-Hall, 1975.

— — —. *Learning Together and Alone, Cooperative, Competitive and Individualistic Learning.* Boston, MA: Alyn and Bacon, 1999.

Johnson, David, Roger Johnson, and Karl Smith. "Academic Controversy: College Instruction through Intellectual Conflict." *ASHE-ERIC Higher Education Report Volume 25.3.* Washington, DC: The George Washington University, Graduate School of Education and Human Development, 1997.

Kegan, Robert. *In Over Our Heads: The Mental Demands of Modern Life.* Cambridge, MA: Harvard University Pres, 1994.

— — —. *The Evolving Self: Problem and Process in Human Development.* Cambridge, MA: Harvard University Press, 1982.

Kegan, Robert, and Lisa Lahey. *Seven Languages for Transformation: How the Way We Talk Can Change the Way We Work.* San Francisco: Jossey-Bass, 2001.

Kent, Orit. "A Theory of Havruta Learning." *Journal of Jewish Education* 76.3 (2010): 215–45.

— — —. "Interactive Text Study: A Case of *Hevruta* Learning." *Journal of Jewish Education* 72.3 (2006): 205–33.

— — —. *Interactive Text Study and the Co-Construction of Meaning: Havruta in the Delet Beit Midrash.* Unpublished doctoral dissertation. Brandeis University, Waltham, MA, 2008.

— — —. "Teaching Havruta in Context." Paper presented at *NRJE.* New York, 2009.

— — —. Kent, Orit, and Allison Cook. "Havruta Inspired Pedagogy: Fostering an Ecology of Learning for Closely Studying Texts with Others." *Journal of Jewish Education* 78.3 (2012): 227–53.

— — —. "Images of the Possible in a Supplementary School: Text Study, Collaborative Learning and Meaning Making." Presented at the

Network for Research in Jewish Education Annual Conference, Toronto: Canada, 2009.

Kepnes, Steven. *The Text as Thou: Martin Buber's Dialogical Hermeneutics and Narrative Theology.* Notre Dame: Indiana University Press, 1992.

Kerdeman, Deborah. "Some Thoughts about Hermeneutics and Jewish Religious Education." *Religious Education* 93.1 (1998): 29–43.

Kessels, Jos, and Fred Korthagen. "The relationship between theory and practice: Back to the classics." *Educational Researcher* 25 (1996): 17–22.

Knowles, Malcom. *Adult Learning.* Houston: Gulf, 1990.

Kosman, Adamiel. *Massekhet gvarim: Rav vehakatzav veod sippurim.* Jerusalem: Keter, 2002.

Krechevsky, Mara, and Ben Mardell. "Four Features of Learning in Groups." In *Making Learning Visible, Children as Individual and Group Learners,* edited by Project Zero and Reggio Children, 284–94. Cambridge, MA, and Reggio Emilia, Italy: Project Zero and Reggio Children, 2001.

LaFountain, Marc J. "Play and Ethics in Culturus Interruptus: Gadamer's Hermeneutics in Postmodernity." In *The Specter of Relativism: Truth, Dialogue and Phronesis in Philosophical Hermeneutics,* edited by Lawrence K. Schmidt, 206–23. Evanston, IL: Northwestern University Press, 1995.

Lamm, Norman. *Torah lishmah: In the Works of Rabbi Hayyim of Volozhin and His Contemporaries.* New York: Yeshiva University Press, 1989.

Lampert, Magdalene. *Teaching Problems and the Problems of Teaching.* New Haven: Yale University Press, 2001.

Langer, Judith A. *Envisioning Literature, Literary Understanding and Literature Instruction.* New York: Teachers College Press, 1995.

Lash, Christopher. *The Culture of Narcissism: American Life in an Age of Diminishing Expectations.* New York: Basic Books, 1978.

Laughery, Gregory J. *Living Hermeneutics in Motion: An Analysis and Evaluation of Paul Ricoeur's Contribution to Biblical Hermeneutics.* Lanham, MD: University Press of America, 2002.

Lave, Jean. "The Practice of Learning." In *Understanding Practice: Perspectives on Activity and Context,* edited by Seth Chalkin and Sean Lave, 3–34. Cambridge: Cambridge University Press, 1993.

Lave, Jean, and Etienne Wenger. *Situated Learning: Legitimate Peripheral Participation.* New York: Cambridge University Press, 1991.

Lawrence-Lightfoot, Sarah. *Respect: An Exploration.* Reading, MA: Perseus Books, 1999.

Levinas, Emmanuel. *Beyond the Verse: Talmudic Readings and Lectures.* New York: Continuum, 2007.

Levisohn, Jon A. "A Menu of Orientations Towards the Teaching of Rabbinic Literature." *Journal of Jewish Education* 76.1 (2010): 4–51.

— — —. "Openness and Commitment: Hans-Georg Gadamer and the Teaching of Jewish Texts." *Journal of Jewish Education* 67.1–2 (2001): 20–35.

Lewis, C. S. *An Experiment in Criticism.* Cambridge: Cambridge University Press, 1992.

Little, Judith W. "The Persistence of Privacy: Autonomy and Initiative in Teachers' Professional Relations." *Teachers College Record* 91.4 (1990): 509–36.

Lord, Brian. "Teachers' Professional Development: Critical Colleagueship and the Role of Professional Communities." In *The Future of Education Perspectives on National Standards in America,* edited by Nina Cobb, 175–204. New York: College Entrance Examination Board, 1994.

Jean-François, Lyotard. *The Postmodern Condition.* Minneapolis: University of Minnesota Press, 1979.

Manguel, Alberto. *A History of Reading.* New York: Penguin Books, 1996.

Meir, Ofra. *The Acting Characters in the Stories of the Talmud and the Midrash.* Unpublished doctoral dissertation. Jerusalem: Hebrew University, 1977. (Hebrew)

— — —. "The Story as a Hermeneutic Device." *American Journal of Scientific Research* 7–8 (1982–83): 231–62.

Michaels, Sarah, Catherine O'Connor, Megan Williams Hall, with Lauren Resnick. *Accountable Talk: Classroom Conversation that Works.* (3 CD-ROM set). Pittsburgh: University of Pittsburgh, 2002.

Michelfelder Diane P., and Richard E. Palmers, eds. *Dialogue and Deconstruction: The Gadamer-Derrida Encounter.* Albany: State University of New York Press, 1989.

Misgeld, Dieter, and Graeme Nicholson, eds. *Hans-Georg Gadamer on Education, Poetry and History.* Albany: State University of New York Press, 1992.

Nietzsche, Friedrich. *A Genealogy of Morality.* Cambridge: Cambridge University Press, 2006.

Noddings, Neil. "Caring and Competence." In *The Education of Teachers*, ed. Edward Griffen, 205–220. Chicago: National Society of Education, 1999.

Noddings, N. *Caring: A Feminine Approach to Ethics and Moral Education*. Berkeley: University of California Press, 2003.

Oakshott, Michael. *The Voice of Liberal Learning: Michael Oakeshott on Education*. New Haven, CT: Yale University Press, 1989.

Paley, Viviane G. "On Listening to What Children Say." *Harvard Educational Review* 56.2 (1986): 122–31.

Palmer, Richard, ed. *Gadamer in Conversation*. New Haven: Yale University Press, 2001.

Parks, Sharon Daloz. *Big Questions, Worthy Dreams: Mentoring Young Adults in Their Search for Meaning, Purpose, and Faith*. San Francisco: Jossey-Bass, 2000.

Pearce, W. Barnett, and Kimberly A. Pearce. "Taking a Communicative Perspective on Dialogue." In *Dialogue: Theorizing Difference in Communication Studies*, edited by Rob Anderson, Leslie A. Baxter, and Kenneth N. Cissna, 39–56. Thousand Oaks, CA: Sage Publications, 2004.

Perkins, David. *Making Learning Whole*. San Francisco: Jossey-Bass, 2009.

Perkins, David. *Smart Schools: Better Thinking and Learning for Every Child*. New York: Free Press, 1992.

Piaget, Jean. *The Psychology of Intelligence*. New York: Harcourt, Brace, 1950.

Raider-Roth, Miriam, and Elie Holzer. "Learning to be Present: How Hevruta Learning Can Activate Teachers' Relationships to Self, Other and Text." *The Journal of Jewish Education* 75.3 (2009): 216–39.

Raider-Roth, Miriam, Vicky Stieha, and Billy Hensley. "Rupture and Repair: Episodes of Resistance and Resilience in Teachers' Learning." *Teaching and Teacher Education* 28 (2012): 493–502.

Ricoeur, Paul. *Freud and Philosophy*. New Haven: Yale University Press, 1970.

———. *From Text to Action: Essays in Hermeneutics II; Studies in Phenomenology and Existential Philosophy*. Evanston, IL: Northwestern University Press, 1991.

———. "Hermeneutics and the Critique of Ideology." In *The Hermeneutic Tradition from Ast to Ricoeur*, edited by Gayle L. Ormiston and

Alan D. Schrift, 298–334. New York: State University of New York Press, 1990.

— — —. *Hermeneutics and the Human Sciences*. Cambridge: Cambridge University Press, 1981.

— — —. *Interpretation Theory: Discourse and the Surplus of Meaning*. Fort Worth: Texas Christian University Press, 1976.

— — —. *Time and Narrative*, Volume 1. Chicago: University of Chicago Press, 1984.

— — —. *Time and Narrative*, Volume 3. Chicago: University of Chicago Press, 1988.

Rodgers, Carol. "Defining Reflection: Another Look at John Dewey and Reflective Thinking." *Teachers College Record* 104.4 (2002): 842–66.

Rodgers, Carol, and Miriam Raider-Roth. "Presence in Teaching." *Teachers and Teaching: Theory and Practice* 12.3 (2006): 265–87.

Rogers, Carl R. "The Interpersonal Relationship in the Facilitation of Learning." In *The Carl Rogers Reader*, edited by H. Kirshenbaum and V. L. Henderson, 304–11. London: Constable, 1990.

— — —. "The Interpersonal Relationship: The Core of Guidance." In *Person to Person: The Problem of Being Human, a New Trend in Psychology*, edited by Carl Rogers, Barry Stevens, Eugene Gendlin, John Shlien and Wilson Van Dusen, 85–101. Lafayette, CA: Real People Press, 1967.

Rogoff, Barbara. *Apprenticeship in Thinking*. New York: Oxford University Press, 1990.

Rosenblatt, Louise. "On the Aesthetic as the Basic Model of the Reading Process." *Bucknell Review* 26.1 (1981): 17–32.

— — —. *The Reader, the Text, the Poem, the Transactional Theory of the Literary Work*. Carbondale, IL: Southern Illinois University Press, 1978.

Risser, James. *Hermeneutics and the Voice of the Other: Re-reading Gadamer's Philosophical Hermeneutics*. Albany: State University of New York Press, 1997.

Rubenstein, Jeffrey L. *Talmudic Stories: Narrative Art, Composition and Culture*. Baltimore: Johns Hopkins University Press, 2003.

Ryken, Leland. "Formalist and Archetypal Criticism." In *Contemporary Literary Theory: A Christian Appraisal*, edited by Clarence Walhout and Leland Ryken, 1–23. Grand Rapids, MI: Eerdmans Publishing Co., 1991.

Scheffler, Israel. *The Language of Education*. Springfield, IL: Charles C. Thomas, 1960.

Schneiders, Sandra. *The Revelatory Text: Interpreting the New Testament as Sacred Scripture*. San Francisco: Harper Collins, 1991.

Scholes, Robert. *Textual Power Literary Theory and the Teaching of English*. New Haven: Yale University Press, 1986.

Scholes, Robert. *Protocols of Reading*. New Haven: Yale University Press, 1991.

Schon, Donald. *Educating the Reflective Practitioner*. San Francisco: Jossey-Bass, 1987.

―――. *The Reflective Practitioner: How Professionals Think in Action*. London: Temple Smith, 1983.

Schwarz, Baruch B. "Students' Havruta Learning in Lituanian Yeshivot: The Case of Recurrent Learning." In *Education and Religion: Between Tradition and Innovation*, edited by Immanuel Etkes, Tamar Elor, and Baruch B. Schwartz, 279–308. Jerusalem: Magnes Press, 2011. (Hebrew)

Segal, Aliza. *Doing Talmud: An Ethonographic Study in a Religious High School in Israel*. Unpublished doctoral dissertation. The Hebrew University, Jerusalem, 2011.

Sheldon Amy. "Conflict Talk: Sociolinguistic Challenges to Self-assertion and How Young Girls Meet Them." *Merrill-Palmer Quarterly* 38.1 (1992): 95–117.

―――. "Talking Power: Girls, Gender Enculturation and Discourse." In *Gender and Discourse*, edited by Ruth Wodak, 225–44. London: Sage Publications, 1997.

Stampfer, Shaul. *Hayeshivah halitait behithavutah*. Jerusalem: Zalman Shazar, 1995. (Hebrew)

Shultz, Kathy. *Listening: A Framework for Teaching Across Differences*. New York and London: Teachers College Press, 2003.

Slatoff, Walter. *With Respect to Readers: Dimensions of Literary Responses*. Ithaca, NY: Cornell University Press, 1970.

Spiegel, Yaakov S. *Amudim betoledot hasefer haivri: Hagahot umagihim*. Ramat Gan: Bar-Ilan University Press, 1996. (Hebrew)

Steiner, George. *Real Presences*. Chicago: University of Chicago Press, 1991.

Sternberg, Meir. *The Poetics of Biblical Narrative: Ideological Literature and the Drama of Reading*. Bloomington, IN: Indiana University Press, 1985.

Stieha, Vicky, and Miriam Raider-Roth. "Disrupting Relationships: A Catalyst for Growth." In *Disrupting Pedagogies and Teaching the Knowledge Society: Countering Conservative Norms with Creative Approaches*, edited by Jullie Faulkner, 16–31. Hershey, PA: IGI Global, 2011.

Stiver, Dan. *Theology after Ricoeur: New Directions in Hermeneutical Theology*. Louisville, KY: Westminster John Knox Press, 2001.

Stodolsky, Susan, Gail Z. Dorph, and Sharon Feiman-Nemser. "Professional Culture and Professional Development in Jewish Schools: Teachers Perceptions and Experiences." *Journal of Jewish Education* 72.2 (2006): 91–108.

Tedmon, Susan. *Collaborative Acts of Literacy in Traditional Jewish Community*. Unpublished doctoral dissertation. Philadelphia: University of Pennsylvania, 1991.

Teomim-Ben Menachem, Esty. *Women Study: Characterizing Conversation and Learning in Women's Havrutot.* (Unpublished doctoral dissertation). Bar Ilan University, Ramat Gan, (forthcoming) (Hebrew)

Theunissen, Michael. *The Other: Studies in the Social Ontology of Husserl, Heidegger, Sartre and Buber*. Cambridge, MA: MIT Press, 1984.

Thiselton, Anthony C. *Hermeneutics*. Grand Rapids, MI: William B. Eerdmans Publishing Company, 2009.

———. *New Horizons in Hermeneutics: The Theory and Practice of Transforming Biblical Reading.*Grand Rapids, MI: Zondervan Publishing House, 1992.

Tracy, David. *Plurality and Ambiguity: Hermeneutics, Religion, Hope*. Chicago: University of Chicago Press, 1987.

———. *The Analogical Imagination: Christian Theology and the Culture of Pluralism*. New York: Crossroad, 1981.

Valdes, Mario J. ed. *A Ricoeur Reader: Reflection and Imagination*. Toronto: University of Toronto Press, 1991.

———. *Phenomenological Hermeneutics and the Study of Literature*. Toronto: University of Toronto Press, 1987.

Vigotsky, Lev. *Mind in Society*. Cambridge, MA: Harvard University Press, 1978.

Warnke, Georgia. *Gadamer, Hermeneutics, Tradition and Reason*. Cambridge: Polity Press, 1987.

Warren, Jeff. "Toward an Ethical-Hermeneutics." *European Journal of Psychology Counseling and Health* 1–2.7 (2005): 17–28.

Weinsheimer, Joel. *Philosophical Hermeneutics and Literary Theory*. New Haven: Yale University Press, 1991.

Welton, Michael. "Listening, Conflict and Citizenship: Towards a Pedagogy of Civil Society." *International Journal of Lifelong Education* 21 (2002): 197–208.

Wentzer, T. Schwarz. "Toward a Phenomenology of Questioning: Gadamer on Questions and Questioning." In *Gadamer's Hermeneutics and the Art of Conversation: International Studies in Hermeneutics and Phenomenology Vol. 2*, edited by Andrzej Wiercinski, 243–66. Berlin: Lit Verlag, 2011.

Zagzebski, Linda T. *Virtues of the Mind: An Inquiry into the Nature of Virtue and the Ethical Foundations of Knowledge*. Cambridge: Cambridge University Press, 1996.

Zeichner, Kenneth M., Daniel P. Liston. *Reflective Teaching: An Introduction*. Mahwah, NJ: Lawrence Erlbaum Associates, 1996.

Index

Printed in the USA
CPSIA information can be obtained
at www.ICGtesting.com
JSHW011458050824
67593JS00009B/383